FUSION

ABSOLUTE STANDARDS
IN A WORLD OF RELATIVITY

FUSION

ABSOLUTE STANDARDS IN A WORLD OF RELATIVITY

SCIENCE, THE ARTS & CONTEMPORARY LIFE
IN THE LIGHT OF TORAH

Edited and prepared for publication by
Dr. Arnie Gotfryd

General Editors
Professor Herman Branover
Rabbi Shalom Lipskar

B'Or HaTorah Publications
in conjunction with
Feldheim Publishers *Jerusalem/New York*

First published 1990
Hardcover edition: ISBN 0-87306-516-6

Feldheim Publishers Ltd.
POB 6525/Jerusalem, Israel

Philipp Feldheim Inc.
200 Airport Executive Park
Spring Valley, NY 10977

Printed in Israel

Library of Congress Cataloging-in-Publication Data

Fusion : absolute standards in a world of relativity / editors,
Herman Branover, Arnie Gotfryd, Shalom Lipskar.
p. 232 cm. 22.2
ISBN 0-87306-516-6
1. Judaism and science. 2. Ethics, Jewish. 3. Philosophy, Jewish. 4. Ethical relativism. I. Branover, Herman. 1931– II. Gotfryd, Arnie. III. Lipskar, Shalom.
BM538.S3F87 1989
296.3'875—dc20

89-38177
CIP

This volume is dedicated to the memory of

Rebbetzin Chaya Mushka, z"l,

wife of the Lubavitcher Rebbe, shlita.

"Her children rise up, and call her blessed; her husband also, and he praises her: Many daughters have done virtuously, but you excel them all."

(Proverbs 31:28-29)

Acknowledgments

Many friends, too numerous to mention individually, helped in the preparation of this book. I am very grateful to my brother, Chanoch, for all kinds of assistance while I labored on the manuscript. Thanks especially to my wife, Leah Hena, for her invaluable support and encouragement.

Arnie Gotfryd
Rosh Chodesh Kislev, 5750
Toronto, Canada

Contents

pendulum is swinging back, as followers of the educational theories of Harvard's Lawrence Kohlberg acknowledge a process of moral development from age five through the late teens.

In contrast, Judaism has never wavered in its emphasis on education as the basis for morality. Moreover, Judaism posits that education begins before birth and continues throughout life.

In discussing methods of teaching morality, the author claims we should not only "practice what we preach" but also "preach what we practice." She links the word *chinuch* (education) to *chanukah* (dedication) and concludes that "Those of us in *chinuch* have a mission: to dedicate ourselves to instilling within our children the moral values found in the Torah."

What is more rational? To believe in God or not to believe? The answer hinges on what we mean by rationality. Dr. Block argues that scientific verification and mathematical proof are useless for querying God's existence because He is neither an empirical hypothesis nor a mathematical theorem. In order to weigh the alternatives, we need a more basic standard of rationality—the criterion of simplicity or unity. That is, when one has competing explanations which are equally plausible, empirically and logically, the rational response is to choose the explanation that is simpler or which displays greater unity.

Countless people from all walks of life have asked, "What is the origin of the universe? Where did it come from?" Ultimately there are only two possibilities. Either God made the universe, or it is eternal and without origin. However, to ascribe eternalness to the universe is to "add on" a property for the sole purpose of explaining the universe's existence, for eternalness is not part of the meaning of the universe, nor is it an empirical property that could be confirmed by experiment or observation. The "eternalness" of the universe serves no purpose other than to "explain" its origin. It is therefore an *ad hoc* explanation. In contrast, the theistic view simpler and more unified, and therefore more rational, than its alternative.

This essay proposes hereditary factors which may underlie the immensely disproportionate number of Jews who have achieved excellence in the sciences.

Professor Domb's argument assumes that the ability for the kind of abstract thinking involved in science has a hereditary association. He then demonstrates that for at least 2000 years, Jewish abstract thinkers have been choosing mates based on familial scholarship. This, he argues, would preserve and enhance any hereditary tendency to outstanding intellectual achievement. Furthermore, even those Jews whose immediate forebears did not choose their mates eugenically would have benefited from the enriched gene pool developed over the ages.

He concludes that such inborn talent is not praiseworthy in itself. It is rather a person's ethical integrity which is of value, and this is not inherited but acquired.

This essay begins with a sharp confrontation between religious and scientific outlooks on why leaves change color in the fall. However, careful analysis of both views leads to the conclusion that these two approaches are not competitive but rather most complementary. The essential difference between religious and scientific explanations of natural phenomena lies in the questions they address: Science is concerned with *how* the world works, while religion attempts to tell us *why*.

To highlight the distinction, the author probes successive layers of scientific study for the "explanation" of changing leaf color. One by one, ecology, physiology, biochemistry, physical chemistry and particle physics are brought to bear, but all these fields merely serve to enrich our *description* rather than to provide an *explanation* of why nature behaves in that way. Even the most reliable laws of nature are purely descriptors of the orderly relationships among things. Indeed the very existence of such orderly relationships is itself something that requires explanation.

One of the greatest wonders of the world is something we automatically take for granted: man's ability to use mathematical equations to predict the course of physical events. This has been considered miraculous by Einstein, Hertz, Planck, etc., for one simple reason. Mathematics is an exercise in mental artistry without any reference to the physical world, and yet the abstract constructions that mathematicians develop are very often applied with remarkable success to accurately describing and predicting phenomena in the real world. Why?

The author points out that, according to Kabbalah, both the human personality and the cosmos are built according to the same ground plan—the Sefirotic Scheme. Since man's creative process mirrors the Divine creative process, the creations of the Divine mind can be grasped by using the creative ideas generated by the human mind.

Throughout its century-and-a-half of development, the science of sociology has been attempting to interpret society using theories which are either so rigidly *absolute* in their bias that they lead to callous intolerance or, at the other extreme, so *relative* that they lack any capacity to address even the grossest violations of fundamental human rights.

Recently a growing minority of sociologists has been developing views which retain flexibility and tolerance but only within the bounds of basic ethical criteria (e.g., the work of Merton, Sapir and Whorf). While this trend is encouraging, the ethical criteria chosen may be arbitrary and therefore limited. This difficulty is transcended by metasociology, a social theory developed by Kranzler, which acknowledges ethical criteria handed down by God. Nonetheless, metasociology retains the best aspects of relativism by allowing one to understand society from widely divergent viewpoints.

Strange as it seems, modern physics and traditional Judaism agree that not only does man depend on the universe but that the universe itself is wholly dependent on the conscious involvement of man.

This essay compares and contrasts secular and religious views on the role and significance of names. Torah teaches that the essence and life-force of a created being is contained in its Hebrew name. Moreover, all properties of any created being are encoded in the Hebrew name, rather like the way genes code for an organism's hereditary characteristics, or, for another example, like the way Dirac's equations tell us everything that is knowable about the physical state of an electron.

To illustrate this, the author explains various types of names: Conventional names merely serve to identify an object; structural names indicate how something's parts are arranged; functional names describe how something works. The Hebrew name includes all these aspects and more—it actually serves as the channel through which the Divine Being continuously creates and sustains the thing named.

A finite human being cannot truly conceptualize God, since He is Absolutely Infinite in all respects. Still, we can gain insights into the Divine creative process by studying those aspects of Torah, in *Chasidut* and Kabbalah, which describe the infinite, intricate and very abstract processes involved in the Creation of the universe by God.

When the author of this essay, a mathematician, first learned about these concepts, he was completely amazed to discover that the infinite, intricate and very abstract ideas he had been developing for years in the cerebral world of mathematics actually had a "real world" application—modeling the process of the Creation of the universe by God.

This essay examines in detail the striking parallels between the two systems, with the result that the reader comes to appreciate the profound beauty and meaning of the mathematical concepts on the one hand, and the rational accessibility of the Divine creative process on the other.

Did the universe come about by chance or was it planned? The question is timeless, but recent discoveries in physics and cosmology have revived Rabbi Akiva's Talmudic "Argument from Design" and catapulted it into the limelight of popular intellectual controversy.

The author's precision instrument for dissecting the issue and resolving the conflict is the idea that there are two kinds of very improbable events: ordinary ones, like holding the winner out of a billion lottery tickets (which some ticket-holder *must* do), and extraordinary ones, like winning three consecutive one-in-a-thousand draws. Even though the odds of this are also one-in-a-billion, the triple win raises eyebrows because it is an unexpected *kind* of event.

One of the new discoveries is that the forces of gravity and electromagnetism within a star are very delicately balanced. A change in *either* force by one part in 10,000,000,000,000,000,000,000,000,000,000,000,000,000 would render the star totally incapable of sustaining life.

Is this by chance or design? As Schlesinger points out, one may believe what he wishes but those who claim to refute the renewed Argument from Design all commit the same inexcusable blunder in their reasoning: They fail to distinguish between those improbable events which are bound to occur in some fashion, and those which are of a totally unexpected kind and hence require explanation.

JACOB I. SCHOCHET *Society's Legal Codes: Pragmatism or Morality? A Jewish View of Natural Law* 157

Legality *per se* has nothing whatever to do with morality. Thus an accepted law may well be immoral and a valid moral principle may well be illegal.

While we naturally aspire toward laws that reflect what is good, right and just, this quest tends to fail. For moral principles (like the Golden Rule) are by definition universal and independent of public consensus, whereas human law is political, and thus as limited and fallible as the human beings who generate it.

On the other hand, Divine Law, being neither limited nor fallible, provides: true moral guidance and justice; precise and just definition of the situations where given rules apply; truly suitable rewards and punishments; rules for internal acts and motives; etc.

While Divine Law includes that which is reasonable to man, it ultimately transcends human intellect since even the rational aspects stem from the Divine Will. Man has freedom of choice not only in the quality of his actions, but also in the quality of his motivation. The best motive for good behavior is not the inherent rationality in such behavior but rather the fulfillment of the Divine Will.

MEIR TAMARI *The Challenge of Wealth: A Jewish Perspective* 173

There exists a distinctive Jewish ethical framework for the conduct of business, within which Jews have always operated. This framework regards wealth as a gift of God, legitimate and useful but operative within the parameters laid down by Jewish law, morality and custom. These parameters forbid the earning of wealth through dishonest means, which include not only theft but also coercion, misrepresentation, unrevealed conflict of interest and the concealment of other relevant facts in business dealings. Corporations are bound by the same moral obligations as their shareholders and therefore what is forbidden to the individual is also forbidden to the corporation.

Because of the national orientation of Judaism, society has, as it were, a share in the wealth of the individual. Private property rights are recognized and protected but are never absolute. This means that possessors of wealth, corporate or otherwise, can be taxed for the social welfare of the community, in order to meet various needs, including charity for the poor and the provision of public services. Furthermore, business may not be conducted in a way that will damage another's property or health, or the ecological quality of life of individuals or of society as a whole.

The legal nature of Judaism ensures that its ethical framework is expressed in terms of law, and the rabbinical courts are obligated to enforce these laws. At the same time, acting beyond the minimal requirements of the law, such as doing one's fellow man an economic favor and voluntarily relinquishing one's property rights, is also part of Jewish religious education.

Torah and science provide different ways of looking at the world. The science "map" is built from observation, inference and testing. Its methods and conclusions are relative to time, place and the observer. The Torah "map," on the other hand, was revealed to man by God and is thus an absolute standard clothed in relative human terms.

The author describes how the biological nature of man limits his knowledge. All living beings are "closed systems" with no way of validating reality except by the fickle and fallible tool, consensus. Still the scientific method helps man achieve an admirable (albeit relative) degree of consistency in describing and understanding reality. But with all this, collective scientific knowledge remains permanently confined within the boundaries of biological and cognitive closure.

Not so Torah. Its origin transcends biology and cognition and it is therefore totally free of their limitations. Moreover, even though Torah is expressed in relative human terms, its absolute truth and validity remain intact while simultaneously being completely compatible with science.

In discussing why the Absoluteness of Torah is a concealed property, the author posits that this ensures that people not observe the commandments blindly, but rather through the maximal exercise of free choice.

Preface

THE FIRST INTERNATIONAL *B'Or HaTorah* Conference took place during Chanukah 5748 (December 20–22, 1987) in Miami Beach. Sponsored by the Aleph Institute, it served several purposes simultaneously.

First of all, it brought together a group of authors and advisors for the *B'Or HaTorah* magazine and enabled them to exchange ideas and clarify problems related to the Torah/Science and Torah/Modern Life interfaces.

Second, being open to the general public, this conference presented a unique opportunity for several hundred non-specialists to listen to scholarly lectures on the above subjects, and to take an active part in the discussions and panel sessions as well.

Third (and perhaps most important), the wide media coverage of the conference conveyed to the resident and visiting populace of Miami the clear and vivid message that strict adherence to a Torah life style is perfectly compatible with creative work and impressive achievement in the sciences and humanities.

A group of twenty distinguished scientists, philosophers and educators from the United States, Canada, England, Australia and Israel actively participated in the conference and contributed to its success. Both the audience and the lecturers were so enthusiastic about the conference that they expressed the hope that the organizers make it an ongoing event every year or two.

A special blessing given to the participants by the Lubavitcher Rebbe, *shlita,* contributed much to the mood of the conference. Beyond his blessing and wishes for great success, the Rebbe also indicated that the subtitle of the conference—"Absolute Standards in a World of Relativity"— could and should be interpreted in a way that provides insight. In fact his interpretation gave a dimension of meaning not even conceived by those who titled the conference in the first place.

"You should realize," the Rebbe wrote, "that the theory of relativity was developed mainly as the result of observing the special features of light. This indicates the special meaning of the time of your conference—the time of Chanukah and the time of the Lights of Chanukah." The Rebbe's comment was hinting at one more profound connection between light, relativity and the subject of the conference: Just as the theory of relativity has its firm foundation in the fact that the speed of light is absolute, so too all the events and ideas of modern life are relative, yet they and even their very relativity are based on a firm and absolute foundation—the eternal Torah and *Halachah.* In fact the Torah is often compared to light in both Biblical and rabbinic writings.

The present volume contains most of the papers presented at the conference. They have been carefully edited and supplemented by lists of references, short biographical notes on the authors and artistic renderings intended to capture some key ideas contained in the articles. Hebrew translations will appear in a number of subsequent issues of the *B'Or HaTorah* magazine.

In conclusion, I would like to sincerely thank all the authors for their contributions and cooperation. It is my pleasant duty to express special thanks to Dr. Arnie (Aryeh) Gotfryd for the enormous work of editing the papers and preparing them for publication. Last but in no way least, we all—participants, authors, and future readers—are indebted to the Aleph Institute and to its spiritual leader, Rabbi Shalom D. Lipskar, who made possible both the First International *B'Or HaTorah* Conference and this subsequent volume.

Herman Branover
Editor, B'Or HaTorah

FUSION

ABSOLUTE STANDARDS
IN A WORLD OF RELATIVITY

"No one has ever seen, felt or measured a wave or particle of gravity."

Arnie Gotfryd
(based on a letter by
the Lubavitcher Rebbe)

Proof for the Existence of the Creator

A TEACHER ONCE wrote to the Lubavitcher Rebbe asking him if there exists convincing proof, palatable to a skeptic, that demonstrates conclusively that God exists. The Rebbe's reply forms the basis of this article. In his letter,[1] the Rebbe uses no religious rhetoric and no polemic. Rather he builds a rationally based scientific argument that leads inexorably to the remarkable conclusion that the Jewish faith is eminently reasonable from a scientific perspective. Moreover the cornerstone and foundation of Judaism, the stand at Sinai, emerges from rigorous scientific scrutiny as the most reliably documented empirical fact in human history.

The question has been raised: Is there a convincing proof for the existence of the Creator that could satisfy skeptics beyond a shadow of a doubt?

ARNIE GOTFRYD earned his Ph.D. in Ecology at the University of Toronto, Canada. He has authored some twenty books and articles on topics ranging from the songbirds of urban forests to the impact of observer bias on environmental assessments. Residing near Toronto, he serves as a consultant to individuals, government and industry on a range of environmental issues. His Torah/Science papers include "On Acknowledging the Creator in Scientific Literature," which appeared in B'Or HaTorah *and in the journal* Canadian Research.

At first glance the question seems simple enough, especially since the concepts are straightforward and the terms familiar. But this apparent simplicity is deceptive, and to address the question properly requires clarity of language and careful definition of terms. In particular, what do we mean by "existence" and "proof" of existence? We must start here because these words mean very different things to different people. For example, that which constitutes complete proof for a young child may be totally inadequate for a meticulous scientist, and vice versa. Furthermore, some say that for children, existence and proof of existence apply only to tangible objects—"Seeing is believing."

Included in this kind of proof is the general idea of a report. This too is a proof based on perception, except that it is someone else's perception. Consider, for example, a person born blind who has never seen the shade of pink called magenta. Does he have convincing proof for the existence of that color? Surely he will rely on the perception of others who tell him that there is such a thing as light, that it comes in various colors, and that these colors come in different shades, one of which is magenta. Although magenta is totally beyond anything in his experience, he has absolutely no trouble believing in its existence because he trusts other people's reported perceptions.

At a more abstract level, another perfectly acceptable kind of proof is reasoning from effect to cause. Everyone acknowledges with complete certainty that everything that happens has a reason and cause for happening. Thus when one sees actions, these themselves are proof of an activating force, even though this is not direct proof and superficially there appears to be room for doubt. A classic example is the existence of electric power. Man is a sentient being; his sense of sight verifies the existence of colors, his sense of hearing verifies the existence of sound, etc. These are considered complete, direct proofs. Yet man has no faculty to perceive electric potential, or voltage. We can sense current but not voltage. We only see its effects, such as a filament glowing or a voltmeter's needle moving, etc. Still, we are certain of our conclusion that there exists some imperceptible force, which we term electricity, that is the reason behind what we do see. This is considered conclusive proof; and in the same way one proves the existence of magnetism and other forces. Electricity is a prime example because its existence is totally accepted beyond any shadow of a doubt.

The scientist's faith in cause-and-effect is so intense that he will accept as undisputed fact the existence of an activating force, even if it plainly contradicts rationality. A case in point is the force of gravity. We are so familiar with the idea of gravity from every science book throughout our school years, that no one would dream of questioning it, even though rationally it is far more difficult to accept than electricity. Electricity is only imperceptible when it is still, but when it flows it can be felt and measured. Not so with gravity; no one has ever seen, felt or measured a wave or particle of gravity. Our only proof that the force of gravity exists is that physical bodies move. But how can a force act from afar with no intermediary whatsoever between the masses? With a remote-controlled garage door or toy, there is a flow of measurable infrared or radio waves, but with gravity there is nothing but the simple faith that every action has a cause.

At first scientists tried to explain the force of gravity by assuming the existence of a fine mediating substance called ether. But the idea had to be abandoned because the proposed medium would have necessarily had so many contradictory properties that it became even more implausible than the alternative absurdity of remote action without any connection.

Anyone in the exact sciences who wonders whether the existence of the Creator can be reliably proven should consider another "standard" concept, derived from the realm of physics. This idea is so intellectually challenging that after many decades of study, even the experts admit it is beyond their comprehension. Nonetheless it is accepted by all exact scientists as a reality, and it is a proven fact in the eyes of the public. The idea referred to is that matter is nothing but a particular form of energy, and that it is possible to transform matter into energy and energy to matter. Superficially it may be hard to see what is so difficult about this notion of relativity, but if one takes a moment to consider the degree of similarity between the light now emanating from his light bulb, and the shoe on his foot, and then tries to imagine converting one into the other and back again, the problem becomes crystal clear. Everything in our experience leads us to think that matter and energy are as fundamentally different as two things can be. Therefore, to say that they are equivalent does not even sound, say, reasonable-but-difficult; it simply sounds ridiculous.

As with gravity, the only compelling proof for relativity is that we see events that have no apparent explanation and if we accept the theory—they are explained. This is considered a scientific proof and, on this basis alone, relativity is accepted virtually everywhere as conclusively demonstrated beyond the faintest doubt, even though from a strictly rational standpoint, the equivalence of matter and energy is not at all compelling.

People act in accordance with their beliefs, and skeptics are no different. Hence it is reasonable to expect that a skeptic will feel free to use as a basis for action any ideas which are shown to meet his criteria of legitimacy. On this basis, there is not only one, but several proofs for the existence of God and, as mentioned, there is no problem if one is forced to say that this existence is not grasped by the senses or the mind, or even if it contradicts rationality. As long as this existence accounts for observed reality and does so better than any other proposition, we have what is usually considered to be conclusive, scientific proof.

In this sense, proving the existence of the Creator is the same as proving anything else, whether in the realm of science or in the context of our daily lives.

Anyone who examines his daily conduct will admit that he doesn't perform a penetrating, thorough analysis assessing the reliability of the information on which he bases his daily activities. If the weather forecast calls for rain, he wears his boots even though he has never met the weatherman or studied meteorology, and furthermore he knows that the weatherman is often wrong. For another example, if Vitamin E is reported to cure baldness, he will take it without knowing for sure how it works or if it works. He'll take it without even knowing what it is. Rather he accepts the word of others who did look into the matter. Only where there is some doubt that maybe the "information" was faked or that the observer was affected by internal or external factors, or that he wasn't sure himself and took someone else's view, etc.... Then one would seek additional evidence. And with every increase in the number of observers, and with every type of variation in position, situation and context relative to the observers, the likelihood of deception becomes more remote and the evidence is strengthened in the form of a scientific and convincing proof. On this basis, the individual and society engage in all kinds of activities and projects, with complete trust that their conclusions are true and established.

So too in our case. The giving of Torah on Mount Sinai was verified, generation after generation, as a fact proven by the presence of 600,000 adult males. If one includes women, children, Levites, men over 60, etc., there were present millions of individuals, including Egyptian emigrants, who saw the events with their own eyes and experienced Divine communication personally and simultaneously.

This is not a testimony restricted to a single prophet, a dreamer of dreams or an elite group. This testimony was transmitted from parent to child, generation after generation, and everyone acknowledges that there was no interruption in the transmission from then until now. Moreover, there have never been less than 600,000 reporters in any generation, people whose characters were dissimilar and who were by no means afraid to disagree on basic issues, as is well-documented from Sinai on. Yet, despite all their differences and arguments, and despite their being dispersed throughout the world for millennia, all the versions of the above historical event that reach us today are similar in every detail. Is there more reliable and precise testimony than this?

There is a second manner of proof which is also based on the premise discussed above—that everything that happens has a cause, that seeing any event or situation is proof positive that some guiding force exists, even if the event was apparently senseless or destructive. This proof is as follows:

Consider any object. Virtually anything that one can imagine is composed of various parts which are arranged and coordinated with remarkable precision. None of the parts has any inherent control over the others and yet we know that the harmonious and unified functioning of the entire system is itself a phenomenon and must be due to some cause. We conclude from this with complete confidence that there is an external power which binds and unifies all the parts. Moreover, the very fact that it binds and unifies the parts proves that it is stronger than they are since it controls them.

For example, if we were to enter a factory where everything was run automatically and we did not see anyone there, we would not doubt the existence and involvement of a great mechanic whose knowledge encompassed all the machinery and component parts and who controlled them—one who was in charge of their functioning among themselves and who maintained the connection between the parts and the control center. On the contrary—the more concealed the hand of man in such a factory, and the more the operations are automated, the more impressed and convinced we are of the mechanic's remarkable skill.

And if this is the case with a factory, where we are speaking of hundreds, thousands, or even tens of thousands of parts, how much more true is this for natural objects, e.g., a piece of wood or stone, a plant or an animal, and—needless to say—the structure of the human body, as Job states, "From my flesh I will envision...."[2] This is especially so from the scientific perspective that every object is comprised of billions of atoms, with each atom containing even more minute parts. One would think, at first glance, that chaos would reign and yield incomparable disorder. But instead, we see an amazing orderliness and a marvelous fitting of the smaller parts to the larger, up to the very largest; we see the fit between microcosmic and macrocosmic patterns and processes, etc., etc. It is therefore clear beyond any shadow of a doubt that there exists a "Mechanic" responsible for all this.

One might say that all this is governed according to the "laws of nature"—but I think it is important to emphasize that such expressions have no *explanatory* content, but rather give a convenient summary or *description* of the existing situation, that is, that natural phenomena are conducted according to definite patterns. But to say that a "law of nature" is a being in and of itself without dependence, and that this being rules throughout Creation, and that there are thousands of beings like it, according to the number of natural laws, is so absurd that there is not one scientist in the field who would say so. Rather it is the case that such laws are merely convenient, summary expressions for describing a situation, so that one should not be forced to duplicate at every turn a lengthy description of the "simple" facts. But however elegant and sophisticated a "law of nature" may be, it is clear and obvious that such an expression provides no explanation whatsoever.

Now to the heart of the matter. To put it plainly, everyone has criteria for what can be reliably considered true. If an idea meets those standards, it is fit to be believed and acted upon. If it does not, then it is not suitable for belief or as a basis for action. But one may not adopt certain truth criteria when it is convenient, and then drop them when it is not. Therefore, it is assumed that anyone who is seeking a proof is not merely doing so for the sake of intellectual exercise, but would indeed live by his conclusions.

In this regard it should be noted that the aforementioned proof is much stronger than all those proofs and evidence by which people conduct their daily lives. What simpler illustration is there than the fact that, when retiring at night, one arranges everything for the morning even though there is no logical proof that tomorrow morning the sun will rise yet again and that all natural systems will continue to function as they did yesterday and the day before. It is only that since the world has been working this way for so many days and years, one trusts that these "laws" will also rule tomorrow and the next day.

And on this basis alone, a person strives and troubles himself to prepare his affairs for the following morning, even though he has no logically compelling reason to do so. On the contrary—if chance or random probabilities were running the show, it would be more reasonable to assume that tomorrow will be utterly unpredictable. The conviction that nature will continue to function as it did today is only logically compelling when it is based on the knowledge that there really is a Master of the world.

Although more could be said on everything that was discussed above and certain points could be explained further, this should suffice and provide enough material for consideration and conclusion. For it is incorrect to maintain that the Creator's existence requires proof, while His Creation itself exists beyond doubt, because in fact the opposite is true! Recent results of scientific research, regarding the existence of the universe and ways to "describe" it, contradict each other in numerous areas and indeed leave room for major doubts. But the most serious, significant and fundamental scientific doubt is as follows:

Who can establish whether the perceived impression of the eyes, of the ears, or of the brain generally, has any reality outside human sensation or thought? This argument poses an insurmountable challenge to the truth of the world's existence but in no way applies to the Creator, nor to the functions of causing events and arranging all Creation. For this, practically speaking, it doesn't matter whether there exists an independent reality or just the impression of such a reality. The primary consideration of the average person, and according to which he lives his whole life, is that for everything in *his world* there is a cause which acts, from within or without.

A further note of importance is that often human nature is such that when one is given a *simple* proof, it is difficult to accept because of its very simplicity. Such irrational rejection is unfortunate because it precludes any effect on personal behavior. And one of the foundations of our faith in the universe's Creator and Director, and in the stand at Sinai and the receiving of the Torah and its commandments, is that the quality of a person's deeds is of primary importance.

NOTES

1. The letter on which this article is based is dated 25 Iyar, 5719, and is published (in Hebrew) in *Emunah U'Mada* (Kfar Chabad, Israel: Machon Lubavitch, 1977), 3-8.
2. *Job* 19:26.

Laya Block

Education as the Basis for Morality

ON APRIL 14, 1912, the fabled luxury liner *H.M.S. Titanic* sank in 13,000 feet of water with a loss of more than 1,500 lives. The sinking of this unsinkable ship has caught the imagination of thousands. Books have been written about it and many attempts have been made to locate the *Titanic*'s remains on the ocean floor. On September 1, 1985, these efforts were rewarded when Robert Ballard and his team found the ship, and subsequently some of the artifacts retrieved from the wreck site were shown on national television. Such has been the interest in the ill-fated ship that it has generated a new term in modern usage. Levine, in a study of American college graduates, concludes that young people have a "Titanic mentality." They think that the ship of society is headed for disaster, but nevertheless they want to travel first class. Their goal is not to better the world as they find it, but to make money, attain social status and live well. This new morality, an ethic of selfishness and egocentrism, has been called by social historian Christopher Lasch the "culture of narcissism."

LAYA BLOCK graduated with top honors from Brooklyn College (B.A.) and Yeshiva University (M.Ed.). Since moving to London, Ontario, she has pioneered Jewish education for students at all levels, including campus programs, the London Hebrew Day School, which she co-founded and directed, and Gan-Gani Nursery, which she founded and has directed since 1964. Mrs. Block is a noted author and well-traveled lecturer on topics pertaining to women and preschool education.

Two other unmistakable trends have been documented in recent years: 1) a steady rise in self-destructive behavior by young people, such as drug abuse, drinking, teenage pregnancy and suicide, and 2) a similar rise in general destructive behavior such as vandalism, violence, cruelty toward peers and juvenile crime.

Viktor Frankl, in his book *Man's Search for Meaning,* writes that "such widespread phenomena as alcoholism and juvenile delinquency would not be understandable unless we recognize the existential vacuum underlying them."[1] He explains that this vacuum occurs when the traditions which buttress man's behavior diminish. "He has no instincts which tell him what to do and no tradition tells him what he ought to do; sometimes he does not even know what he wishes to do."[2] Modern man feels that his life is ultimately meaningless.

It seems clear that the teaching of morality is needed today. Principles of self-respect and respect for others are essential to offset the pattern of self-destructive and destructive behavior. Man needs guidelines and rules of conduct on how to live as a responsible, contributing member of society. The knowledge that everyone has a contribution to make can help put meaning back into a person's life. It is interesting to note that until the mid-nineteenth century, philosophers and educators assumed that one of the goals and aims of education was to teach morality.

Kant wrote that man must improve his moral sense. "Man's duty is to improve himself; to cultivate his mind, and when he is evil, to develop moral character. Upon reflection we shall find this very difficult. Hence education is the greatest and most difficult problem to which man can devote himself."[3]

Pestalozzi felt that education could not be separated from ethical instruction. He wrote, "Do not hesitate to touch on the difficult questions of good and evil, and the words connected with them. And you must do this especially in connection with the ordinary events of every day, upon which your whole teachings in these matters must be founded, so that the children may be reminded of their own feelings, and supplied as it were with solid facts upon which to base their conceptions of the beauty and justice of moral life."[4]

In the second half of the nineteenth century, a dramatic shift occurred. Herbert Spencer and Thomas H. Huxley, among others, felt that the most important knowledge was scientific knowledge. In this new era, there was no infallible authority, no absolutes and the teaching of morality was removed from the schools.

As we moved into the twentieth century, a vacuum was created in the field of moral education. What came to fill this gap was the theory of moral development, as introduced by Lawrence Kohlberg of Harvard University. According to this theory, man's moral development begins at about age five or six and continues until his late teens. As the young person develops rational skills, he progresses through stages that are "invariant, sequential and hierarchical." Aided by discussions of values and hypothetical dilemmas, the child goes through six stages until he reaches the highest stage of moral judgment. At stage 1, the physical consequences of action determine its goodness or badness regardless of the human meaning or value of these consequences. At stage 6, right is defined by the decision of conscience in accord with self-chosen ethical principles appealing to logical comprehensiveness, universality and consistency. Kohlberg's ideas and theories are the center of much discussion and a great amount of research continues to be done in the field of moral education.

What does Jewish education—*chinuch*—have to say on the question of teaching morality? I am reminded of the bumper sticker popular in the 1970s which read "I Found It," and of the countering sticker put out by Chabad which read "I Never Lost It." Throughout the ages, discussions of absolutism and relativism, on teaching morality or not, have never entered the province of *chinuch*. Jewish education is today and always was the basis for morality, and absolute values are found in the Torah. As we look back in our history, to its very beginning, we are allowed to listen to God's conversation with Himself before executing judgment on Sodom and Gomorrah: "And the Lord said, Shall I hide from Abraham what I am doing?"[5] At this moment Abraham is chosen to come within the intimate counsels of Hashem. Why was he chosen? The verse reads: "For I have known him to the end that he may command his children and his household after him to keep the way of the Lord, to do righteousness and justice..."[6]

Rashi explains that "knowing" here implies not merely cognition, as in many other places in the Bible, but indicates a closeness of relationship to the thing known. Abraham was chosen because the Lord had become close to him, had become fond of him, because, as Hashem says, he commands his children to keep My ways. What are the ways of the Lord? Righteousness and justice.

In the writings of Kohlberg and other moral educators, education is limited to schooling. In the Torah we see that Abraham, our first father, is beloved of Hashem and rewarded because he teaches his children morals. Shelomo *Ha-Melech* writes in *Proverbs*: "My son, hear the instruction of your father and forsake not the law of your mother."[7] Parents are the first teachers of the child and bear the basic responsibility for guiding their children and instilling in them proper attitudes and values. This is a great responsibility and the method is one which is easier said than done. The best way to teach is by example. No matter how much you talk about the virtue of honesty, if your child hears you boasting about how you falsified an insurance claim, you can't blame him if he cheats on an exam. There is also the other side of the coin—if the child lives in a home which is always open to guests, don't blame him if he invites the mailman to supper.

Bruno Bettelheim put it succinctly when he wrote, "Unfortunately the maxim 'Do as I say and not as I do' won't work with children. Whether they obey our orders or not, deep down they are influenced less by what we tell them than by who we are and what we do."[8]

Bettelheim details a study conducted in Sweden which demonstrated how persuasive the example set by the parents can be to a child. Some years ago, the Swedish government became concerned because alcoholism, vandalism, drug use and criminal behavior had become prevalent among Swedish teenagers. To find out why some children became troublesome and others did not, researchers compared the homes of law-abiding teenagers with those of delinquents. They found that neither material assets nor social class exercised a statistically significant influence on the behavior of these young people. Instead, what was decisive was the emotional atmosphere of the home. Teenagers who behaved well tended to have parents who themselves were responsible, upright and disciplined—who lived in accord with the values they professed and encouraged their children to follow suit. He concludes that "children form themselves in reaction to us: the more they love us the more they emulate us and the more they respond positively to our consciously held values and to those of which we are not conscious but which also influence our actions."[9] Viktor Frankl writes that "man does not behave morally for the sake of having a good conscience, but for the sake of a cause to which he commits himself, or for a person whom he loves, or for the sake of his God."[10]

I could quote many other studies which link parental warmth, love and nurturance to children's moral development, but I would rather take the time to tell you a story about the founder of Chabad *Chasidut*—the Alter Rebbe....

The Mitteler Rebbe and his father the Alter Rebbe lived together in the same house, each occupying different floors. One day the Alter Rebbe, who was engaged in Torah study on the upper floor, heard his infant grandson crying downstairs. He continued studying, assuming that his son, who was downstairs, would attend to the baby. However, the child's cries became louder and more insistent, with no signs of abating. The Alter Rebbe closed his *sefer* and quickly descended the stairs separating their apartments. Imagine his surprise when, upon entering the room, he found the Mitteler Rebbe wrapped in his *tallit*, praying fervently, while right beside him his infant son lay howling in his cradle, his face red and flushed. The Alter Rebbe immediately picked up the baby and soothed him until his cries stopped. The Rebbe then chastised his son, telling him that no matter what one is engaged in, one must always heed the cry of a child. We parents and teachers must always be sensitive to a child's needs and feelings and show him our love and concern.

The story is told of the mother of a newborn infant who was very anxious to bring up her child correctly. She went to a Rebbe and asked him when she should start teaching her child. The Rebbe inquired how old the child was. When he was told that the baby had recently been born, the Rebbe answered gently, "My daughter, you are nine months too late." Contrary to Kohlberg, who says that moral development starts at age five or six, Torah teaches us that learning starts at the moment of conception and that the child's first three years are crucial to his development. The Rebbe, *shlita,* gives us the example of a tree: a nick made in a tiny seedling can cause the tree to be deformed as it grows. What we teach a child when he is young can affect his future growth.

Parents and teachers are partners in the child's learning adventure, particularly in the younger years. A mother of one of my preschool students recently mentioned to me that her son had told her that he loved Hashem more than her. I thought long and hard to discover where this feeling had come from. I certainly had not taught my students that they should love God more than their parents. After reviewing in my mind the structure of the class routines and the format of the lessons, I concluded that indeed these things might have contributed to David's remark. When we say the prayer *V'ahavta,* we put our hands on our hearts to signify loving Hashem. We talk about how Hashem watches over us when we sleep. We thank Hashem for the food that we eat. We learn about how Hashem made the world and all the beautiful things in it. Ours is a very God-centered program and somehow David had internalized this ultimate Jewish value—the love of Hashem.

This incident made me think of Ilana, another child who had a unique relationship with Hashem. We had just finished learning about the *mezuzah.* We had talked about the three letters on the cover of the *mezuzah*: *shin, dalet,* and *yod,* and how they stood for the words *Shomer Delatot Yisrael*—Guardian of the Doors of Israel. Ilana thought about this for a moment, then turned her head upward and said, "Hi, *Shaddai,* up in the sky!" This little girl had felt so close to Hashem that she could turn to him as a friend and call out, "Hi, *Shaddai!*"

What have I said so far? Nothing revolutionary. I have only pointed out some very obvious things. We teach by setting good examples. We foster love and a desire to emulate us in our children by showing them love and respect. We provide an environment that is conducive to the development of good moral traits.

Let me add yet another—one that has been with us throughout our history. We teach by telling. Not only do we have to practice what we preach, but we must also preach what we practice. Research on this issue concludes that parents who frequently moralize—point out the moral issues in a situation—have children who are more advanced in their moral reasoning than children of parents who do not do this kind of teaching.

It is interesting to note the results of London's research on the backgrounds of "rescuers"—people who risked their lives and/or their fortunes to save Jews. His study revealed that rescuers consistently remembered their parents as strong, good people who both preached and practiced morality. London quotes one man, who was involved in the rescue of more than 200 Jews over a four-year period, as exemplifying this pattern. "You inherit something from your parents, from your grandparents," he explained. "My mother used to tell me when we were small, and even when we were bigger, 'Regardless of what you do with your life, be honest. When the day comes that you have to make a decision, make the right one. It may be a hard one, but even the hard ones should be the right ones.' "[11]

I would like to conclude with one of my favorite stories. Mr. S. was telling his family about his difficult childhood in Siberia. "When I was a little boy of six, and I lay down to go to sleep every night in the woods, the stars and the sky were my ceiling and the snow was my blanket." He told his family how his father and brothers had died of hunger.

His wife asked him, "Your father and your big brothers were gone, you had no yeshiva and no rebbe to teach you—how then were you able to observe the *mitzvot*? How? What gave you the strength?"

Mr. S. was thoughtful for a while and then he spoke. "It was my mother," he said. "Yes, my mother and all her stories around the fire. That's what kept us going. She talked to us a lot. She liked to tell us about a man who had his best clothes packed in a special suitcase, all ready and waiting for *Mashiach* to come. I remember," he continued, "how my mother used to say, '*Kinderlach,* every time you make a *berachah,* every time you do a *mitzvah,* you bring *Mashiach* one step closer.' "

This conference is taking place during the days of Chanukah. It would therefore surely be remiss not to connect my topic of *chinuch* with this Festival of Lights, especially since both words come from the same Hebrew root. Chanukah, as we know, means dedication. Those of us in *chinuch* have a mission: to dedicate ourselves to instilling within our children the moral values found in the Torah. We should strive to change the "Titanic mentality" of the "me" society to the "*Hakhel* mentality" of the "we" community, and through this unity maybe we will bring *Mashiach* one step closer.

NOTES

1. Viktor Frankl, *Man's Search for Meaning* (New York: Simon and Schuster), 107.
2. Ibid., 106.
3. Immanuel Kant, *Pedagogy*.
4. Pestalozzi, Letter on his work at Stanz.
5. *Genesis* 18:17.
6. *Genesis* 18:19.
7. *Proverbs* 1:8.
8. Bruno Bettelheim, "Punishment versus Discipline," *The Atlantic Monthly* (November 1985): 57.
9. Ibid., 57.
10. *Man's Search for Meaning* (New York: Simon and Schuster), 99-100.
11. P. London, "The Rescuers," in *Altruism and Helping Behavior*, J. Macauley and L. Berkowitz, eds., 245.

Yitzchok Block

Rationality and God

DEBATES ABOUT whether belief in God is rational usually begin *in medias res*, i.e., in the middle. Everybody assumes that it is clear what constitutes rational belief, and the question is simply whether belief in God falls into that category. This is difficult, if not impossible, to determine, for there are as many notions or conceptions about what is rational as there are different ways of going about life and living. That there should be some absolute criterion for rationality is remote. This is much like asking whether there is some absolute standard of beauty by virtue of which various things are called beautiful. What is it by virtue of which a painting, a song or a mathematical equation is called 'beautiful'? There probably is no one criterion. What makes a painting beautiful is not what makes a song or an equation beautiful. To say that they all display harmony is no more enlightening than to say that they all display beauty. The point is that what one means by beauty varies according to the subject.

Similarly, there is no single criterion of rationality. A rational move in a game of chess is something quite different from a rational way

---

YITZCHOK BLOCK earned his M.A. and Ph.D. in Philosophy from Harvard University. For several decades, he has served in London, Canada, as emissary of the Lubavitcher Rebbe and as Professor of Philosophy at the University of Western Ontario. He has written numerous articles on Aristotle and Wittgenstein and has edited a book entitled Perspectives on the Philosophy of Wittgenstein, *published by Blackwell.*

of marketing a product, and both of these differ from a rational way of dealing with a terrorist. There is no single criterion of rationality that will help one play chess, market a product and deal with a terrorist. Each has its own rationale. There are, no doubt, methods or procedures in each of these cases which it is rational to follow, but the procedures are not the same.

When one asks if belief in God is rational, one usually has certain criteria of rationality in mind; but these criteria are taken from fields of study or inquiry that have little to do with God. They are usually taken from mathematics or the empirical sciences. However, God is neither a mathematical theorem nor an empirical hypothesis. It is no wonder then, that belief in God does not satisfy the criteria of rationality of either mathematics or the empirical sciences.*

What many people assume is that the criteria of rationality in these fields of inquiry are the only valid ones, or are at least the most important ones. Thus deductive proof or empirical confirmation are said to be the *sine qua non* of a rational belief. This is like saying that beauty is to be defined in terms of harmonic tones or blending of colors—these are proper for music or painting, but what is the criterion for beauty *per se*, which is not the specific beauty of a particular object or fact? There is none. Similarly, there is no definition of rationality *per se*. There are rational procedures in science and there is a rational way of constructing a deductive argument; but to insist that all forms of knowledge must conform to one of these procedures is not only dictatorial but also counterproductive.

The question of God's existence is not a question that science or mathematics can answer. It is, if you wish, a metaphysical or, even better, a philosophical question; and answers to such questions cannot be decided on the basis of empirical confirmation or deductive proof. There is, however, a sense of rationality that does apply to such questions, and if I am not mistaken it is a sense of rationality that is more basic than the ones employed in either mathematics or science.

One way of expressing this sense of rationality is as follows: of

* However, see Gotfryd, "Proof for the Existence of the Creator," in this volume.

two competing beliefs, all other conditions being equal, it is more *rational* to accept as true that belief which displays greater simplicity and unity. However, if in fact we should observe that the less simple and less unified belief is true, we will throw rationality to the winds and follow our eyes and ears. In that case it would be more rational to *reject* the simpler theory. This is a conception of rationality that is relevant to science and to our ordinary beliefs about the world. No matter how simple or neat a theory may be, it is the empirical observation that settles the issue of truth, and it is irrational to reject evidence on the basis that it does not support the simpler view.

For example, if one has had dreams every night for the past six months about which horse would win the race the next day, and that horse actually wins the race, it would be irrational not to bet on that horse, even though this may go counter to other rational considerations, such as which horse in the field has the best record or which horse is being ridden by the best jockey. These considerations are more rational, but in the face of such evidence as these dreams, one would be justified in ignoring such considerations and acting in accordance with the dreams.

However, beliefs that are not empirical in nature—such as belief in the existence of God—should not be made subject to empirical confirmation, and any attempt to do so is simply a mistake. Belief in God is, I believe, *a priori*, as are other metaphysical or philosophical conceptions. That is, they are views whose truth we accept, independent of empirical confirmation. To qualify for this category, a belief must be one that cannot in principle be confirmed or denied by empirical evidence. I have in mind specifically the kind of belief that provides one with an outlook or viewpoint from which one views the world or events as a whole. Viewing the world as a whole is part of what we mean by being rational. That is, our rational instincts seek a single explanation for all of reality, not just for part of it. This is what we mean by simplicity.

That such an explanation should be a single explanation, and not two or three different ones, is what we mean by unity. It is the rational instinct of the human mind to seek an explanation of the world as a whole, that is single and unified. Our minds balk at the idea that reality, or the world, might be subject to radically different kinds of laws that do not overlap or impinge on one another at any point. What human rationality seeks is a comprehensive view of the world as a whole, with nothing left out. This is what those first scientists and philosophers, the pre-Socratics, sought in their speculations—a single scheme or explanation of the world as a whole. This is the ultimate, rational goal of man, whether it can be realized or not.

Since what I call here a metaphysical view is a view about the nature of reality as a whole, leaving nothing out, it follows that no metaphysical view can be empirically verified or disproved. To do so, one would have to have experience of everything, and know that it was everything, with nothing left out—and there is no way that anyone could know that empirically.

However, not every metaphysical view is a religious one. For instance, many materialists hold a certain metaphysical view which I call metaphysical materialism. This view holds that only material forces exist, i.e., there are no non-material or spiritual forces. The reason this can be called a metaphysical view is that it is a view about the nature of reality as a whole. There can be no empirical verification of this view; it simply represents one way of viewing the world and reality.

This is to be distinguished from another view which may appear similar, but is vastly different. This is a position that I call empirical, or scientific, materialism. It says that as far as scientific or empirical knowledge of the world goes, only material forces exist. This indeed is nothing more than a tautology. It is similar to saying that fishermen catch only fish. They may indeed catch other things, but they don't take the trouble to bring them back to port—they throw them overboard. Fishermen are interested in fish, and scientists are interested in an empirical description of the material world. To achieve this description it is not necessary to indulge in metaphysics. One can keep one's nose in the test tubes and forget about the rest of the world.

Part of the claim of this paper is that to wonder about the nature of reality as a whole is to follow our rational instincts. When we devise an answer to this question, we formulate what I call a

"Other things...they throw overboard."

metaphysical view of the world. Thus the formulation of a metaphysical view is a response to the innate rationality of the human mind. "Nine-to-five" scientists, who refuse to speculate on the nature of reality as a whole, are thwarting a basic rational requirement. As one who goes on a diet, or denies the body its basic needs, will inevitably rectify this need through some form of compensation, so will a man who abjures all metaphysics seek a substitute. This substitute is what I call metaphysical materialism, and what the materialist will simply call materialism. When someone says that he is a materialist and doesn't dabble in metaphysics, what he means by materialism is what I call here metaphysical materialism. Such a materialist is unaware that he is really enunciating another form of metaphysics, even though he may be adamant in his insistence that he does not believe in metaphysics but in hard-nosed science. This is like a man who insists that he is on a diet, but gorges himself when no one is watching—he is only fooling himself.

One who truly rejects metaphysics will have nothing whatever to say about reality as a whole, but will simply insist that as far as human knowledge goes, only material forces *can be known* to exist. What is beyond the ken of human knowledge, God only knows. The basic categories of human understanding, such as space, time and causality, are geared to the material world. But is that all there is to reality? This is the metaphysical question that the natural rational instinct of man wonders about. The materialist can either sweep the question under his scientific rug and get back to work, or he can follow his rational instincts and declare himself a materialist, i.e., one who proclaims that material forces susceptible to scientific investigation constitute the whole of reality. What I would now like to argue is that, of the two competing metaphysical views, theism and materialism, theism is the more consistent, simpler and unified view and therefore the more rational view.*

For explaining the origin of the world, what are the alternatives to God? There are only two. Either the world had no beginning and is eternal, or the world came from nothing—that is, it just popped into existence from absolute nothingness. One cannot say that the world came from some force or power that is not God, for one can then ask what is the explanation of that force or power itself. Thus if one is prone to adopt a Big Bang theory of the origin of the world, one cannot point to some possible previous world or force as the origin of the Big Bang, for one can ask for an explanation of that world or force, and so on *ad infinitum*. The only possible explanation which could satisfy the question, "What is the origin of the world?" is a cause that, by definition, is itself uncaused, i.e., a Being Who is eternal—which is what we mean by God.

Let us rule out the possibility that the world just suddenly popped into existence for no reason whatsoever, because this flies in the face of the Principle of Sufficient Reason, which states that everything has some cause or explanation of why it exists. If the world did come from nothing, then the origin of the world is irrational—it defies the Principle of Sufficient Reason. However, why should one admit this possibility as long as more rational alternatives are available? The alternatives are that the world has no origin and is itself eternal, or that God is the explanation of the world. Which of these two alternatives is it more rational to believe?

The first question to consider is why anything should exist rather than nothing. The existence of nothing requires no explanation. An explanation is required only for things that exist. The fact that there

---

* For further elaboration of this, see "God and Rationality Revisited," *B'Or HaTorah*, vol. 6: 114-116.

is a world, therefore, calls for an explanation of how it came about or what brought it into existence.

Some philosophers have argued that no explanation is required for the world in its totality. The Principle of Sufficient Reason might apply to particular events or objects in the world but not to the world as a whole. The reason they say this is similar to the reason we are not inclined to ask for the explanation of some objects or things in the world. For instance, if you are walking in a forest and see an arrow carved into a tree, you will wonder why that arrow is there, but you will not wonder why the tree is there. It is perfectly normal to find trees in forests, but it is not normal to find arrows carved into them. This is not to deny that there is *some* explanation for the tree being there, but it is not an explanation that anyone would seek out or ask for. It is not something to wonder about, whereas the arrow is. Thus, explanations are required for deviations from a normal pattern, but the normal pattern itself calls for no explanation. In fact there must be some background that is taken for granted before you can wonder about anything. Trees have to be taken for granted before you can wonder about the arrows carved into them.

In a different context, a forester or geologist might wonder why that forest is there, or even why this particular tree is there, but he will have to take other things for granted in his explanation, such as the germination factor of seeds, soil composition and climatic conditions. In a wider context, a biologist or weatherman may be interested in explaining the germination of seeds or the weather, but these explanations require other things we take for granted such as molecular structure, the rotation of the Earth, the angle of the tilt of the Earth's axis from the sun and the distance of the Earth from the sun. It is impossible to explain everything, for then there would be nothing fixed or taken for granted in terms of which everything could be explained. This "everything" is the world (universe) in its entirety. Therefore, it is impossible to give an explanation for the world as a whole, and thus the Principle of Sufficient Reason does not apply to the world. This being the case, it is not possible to ask for an explanation of the world, and one can assume without any qualms that the world is eternal. One then does not need God in order to explain the world, for the world requires no explanation. The existence of the world is what one must assume before one can explain anything in the world.

I think there is a good deal of truth in this. Surely the kind of explanation we are asking for when we wonder why that tree is there or why an arrow is carved in the tree is very different from the kind of explanation we seek when we ask why there is a world at all. To the latter question we don't expect an answer in terms of laws of nature, seeds and climate, nor in terms of desires or wants that any person could understand, for who can understand the mind of God? "My thoughts are not your thoughts, nor your ways My ways, says God" (*Isaiah* 55:8).

Perhaps there is a message relevant to man that one can find in the Torah. God wanted a place to dwell in the world below, or God created man in order that man could come to know God; but why does God need a place in this world and why does God need man to know Him? Indeed why should God require anything other than Himself since He above all else is absolutely self-sufficient and requires nothing?

When one talks about God wanting or needing anything, this is to be taken with a grain of salt. We speak analogically for, as we say, who can understand God? When the biologist or soil scientist explains how seeds germinate or how climate affects the growth of plants and trees, we say, "Now I understand." But there are, no doubt, elements in the explanation that are not really understood.

There are no perfect explanations that explain everything, for the reasons mentioned above. Nonetheless, there is a lot to learn about biology that could take a lifetime to master. However, when one asks why there is a world and in reply is told that God created the world, does one then understand *how* the world was created? Could one study this for any length of time? After one has said that God made the world, is there anything left to add which will enable one to understand it better? It seems not. For these reasons there is something to be said for the arguments of those philosophers who claim that the world neither has nor requires an explanation for its existence, in the sense that one can understand how it came about.

In spite of all this, there is something important that the philosophers have left out of their analysis. This is the simple fact that people *do* wonder where the world came from. The human mind *is* capable of asking such transcendental or ultimate questions, even though there may be no clear answers of the kind we expect for such questions as where that tree came from. The philosopher says that such questions have no answers so it is better not to ask them; but the minds and hearts of men do not always obey the decrees of philosophers. Furthermore, this is not some technical or abstruse question which one could ask only after having studied philosophy for a few years, as are many questions asked in philosophy. It is a question asked by simple folk as well as the most learned, and it is a question that is important to them. It could affect how they live their lives and their whole attitude towards life and the world. They could become different people according to how this question is answered. The existential implications are considerable. This is not the case with many questions in philosophy today which have as much relevance to human life as the proverbial, irrelevant medieval question of how many angels can dance on the head of a pin. The question of how the world came about, and why, is a real question that almost every human being asks, and it will not go away because some philosophers call it "transcendental" and turn thumbs down on it. In other words, though the question may have no answer that we can understand, this will not prevent us from asking it.

It is part of the human condition to wonder about this as well as other transcendental questions. We are arguing here that once one poses this question, the most rational answer is God. The atheist will choose not to ask the question in the first place. This is what he is doing when he says the world itself is eternal, and he will support this with arguments of the kind spelled out above. However, none of these arguments removes wonder about the origin of the world from the minds of the vast majority of people. The atheist must consider himself one of those select few who have succeeded in ridding themselves of the question and thus of any need to supply an answer.

Insofar as one is troubled by this question at all, God is the only reasonable answer.

Many materialists will challenge this claim and argue that what I have called metaphysical materialism is a more rational view to hold than belief in God. I will now present an argument that I think undermines such a view.

If materialism were true, the only way to account for the world would be to declare that the material world itself is eternal and never had an origin. However, the eternalness of the material world is not an empirical property, i.e., it could never be empirically demonstrated that the world as a matter of fact is eternal or is not eternal. On the other hand, the eternalness of the material world is not part of the definition of what we mean by the material world. Thus it seems that the eternalness of the material world is something *ad hoc* that we add to it to give it the appearance of a coherent idea. The fact is that it is not a coherent idea at all, for the eternalness of matter is a property or description that is neither *a priori* nor *a posteriori*. That is, it is a property that is neither an empirical property to be confirmed by evidence, nor is it one which follows from the meaning or definition of the material world. It is simply added to the notion of materiality, in order to account for the origin of the world. There is nothing in the notion of materiality itself that would lead one to expect that matter is eternal. The only case for thinking that matter is eternal is if there is no other explanation for it. But there is no other explanation only if one rejects God.

The very idea of God is that of an infinite, eternal Being which is the ultimate unity of all things. It is not that eternalness is added to God in order to account for the world. Eternalness is part of the meaning of God. If God were not eternal He would not be God. One cannot say this about matter. If matter were not eternal it would still be matter.

This conception is close to the formulation of God as the most perfect Being, or as a Being greater than whom it is impossible to conceive—an idea with which we are familiar from the ontological argument for God. Although I am not defending this particular argument here, it nonetheless serves to clarify what is meant by God in monotheism. When this is clarified, it is evident that eternalness and oneness or unity are part of the essence, or very meaning, of the term God. The monotheistic idea of God thus fulfills the demands of our rational faculty in seeking a metaphysical view of the world in its totality, with nothing left out. Reason demands that the essence of reality be a unity that never came into being and will never cease to be. This is what is meant by saying that God is the simplest "explanation" of the world.

This demand of reason is not proof of the existence of such a Being because it does not follow from the rationality of a belief, that it is true. There is no contradiction in the idea of the world popping into existence from absolute nothing, nor in the eternalness of the material world itself; but neither of these alternatives to God satisfies the natural, rational pursuit of unity and simplicity. Both of these views are "hard pills" for the rational mind to swallow, though swallow them we would if they turned out to be true. The problem is that if either of these alternatives were true, there could be no evidence, observations or science that could prove them true. This is because these alternatives to God are themselves metaphysical theories and as such cannot be confirmed or denied by empirical evidence. The only thing one has to go on in judging competing metaphysical views is the appeal to rationality; and on this level it seems to me that God wins, "hands down."

Note that in this discussion we have said little about Creation, and indeed this argument for God, that I call the Argument from Unity, implies nothing about Creation. All that is required for the being and existence of the world is the existence of God. God's Creation of the world is another matter.

This, I believe, is consistent with Maimonides' discussion of God, both in the *Guide for the Perplexed* and the *Code*. The first few paragraphs of the *Code*, which outline the dependency of the world on God, say nothing about, nor do they require, God's Creation of the world. God's Creation of the world is a miracle that defies human comprehension and there can be no proof for this. Indeed Maimonides does bring arguments in the *Guide* to support Creation, but these arguments never amount to a proof in Maimonides' view. Ultimately one must appeal to revealed Scripture as a "proof" for Creation.

I personally think that there are strong arguments that support Creation; but this is a topic for a different paper. As far as this paper is concerned, we repeat that God is the simplest explanation of the world, and thus satisfies the rational instincts of the human mind more adequately than any other metaphysical alternative.

"One would like to know more about the Jewish gene pool."

Cyril Domb

Jewish Distinction in Science

AS A THEORETICAL physicist who has traveled extensively to international conferences all over the world, I have noted with surprise that an unusually large percentage of participants—usually 25 to 30 percent, but sometimes even 50 percent—were of Jewish origin. Most of them were not practicing Jews, but if one went back one or two generations, one would find that the parents or grandparents were active members of the Jewish community. When one considers that Jews constitute perhaps 2 percent of the population of advanced Western societies, these figures are amazing.

Even more extraordinary are the statistics of winners of the Nobel prize in physics, chemistry and medicine, an honor which represents the highest level of scientific achievement in contemporary society. *The Jewish Chronicle Year Book* lists Jewish Nobel prize winners, and

---

CYRIL DOMB is currently Professor of Physics at Bar-Ilan University and Academic President of the Jerusalem College of Technology. Before settling in Israel in 1981, he served for many years as Maxwell Professor of Theoretical Physics at King's College, London. Previously he had held Faculty Appointments at Oxford and Cambridge Universities. He is a Fellow of the Royal Society and a past President of the British Association of Orthodox Jewish Scientists.

His Torah publications include the classic compendium, Challenge: Torah Views on Science and Its Problems, *which he edited with Aryeh Carmell, and* Maaser Kesafim: Giving a Tenth to Charity.

although the lists are not completely accurate, they provide a reasonable first approximation. They suggest that about 20 percent of Nobel prize winners have been Jewish.

A few years ago Stanislaw Ulam, a Polish Jewish mathematician who had emigrated to the United States, published an autobiography entitled *Adventures of a Mathematician.* He had spent many years in Los Alamos working on the atomic- and hydrogen-bomb projects, and his recollections of the dramatic controversy surrounding the hydrogen bomb were particularly fascinating. Again, many of the leading characters in this adventure were Jewish: Oppenheimer, Teller, von Neumann, Bethe, Ulam, Feynman, Frisch, Weisskopf.

I understand from Moshe Gitterman that the situation in Russia is very similar. For example, among top-level scientists the following full members of the Soviet Academy of Sciences are (or were) Jewish: Landau, Ginzburg, two Lifshitz brothers, Zeldovitch, Pomeranchuk and Migdal. Gitterman regularly attended the Moscow seminars of the Kapitza Institute of Physical Problems, and the Physics Institute of the Soviet Academy of Sciences. Perhaps 100-200 people would attend from all over Russia, and the percentage of Jewish participants was so high that he sometimes felt as if he were in a synagogue.

The world of physics has been very excited recently at the prospect of a grand, unified superstring theory which might be able to account for all the forces in nature, including gravitation. In a recent lecture on this topic, Prof. Yuval Ne'eman drew attention to the substantial percentage of Jewish contributors to this development.

The above facts are sufficiently striking to merit an explanation. Some people have suggested that, because of prejudice and discrimination, Jews have always tried harder to succeed. Such a theory might account for progress in the business world, where zeal and industry alone can produce exceptional results. It cannot explain, however, the achievement of Nobel prizes, which requires a special type of ability, in addition to energy and enthusiasm.

Previous Discussion

The first person to comment in public on the above facts was the distinguished writer, C.P. (Lord) Snow. In a lecture delivered in New York on March 31st, 1969, upon being awarded an honorary degree by a Jewish institution, Snow pointed out that genetic inheritance is far more important than environment or good fortune in establishing a man's ability to achieve. In regard to the Jewish people he continued as follows:

> Take any test of achievement you like—in any branch of science, mathematics, literature, music, public life. The Jewish performance has been not only disproportionate, but almost ridiculously disproportionate. The record is remarkable, and quite outside any sort of statistical probabilities.
>
> This isn't arguable. The facts are plain. But why is it? One answer is, of course, that the Jewish environment makes for the utmost use of talent. Apart from the Jewish respect for education, the very obvious truth that a Jewish person starts with two strikes against him means that he will struggle when others don't. In that case, in countries like the United States and the United Kingdom, where the environment is presumably less oppressive than at any time since the Babylonian captivity—or perhaps short interludes in Moorish Spain—one would expect this explosion of talent in due course to lose its force.
>
> What will happen? Or is there something in the Jewish gene pool which produces talent on quite a different scale from, say, the Anglo-Saxon gene pool? I am prepared to believe that that may be so. One would like to know more about the Jewish gene pool.

There was a considerable negative reaction to this lecture in some circles. Edward Short, the British minister of education, said that it was reminiscent of Dr. Goebbels. Among the strongest critics were Anglo-Jews, who may have been motivated (perhaps subconsciously) by the fear of anti-Semitism. Arthur Jensen, a psychologist at the University of California, had previously claimed that Negro children inherit lower intelligence levels than white children, and the subject therefore had political and racial overtones. Now, perhaps, we can look at the matter with greater detachment. The idea that a specific group has a particular talent for some human activity—athletics, music, mathematics, etc.—has no moral implications and can be subjected to experimental test. It is vital to emphasize that having a particular talent does not convey any moral superiority.

A historical example will help to illustrate this point. One of the most distinguished families in the history of mathematics and science was the Bernoulli family of Switzerland, which, from the late seventeenth century until the mid-nineteenth century, produced an unusual number of capable mathematicians and scientists.[1] This represents persuasive circumstantial evidence of hereditary mathematical talent; at the same time, Johann Bernoulli, one of the most distinguished members of the family, was known as a jealous and cantankerous man.

Douglas Villiers edited an interesting book[2] devoted to an account of Jewish achievements in various fields. The chapter on twentieth-century physics was written by Sir Rudolf Peierls, who presented brief biographical sketches and summarized the contributions to science of a number of Jewish physicists: Albert Einstein, Niels Bohr (whose mother was Jewish), Robert Oppenheimer and Lev Landau; he also mentioned the experimentalists Heinrich Hertz, James Franck and Otto Stern. These were examples of the surprisingly large number of Jews among the leading physicists. He then sought reasons for this preeminence:

> What could be the reasons for the prominence of Jews in science, and in particular in physics? The suggestion has been made that the intricate arguments of modern physics have some resemblance to Talmudic studies, and that people who grow up in an environment in which such studies are traditional find this mode of thought natural. However, quite apart from the question of how real or deep is such a resemblance, one notices that a large proportion of twentieth-century Jewish physicists came from families in which religious customs have not been observed for generations. Perhaps this attitude was bred by a kind of natural selection, since it was for many generations a cause of pride for a family if a daughter married a learned scholar. One could judge this hypothesis better if more were known about the genetic character of intellectual traits. It sounds just possible, but a little farfetched.

In the forthcoming sections of this article we will endeavor to explain the disproportionate Jewish contribution to science by:

(1) Assuming as valid Snow's reasonable assumption that ability for the kind of abstract thinking involved in science has a hereditary association.

(2) Bringing evidence from halachic discussion in the Talmud that ability in abstract thinking was widespread among Jewish scholars nearly 2000 years ago, so that a gene pool was already in existence then.

(3) Demonstrating that the common tendency to eugenic practice which has been adopted by many traditional Jewish families throughout the ages has served to enhance this gene pool significantly.

(4) Reasoning that the common practice of selecting a marriage partner based on familial scholarship would naturally preserve and enhance any hereditary tendency to outstanding intellectual achievement.

Halachic Discussion in the Talmud

Rabbi J.B. Soloveitchik, in a remarkable article[3] in Hebrew entitled "Ish haHalachah," published in 1944 and translated only recently into English under the title "Halachic Man,"[4] draws attention to a close analogy between the corpus of *Halachah* and mathematics or theoretical physics. *Halachah* creates an idealized logical framework. Some of its concepts may be far removed from practical reality. Its application to the real world is very similar to the application of pure mathematical geometry to practical engineering problems. The following quotation illustrates the thesis:

> All halachic concepts are *a priori*, and it is through them that halachic man looks at the world. As we said above, his world view is similar to that of the mathematician, *a priori* and ideal. Both the mathematician and the halachist gaze at the concrete world from an *a priori*, ideal standpoint, and use *a priori* categories and concepts which determine from the outset their relationship to the qualitative phenomena they encounter. Both examine empirical reality from the vantage point of an ideal reality. There is one question which they raise: Does this real phenomenon correspond to their ideal construction?

> And when many halachic concepts do not correspond with the phenomena of the real world, halachic man is not at all distressed. His deepest desire is not the realization of the *Halachah* but rather the ideal construction which was given to him from Sinai, and this ideal construction exists forever. "There never was an idolatrous city and never will be. For what purpose, then, was its law written? Expound it and receive a reward! There never was a leprous house and never will be. For what purpose, then, was its law written? Expound it and receive a reward! There never was a rebellious son and never will be. For what purpose, then, was his law written? Expound it and receive a reward!"[5] Halachic man is not at all grieved by the fact that many ideal constructions have never been and will never be actualized. What difference does it make whether the idolatrous city, the leprous house, and the rebellious son existed or didn't exist in the past, will exist or won't exist in the future? The foundation of foundations and the pillar of halachic thought is not the practical ruling but the determination of the theoretical *Halachah*.

Later on Rabbi Soloveitchik pursues in more detail the analogy between *Halachah* and mathematics and modern physics:

> Halachic man's ideal is to subject reality to the yoke of the *Halachah*. However, as long as this desire cannot be implemented, halachic man does not despair, nor does he reflect at all concerning the clash of the real and the ideal, the opposition which exists between the theoretical *Halachah* and the actual deed, between law and life. He goes his own way and does not kick against his lot and fate.
>
> Such is also the way of the mathematician! When Riemann and Lobachevski discovered the possibility of a non-Euclidean space, they did not pay any attention to the existential space in which we all live and which we encounter with all our senses, which is Euclidean from beginning to end. They were concerned with an ideal mathematical construction, and in that ideal world they discovered certain features of a geometric space different from ours. Afterward, physicists such as Einstein and his circle appeared, and they utilized the concept of a non-Euclidean space in order to explain

> certain physical phenomena. The ideal-geometric space then found its actualization in the real world.*

The rest of this section is devoted to illustrating generally how some legal and philosophical arguments in the Gemara closely resemble (*l'havdil*) the type of intellectual abstraction involved in rigorous scientific and mathematical thought.

Anyone who has studied the Gemara *Sukkah* is familiar with concepts related to sophisticated geometrical constructions. When a wall of the *sukkah* does not reach the ground, it can in certain circumstances be conceptually stretched down (*gud achit*), and when the wall does not reach the ceiling it can in certain circumstances be conceptually stretched up (*gud asik*). If the correct *sukkah* covering does not reach the wall and part of the incorrect covering intervenes, it can, in certain circumstances, be treated as a "bent wall" (*dofen akumah*). If the correct covering has been put on an exadra (an open space surrounded by a railing), the edge of the roof can be conceptually extended vertically to the ground (*pi tikrah yored v'sotem*).

In projective geometry it is an important hypothesis that any two lines in a plane meet at a point. But in real Euclidean space, two lines may be parallel and never meet. By extending the lines indefinitely and introducing a *point at infinity*, the hypothesis is used for practical problems. Again, one of the most fruitful concepts introduced by Michael Faraday in his description of electromagnetism was that of lines of force. For the electric field lines of force start and end on electric charges, while magnetic lines of force form closed loops around electric currents. Lines of force have no real existence, and are conceptual geometric constructions; but they led Clerk Maxwell to the theory of the electromagnetic field, one of the greatest discoveries in the history of science.

Similarly there are abstract concepts associated with the practical laws of Shabbat. The term *melechet machshevet*—a significant act—enunciates generally what is forbidden, and several of the theoretical discussions are introduced to define precisely what is, and what is not, significant. The Gemara lists 39 categories of ac-

---

* Compare the articles by Saks and Hasofer in this volume.

tivity, the performance of each of which constitutes a major infringement of the Shabbat. For each category there is a minimum performance below which the act is classified as not significant. Writing is one of the categories for which the minimum is two letters which must be written in a manner in which they can be put together. Thus, if the letters are written on two separate walls, there is no liability. But if they are written on moveable boards, even if they are miles apart, they do have the *potential* to be put together even if they are *actually* apart, and the act is considered significant.

Mathematics and physics are full of problems in which the *actual* value of a correction parameter is small, but the *potential* influence on the character of the solution is extremely large.

Carrying from a private to a public domain (or vice versa) is the last of the 39 categories. The minimum quantity to be carried, which will be considered significant, depends on the purpose of the act of carrying. If grain is carried for sowing, a minimal amount suffices, but if it is required for eating, the minimum amount is an olive's bulk (*kazayit*). There are two essential conditions for an act of carrying to be complete: picking up in the first domain, and putting down in the second. Suppose one picked it up with the aim of sowing and changed his mind en route? A more theoretical question considered in the Gemara is the case in which an object started below the minimum size and expanded en route. It would obviously be extremely difficult to undertake a precise measurement to determine whether this had happened, and in the time of the Talmud, equipment was not even available to measure an olive's bulk to high accuracy. But this does not prevent theoretical study.

Newtonian mechanics makes considerable use of theoretical abstractions unattainable in practice, e.g., media which offer no resistance to motion, strings which have no weight, surfaces which have no friction. Mechanical problems which occur in nature are too complex to solve. By using abstract theoretical concepts, simple and beautiful laws can be formulated, and problems relating to them can be solved. The adaptation of those solutions to problems in the real world is a separate issue.

The Gemara in *Menachot* 37a quotes a very academic question put by Phelimo to his teacher, Rabbi Yehudah *ha-Nasi* (Rabbi): If a man has two heads, on which of them does he put *tefillin*? Rabbi had no patience with him, and wanted to suspend him from the *beit ha-midrash*. At that moment, a man arrived with the message that his wife had given birth to a firstborn with two heads, and he wished to know whether he was obliged to pay the *kohen* one or two redemption fees.

There are many instances in physics of problems which were formulated and solved with no practical application in mind, e.g., because they used models of molecules which were considered not to correspond to reality, or because they related to 4-dimensional space in a 3-dimensional world. But new problems arose later, for which they unexpectedly provided a valid representation.

There are, of course, Talmudic discussions directly related to mathematics. The organization of the lunar Jewish calendar and its adjustment to the solar calendar by suitable intercalations of months involve some detailed knowledge of mathematics and astronomy. In the earlier Talmudic period the adjustment was made by practical observation, although it is fairly clear from the discussion in the Gemara *Rosh Hashanah* that Rabban Gamliel was closely familiar with the lunar orbit. When the calendar was finally fixed by the *amora*, Hillel, the plan he devised was so accurate and comprehensive that no changes were needed in the subsequent 1500 years.

Rabbi Nahum Rabinovitch[6] has drawn attention to a number of problems in Talmudic and Rabbinic literature in which reasoning of the theory of probability enters. Permutations and combinations arise in relation to problems connected with firstborns. There are laws in the Torah relating to firstborn children, firstborn animals, and firstborn donkeys (which must be redeemed by lambs). But quite complicated situations can arise when a number of births have taken place and the order is unknown; for example, if a primiparous ass bore a male and a female and it is not known which was first, or if two she-asses, one primipara and one not, bore a male and a female and it is not known which belongs to which.

The classic Talmudic location for permutations and combinations is the Mishnah tractate *Kinnim* whose subject is the laws pertaining to sacrificial birds. Very complex problems arise when the priest confuses the birds of different offerings. The statement of

Rabbi Elazar Hisma in *Avot* 3:23 indicates that these problems, together with those arising from sorting out the *niddah* and *zavah* aspects in the purification of women, were complex but important.

Finally, attention should be drawn to the logical structure of *sugyot*, i.e., in-depth discussion of themes, in the Talmud. This can be illustrated by reference to the first *sugyah* which youngsters encounter when they begin to study Gemara, *Yiush Shelo Mi-da'at* in *Bava Metzia* (21b-22b). A Jew is obligated by the Torah to restore lost property to its owner. But this obligation applies only when the one who lost it has not given up on finding it. *Yiush* denotes the mental process by which such a relinquishment takes place. What if a person is unaware of his loss? Suppose he has lost something of which we can be sure that, if he becomes aware of his loss, he will relinquish ownership (e.g., if it has no identifying features). But if he does not yet know of his loss, shall we say that *Yiush* (and therefore "finders keepers") applies or does not apply? Two leading *amoraim*, Abaye and Rava, take opposite points of view: Abaye maintains that it does not apply, and Rava says that it does.

The Gemara quotes a number of different established *halachot* to try to decide between the two views. The cases quoted include various kinds of lost property which may be retained: gleaning during harvest-time by the poor, stolen property, property picked up by flood waters and deposited elsewhere, the separation of *terumah* (priestly agricultural gifts), and the preparatory process by which agricultural products can become unclean (*tamei*). The abstract question uniting all of these diverse cases is whether a thought which we know is going to occur in the future can be considered to be operating already in the present. Each case requires a logical analysis, and the challenge to one or the other view is refuted. Eventually the view of Abaye prevails.

These examples could readily be multiplied a hundredfold. They illustrate the degree of sophistication which logical argument and analysis had reached in the Talmudic era.

Eugenics in Torah Society

For several millennia, it has been common Jewish practice to select a spouse with attention to the in-laws' stature in Torah scholarship and refinement of character.

In the Book of *Shemot* (6:23) we are told that Aaron the High Priest took as his wife Elisheva, daughter of Aminadav, *sister of Nachshon* (the prince of the royal tribe of Yehudah). Our Sages take this as an example to emulate—a person who contemplates marrying a woman should examine her brothers.[7] A number of Talmudic rabbis were married to sisters of their colleagues: Rabbi Eliezer was married to the sister of Rabban Gamliel; Resh Lakish was married to the sister of Rabbi Yohanan.

Another important Talmudic maxim for anyone contemplating marriage is the following:[8] "A man should sell everything in his possession in order to marry the daughter of a scholar (*talmid chacham*)." It was common practice for the best student to marry the daughter of his teacher. Rabbi Hisda had two distinguished disciples, Rami bar Hama and Rava.[9] When his daughter was young he asked her jokingly, "Which of the two would you like to marry?" "Both," came the reply. "Then I would like to be the second," responded Rava quickly. This is exactly what happened.

Rabbi Yohanan tried hard to persuade his disciple Zeiri to marry his daughter.[10] But Zeiri, who came from Babylon and considered himself of distinguished birth, was doubtful about the family pedigree (*yichus*) of those living in *Eretz Yisrael*. Rabbi Yohanan commented wryly, "My Torah teaching is good enough for him, but not my daughter."

These practices seem to have continued in centers of Torah scholarship after the close of the Talmudic era and unto the present day. Two daughters of the great medieval commentator Rashi were married to his leading disciples, R. Meir ben Shmuel, and R. Yehudah ben Natan; their talented children were leaders of the school of Tosafists. R. David Halevi (author of the *Taz* commentary on the *Shulchan Aruch*) was married to the daughter of R. Yoel Sirkis (author of the *Bach* commentary on the *Tur*). R. Moshe Sofer (author of *Chatam Sofer*) was married to the daughter of the outstanding Talmudic scholar R. Akiva Eger.

The most detailed information available, which indicates how widespread the practice is, relates to the present-day yeshiva world. The granddaughter of the *Natziv* (R. Naftali Zvi Yehudah Berlin), the famous *Rosh Yeshiva* of Volozhin, was married to the son, Haim, of his colleague, R. Yoshe Ber Soloveitchik. R. Haim Soloveitchik (better known as R. Haim of Brisk) is regarded as the most original thinker in the last few generations of the Lithuanian yeshivot. He established a Soloveitchik dynasty which could be compared to the Bernoulli family in mathematics. Among the famous descendants were his sons, R. Velvel and R. Moshe, his grandson Rabbi J.B. Soloveitchik of New York, and many other learned *Rashei Yeshiva* following the "Brisker" path. R. Aharon Kotler, founder of Lakewood Yeshiva in the United States, was the son-in-law of R. Issar Zalman Meltzer, head of the Yeshiva Etz Haim in Jerusalem. R. Avraham Yitzhak Kook was married to the daughter of the *Aderet*, R. Eliyahu David Rabinowitz-Tumim, former *Rav* of Jerusalem. R. Yitzhak Herzog was the son-in-law of R. Shmuel Hillman, *Rosh Beth Din* of London.

R. Ya'akov Kanyevsky, the Steipler, was married to the sister of the *Chazon Ish*. In the Mir Yeshiva, R. Haim Shmulevitz was married to the daughter of R. Eliezer Yehudah Finkel, and took over from him the running of the yeshiva. Two outstanding contemporary Talmud scholars, R. Haim Kreiswirth and R. Shlomo Wolbe, married the daughters of the *mashgiach* of the Slobodka Yeshiva. R. Mordechai Gifter, the present *Rosh Yeshiva* of Telz, married the daughter of the previous *Rosh Yeshiva*. The present Lubavitcher Rebbe married the daughter of the previous Lubavitcher Rebbe. All of the abovementioned personalities are from the top rank of Talmudic scholars of their generation.

If, as we have tried to indicate, special genes were present among the scholars of the Talmudic era, there could have been no better way of preserving and enhancing them than by the above eugenic pattern of marriage. To support this claim, one should consider the two alternative genetic mechanisms for inheritance of ability in abstract thinking: (1) If the ability is associated with one or more genes on one chromosome, then one would have to assume a marginally greater reproductive success for the great minds, in order to build up over generations the observed high frequency of great Jewish intellectuals. Although this is a reasonable and defensible assumption, it is impossible to prove. (2) But if, as biologists believe, intellect is transmitted through the combined contributions of many genes on several different chromosomes, then it is clear that selective mating practices would certainly lead to disproportionately high numbers of Jewish intellectuals, even without the assumption of more babies to the bright.[11]

There are two additional features of the Talmudic era to which attention should be drawn. Many Gentiles of high ability, who were contemporaries of the Talmudic rabbis, were attracted to Judaism and became proselytes. In the Mishnaic period we can mention the proselytes Onkelos and Akilus, as well as the descendants of proselytes, Shemayah and Avtalyon, R. Akiva, and R. Meir, who reached the highest rank of Talmudic society. This added an external positive contribution to the gene pool.

The social outlook of Torah society, which reveres scholarship no matter how humble its origin, gives opportunity for those with intellectual ability to rise to the rank of leadership. "Take particular care of the children of the poor: from them Torah will go forth.[12]

Elitism in a Torah Society

From the last remark the conclusion can reasonably be drawn that Torah society is elitist, in the sense that every opportunity is given to people with a special intellectual gift to develop and make use of their gift. But at the same time, gifted people are continually reminded of their special responsibilities, that more is expected of them, and that their moral standards must measure up to their intellectual standards. In the words of *Pirkei Avot* 3:11, "Anyone whose fear of sin precedes his wisdom (i.e., his moral conduct is more significant than his learning), his wisdom will endure; anyone whose wisdom precedes his fear of sin, his wisdom will not endure."

People who are not gifted are in no way inferior, and if they require extra effort to achieve a particular degree of Torah knowledge, they will be given special reward for their efforts—"the reward is given according to the effort" (*Avot* 5:26).

A story in *Bava Kama* 117a gives some insight into the encouragement given to scholars of ability. R. Kahana, a brilliant disciple of Rav, went from Babylon to *Eretz Yisrael* to join the school of R. Yohanan. Rav made him promise not to intervene in any of the lectures of R. Yohanan for seven years (since he did not wish R.

Yohanan to be embarrassed). When R. Kahana arrived he was given a seat in the front row. But every time he failed to participate in the discussions he was moved back, until he had moved back seven rows (from this we learn of the custom to move forward pupils who did well, and vice versa). R. Kahana prayed silently that the seven rows which he had moved back should be considered as equivalent to seven years, and he then began to exercise his talents. He pointed out difficulties in R. Yohanan's arguments and was gradually moved forward until he reached the front row. R. Yohanan, who sat on seven cushions, removed one cushion each time a difficulty was pointed out to him, until all the cushions had been removed and he was left sitting humbly on the ground!

But as a counter to this story, we read in *Eruvin* 54b of R. Preida having a slow disciple with whom he needed to study a *halachah* 400 times before his pupil could master it properly. One day R. Preida was called to perform a *mitzvah*, but before he left he noticed that his pupil was even slower than usual, and had failed to master the material even after 400 times. When he asked why, he was told that the pupil could not concentrate, since he expected that at any moment his teacher would have to go away. After setting the pupil's mind at rest, he went over the *halachah* with him another 400 times.

Many other examples could be given from Talmudic and post-Talmudic Torah scholars to illustrate these points. In *Pesachim* 66a we are told that the children of Beteira stepped down from the privileged position of *Nasi* (president) in favor of Hillel when they found that his knowledge was greater than theirs. R. Meir was one of the most brilliant of the *tannaim*. He had an amazing memory, and it is related (*Megillah* 18b) that when he visited a Jewish settlement where there was no *megillah*, he wrote one out from memory. In addition to his exhaustive knowledge of Torah, he was well-versed in matters of general scholarship. But at the same time he was scrupulously careful not to cause public embarrassment to anyone. When a woman came to complain that one of his students had betrothed her by means of sexual relations, R. Meir wrote her a *get* himself, and all his disciples followed suit (*Sanhedrin* 11a). When a woman who regularly attended his lectures arrived home late once, to the annoyance of her husband, the latter threatened to divorce her unless she spat in R. Meir's eye.

When R. Meir heard of this, he immediately told her that he had an eye infection which he had been told could only be cured if a woman spat in his eye seven times. She was able to go home and tell her husband that she had done much more than he asked.

This is the pattern of Torah elitism. In our own times there have been similar examples of brilliant feats of memory. When the Mir Yeshiva was in Shanghai during the war years, the only available copy of the *Ketzot Ha-Choshen*, a *sefer* widely used in yeshiva studies, had several pages missing. The *Rosh Yeshiva*, R. Haim Shmulevitz, reconstructed them from memory. Likewise, the Chibiner *Rav*, R. Dov Berish Weidenfeld, when in exile in Siberia, gave many halachic responsa quoting sources from memory, since he had no books at his disposal. But the above two personalities became famous for their great moral attributes as well as for their brilliant minds.

In comparing the brilliant Torah scholars mentioned in the past two sections with their scientific counterparts of the first section, we can accept the hypothesis that the genes which gave rise to top-class intellectual ability have a common source. But those who remained in the Torah fold added a top-class moral commitment to their intellectual excellence. This is not inherited but acquired.

* * *

Acknowledgment

The author is grateful to Prof. Yuval Ne'eman for drawing his attention to Lord Snow's lecture, and to Mr. Joseph Finkelstone of the *Jewish Chronicle*, London, for supplying detailed information from his files on the content of the lecture. He is also grateful to Rabbi Aryeh Carmell for helpful suggestions which have been incorporated into the text, and to Mr. Menachem Goldberger for information relating to section 4.*

---

* After this manuscript had been completed, Professor Joe Gillis, a mathematician at the Weizmann Institute, informed the author that he had learned from a contemporary member of the Bernoulli family that the original family name had been Abarbanel. This indicates that they were descended from the distinguished fifteenth-century Jewish scholar and statesman of that name.

NOTES

1. See Howard Eves, *An Introduction to the History of Mathematics*, Fifth Edition (New York: Saunders College Publishing, 1983), 321.
2. *Next Year in Jerusalem* (London: Douglas Villiers Publishing, 1975), 295.
3. J. B. Soloveitchik, "Ish haHalachah," *Talpiot* 1 (1944):651-735.
4. J. B. Soloveitchik, "Halachic Man," translated by Lawrence Kaplan (Jewish Publication Society, 1983).
5. *Sanhedrin* 71a.
6. Nahum Rabinovitch, *Probability and Statistical Inference in Ancient and Medieval Jewish Literature* (Toronto: University of Toronto Press, 1973).
7. *Bava Batra* 110a.
8. *Pesachim* 49b.
9. *Bava Batra* 12b.
10. *Kiddushin* 71b.
11. D. S. Falconer, *Introduction to Quantitative Genetics*, Second Edition (Longman House, 1981).
12. *Nedarim* 81a.

Arnie Gotfryd

Beyond Description: The Boundary between Science and Religion

DURING AN AUTUMN stroll, a mother and her school-aged daughter were admiring the beautiful array of colored leaves. They were discussing what lay behind this quietly spectacular transformation.

"Mom, why do the leaves change color?"

"Well, dear, in the spring and summer, the leaves make food for the tree. Inside each leaf, there are millions of tiny green molecules called chlorophyll. The chlorophyll makes the food by collecting light from the sun, carbon dioxide from the air, and water from the ground. Then it puts them all together to make sugar and starch. In the autumn, the tree stops making food because it doesn't need any in the winter. When that happens, the chlorophyll breaks down, and with it goes the green color. By that time, other molecules in the leaf become more obvious and they give off the red, orange and yellow colors that we see today."

"That's not what Grandma says," commented the little girl.

"No? What does she say?"

"She says God paints them… one at a time."[1]

A biographical note on the author appears on page 1, with his article "Proof for the Existence of the Creator."

Whom should the child believe? Mom? Grandma? Both? Neither?

Grandma's Right, But...

Those who side with Grandma are to be admired for their piety. Still, it is unfair to totally reject Mother out of hand. Is it not possible that the scientific explanation has some truth and some value? If so, it is unwise to reject it out of ignorance. It would amount to saying, "Religion, I know and like; but science, I don't really understand. Therefore religion is better."

Sometimes people reject a scientific explanation because it seems to conflict with the religious view. True, there is nothing wrong with accepting one view over another, but on what basis? Can one rule out an explanation based on direct observations and plain logic? After all, one trusts observations and sound reasoning in other areas of life; why not here? Faith is fine, but there is a problem with "blind faith" that ignores the observed facts and rational deductions of science.

Mother Knows Best, But...

Those who side with Mother are to be praised for their sophistication. Still there may be more to Grandma than meets the eye. One should at least know whether religion provides insights into the natural world, before rejecting it. It is unfair to say, "Science, I know and like; religion, I don't really care to understand. Therefore science is better."

Rejecting religion out of ignorance is no better than rejecting science out of ignorance. To illustrate from a true story, a rabbi and a scientist once wound up seated together on a transcontinental flight out of Los Angeles.

"You must be a rabbi," opened the scientist.

"Yes, I am," confirmed his neighbor.

"I know all about Judaism,"quipped the scientist.

"Do you really?" the rabbi responded, a little piqued.

"Sure: Do unto others as you would have them do unto you."

"I see. And what, may I ask, is your occupation?"

"I am an astrophysicist."

"Oh, really?" The rabbi paused a moment, then countered, "I know all about astronomy."

"Come now, rabbi. What do you know about astronomy?"

"Tvinkle, tvinkle, little stah."

Some would reject the religious view in the leaf color debate because they imagine God to have human dimensions and features. They envision Him as an invisible, bearded baritone holding a nylon paintbrush, a tin of latex paint and a stopwatch to make sure all those leaves get done on time. Of course they reject the religious explanation of natural events as a childish fantasy. On those terms, who wouldn't?

But what if "He" is an Absolutely Infinite Being using the brush of photoperiodically-induced cellular physiology dipped into pigments like chlorophyll and carotene? Surely if the Creator is capable of making something from nothing, He can also regulate existing chemicals and processes.

"Surely if the Creator is capable of making something from nothing, He can also regulate existing chemicals and processes."

No Need to Fight—They're Both Right

By now you may well have guessed where I stand on whether the child should believe Mother or Grandma. She should believe them both. Neither science nor religion is as stiff and boxed-in as many people think. Science has room for the Creator, and religion has room for science. Individual scientists or theologians, or even whole sects of them, may be too biased or uninformed to recognize this, but authentic science and authentic religion are quite compatible and even complementary.[2]

The Boundary of Science

It is important to articulate precisely the basic difference between scientific and religious explanations of events. Followers of either system accept the validity of our sensory experiences.* So too will they agree pretty much on what they observe in terms of temperature, weight, volume, brightness, duration, etc. They should also agree on the validity of sound, logical proofs and deductions. Where they differ is in the questions they answer.

Essentially science is concerned with *how* the world works, while religion addresses *why*.[3] This distinction will become clear through (1) a brief review of the scientific method as it has been practiced for the last few centuries and up to the present day, and (2) an analysis of the modern scientific view on why leaves change color.

The Scientific Method

This section is an informal description of how scientists work and how they derive knowledge. It is based on my own experiences, those of my colleagues, and published scientific literature. When a scientist wants to understand any system, the first step is always to observe. What are the system's physical properties and what is it doing? This step is purely descriptive and is based on sensory information: sight, sound, etc. The recorded perceptions are called data.

Science today has extended its perception by using sophisticated equipment. In the optic sphere, we can now "see" down to nanometers and up to zillions of kilometers. Even the light spectrum itself has been broadened to infrared, ultraviolet, and beyond. Similar re-

---

* Although both camps accept sensory experience as a necessary and integral aspect of daily life, both science and religion also recognize that the senses are subjectively biased and even fickle. Therefore the senses cannot yield a "bottom line" definition of reality.

finements have occurred for our perception of mass, distance, and time. With the aid of particle accelerators, nuclear clocks and electron microscopes, we can detect the orderly behavior of thousands of minuscule events that happen within the blink of an eye.

Although these advances help us see more things more precisely, we are still merely recording data which describe nature. The scientist's goal, however, is not just to describe, but also to discover *why* the system is like that. Finding the cause is detective work. The data are put in numerical form in order to discover how changes in one part are correlated with changes in another. For example, blood pressure increases with cholesterol levels, and the likelihood of getting AIDS increases with homosexual activity. Red herrings and other confounding factors are removed from the data by the use of analytical tools like multivariate statistics, matrix algebra, and computer algorithms. In this way, hidden patterns are revealed among diverse parts of a system. But these patterns are still correlations, and the scientist at this stage has not yet found out what *causes* the observed patterns.

To answer this, the researcher then sits back and reflects on the system under study and reviews other people's thoughts over the years until he comes up with some explanation of why the system works in the way that it does.

Now, in order to determine whether he is right or wrong, he tests the truth of his ideas by experimenting or making more observations on a new system. But before he makes these new measurements, he must make a prediction based on his theory. If his prediction is correct, his theory is supported. If not, his theory is proven wrong and he is back to figuring out a cause.[4]

This is the scientific method and as a result of its application, our understanding of the universe has increased enormously over the course of a mere few hundred years.

It is important to note that an explanatory theory is always tentative and never certain, because new observations can always be made which will disprove the theory. This happens all the time in science. For example, we used to think that matter and energy were essentially different; but since Einstein we have seen the fusion of these concepts. Similarly, relativity is not the last word on matter and energy either. Besides these changes in scientific opinion over time, there is also much conflict among contemporary experts at any given time, and especially in our day.

This inability of science to clearly determine cause is built into the scientific method, and thus applies equally to the entire spectrum of scientific inquiry.

Even where our mental models gain consensus and withstand the test of time to become accepted "natural laws," these laws are still purely descriptive. Laws like $F=ma$ in physics, $PV=NRT$ in chemistry, or $dm/dt = D\ A\ dc/dx$ in membrane physiology,* do not explain why the system under study behaves in that particular fashion. Such laws only provide a convenient summary of the existing arrangement, to avoid voluminous redundancy in describing the state and behavior of each part. Yet, however well they summarize, natural laws do not cause the system's behavior at all, and there is not one scientific expert who would claim so.** Thus, however refined our scientific perceptions become, firm explanation of anything natural continues to elude the scientist.

Seeing the Forest

To illustrate the above, let us return to the autumn woods. Why *do* the leaves change color? This question is actually made up of three smaller questions: Why are leaves green? Why are they orange? And why do they change from one to the other? Let us start with the simpler question of why they are green in the first place. First

---

* The Newtonian equation tells us that the force exerted by an object is a product of its mass and its acceleration. The "Ideal Gas Law" says that the pressure exerted by a given gas increases with increasing temperature and number of molecules, and it decreases as the space containing the gas increases. Fick's Equation describes how various factors act together to determine the rate of diffusion of a chemical across a membrane. For example, the amount of oxygen going from your lungs into your bloodstream (*dm/dt*) will depend on how much oxygen is on either side (*dc*), as well as the density (*D*), area (*A*), and thickness (*dx*) of the membrane.

** See in this volume, "Proof for the Existence of the Creator," based on a letter from the Rebbe, *shlita*.

of all green leaves are not really green at all. They are actually every color except green. The whole spectrum of colors in sunlight strikes the leaf and nearly all are absorbed except green, which is reflected away to be caught by our eyes. This serves to describe *how* the unused light reflects off the plant surface; but *why* is this wavelength perceived by us as green? Consider how one comes to see a leaf as green. Light travels from the leaf, through the lens of the eye and onto the retina, where a focused image is formed. There the light stimulates color-sensitive cells called cones. These release chemicals which are picked up by nerves behind the retina. Each nerve responds by emitting a series of electrical impulses which in turn lead to the release of chemicals to an adjacent network of nerve cells bundled into clusters called retinal ganglia. A new pattern of impulses from the ganglia is passed down the optic nerve to the visual cortex at the back of the brain.[5]

It is here that vision is experienced. The odd thing is that the perception of light takes place in a completely dark place, in a mass of tissue deep within a light-tight box of a skull, where light neither penetrates nor is generated.[6]

How can the brain see light without light? Is this fact really explained by describing, as above, how light energy stimulates several steps leading to neural and chemical impulses in the brain? Augros and Stanciu (1986) address this question by using an analogy:

> This double translation amplifies the wonder of sense perception. That such a chain of physical-chemical translations should result in the particular sensory experience "green" is no less startling than a person suddenly understanding a text when it is translated from one language unknown to him into another language unknown to him.[7]

Seeing the Trees

To explain why the leaves change color, science breaks the leaf down into its component parts and processes. This reductionist method leads us through progressively finer descriptions, but leaves the original question of "why" unanswered. Furthermore, many new questions arise at each level of study as the focus shifts from sense perception to plant physiology to biochemistry to physical chemistry to particle physics and beyond.

The first level of analysis seeks to explain leaf color in terms of chlorophyll. Essentially we want to say that the leaf is green because chlorophyll is green. But all this does is transfer the question from the leaf to chlorophyll. To explain chlorophyll's coloration, we study what it does: photosynthesis. We want to say that chlorophyll is green because of how light is used in the manufacture of sugar by plants.

Superficially this is satisfying. Plants are green because photosynthesis needs red, blue and violet, but not green light. Problem solved. Or is it? After all, one may yet ask why photosynthesis requires precisely those colors and not others. This is just as legitimate as asking why leaves or chlorophyll look green. The plant physiologist will acknowledge the validity of the question, but will tell you that the answer is not found in physiology but in the branch of science which underlies it—biochemistry, the study of how complex molecules carry out life's processes.

Many volumes have been published on the molecular intricacies of photosynthesis.[8] It is among the best documented of biochemical processes. The mechanism is also quite well agreed upon by the experts. Thus it is reasonable to expect that here we could find out why leaves are green.

The major steps in photosynthesis are: (1) photolysis, where light splits water into hydrogen and oxygen; (2) photoexcitation where electrons absorb different colored lights, leap off chlorophyll, and flit among various other large molecules, until they finally settle on the oxygen produced by the splitting of water; and (3) carbon fixation, where leftover energy from step (2) helps fuse carbon dioxide with a 5-carbon sugar to make an unstable 6-carbon substance. This rapidly splits into 3-carbon molecules, some of which rejoin to eventually form glucose, while the rest rearrange to again form the original 5-carbon sugar, which meets the next carbon dioxide molecule and brings it into the manufacturing process.

The biochemistry of photosynthesis is actually far more complex than what is outlined above. Light's role alone has been intensively studied for the past century, since Engelmann observed that bacteria clustered around algae that were lit with red, orange, blue and violet light, but did not cluster around algae lit with green or yellow. Biochemistry has still not revealed why only those wavelengths are usable, and therefore we have not yet answered the question of why chlorophyll is green or why leaves are green. Thus we still do not have an explanation of why leaves change color. In addition to this, there remains the mystery of visual perception altogether, as detailed above.

Another major question emerges from this whole story. The entire biochemical system involved in photosynthesis is an incredibly ordered process. Hundreds of chemical types, each comprised of a multitude of atoms, are matched and linked together with remarkable precision, and all these parts continually interact in a non-random way. In fact, not only is the biochemical system not random, but it is obviously all geared toward a single function—the transformation of light energy into chemical energy in the form of sugar.

The question is: What is organizing this system? What is keeping all these parts working together? Is it sugar? Obviously not.

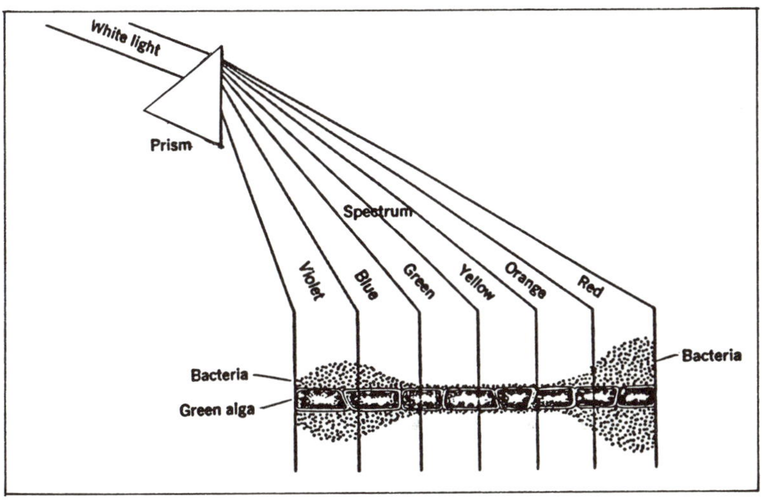

"Plants are green because photosynthesis requires red, blue and violet, but not green light."

Is it light? Impossible.

It is unreasonable to think that *any* single part of the system can organize the behavior of all the other parts. For a while, many scientists thought to explain the control of cells and organs in terms of DNA. However, this view too is becoming less popular as leading biologists continue to discover more basic life processes that are quite beyond the control of the cell nucleus.

The chemical components are by nature independent, without power over each other, and quite unaware of their role in manufacturing sugar. Hence, it must be that the controlling factor is outside the chemical system and more powerful than any of its parts, since it guides the behavior of each part. The greatness of the "mystery factor" controlling photosynthesis is emphasized when one considers that the chemistry of photosynthesis in a leaf is just one aspect of a much larger, integrated picture. The behavior of these molecules is thoroughly interwoven with the rest of the plant as well as with sunlight, air, water, soil, other plants, animals and people. After all, photosynthesis provides food for virtually all life on this planet.

From the Torah perspective the answer is obvious. There is only one factor that can be beyond every system and yet control all the parts. But the hard-nosed reductionist keeps searching, hoping that maybe, when we take those molecules apart, the explanations to all these questions will surface.

Let me tell you about my first exposure to the science which underlies biochemistry—physical chemistry. It was an introductory lecture, so it only dealt with the basic concepts. Still I was confused as to what the lecturer was talking about. The renowned professor responded to my questions after class: "I don't really know what it all means. I don't think anyone does." At the time I felt horror and relief—horror that hundreds of students were going to spend half a year listening to a man who admits he doesn't know what he's talking about, and relief because I found out before wasting too much effort. At the time, I thought he was a fraud. Now I respect him for his honesty, as well.

The most basic of the exact sciences is particle physics. But in fact, it is not nearly so exact as it used to be. There was a time when matter was hard, when space and time were fixed, and when there were only three basic particles: protons, neutrons and electrons. But with our refined instrumentation and experiments, many strange results have shaken our materialistic view of nature.

Now matter is just a special form of energy, space is curved and time passes at different rates in different reference frames. Matter is now made up of a multitude of unknowable* particles (or waves, depending on how you look at them), including leptons, muons, gluons, mesons, and quarks, having odd properties like spin, flavor and charm. Even more surprising, these "particles," which are the basis of everything physical, have the remarkable habit of continually disappearing and coming into existence in random locations and at random times.[9]

Has particle physics answered why leaves are green or any of our other questions? No. Furthermore, we now have the new question of how atoms can be stable (and they do seem to be) while their parts are so ephemeral. Such problems have led Paul Davies, a prominent physicist who is a self-avowed atheist, to remark in a recent article that "the new physics... seems to demand some guiding influence located, as it were, above nature, sustaining all of existence."[10]

Can you imagine the headline? "Atheist Physicist Discovers God."

It is here that science and Torah really converge. There is no difference between what Davies is saying in the name of physics and what Jews have been saying since Abraham.... There is a Divine Providence that continuously sustains and orders the entire universe,** and not just at the cosmic level, or on the grand general scale. Modern physics sees supernatural guidance operating at the most minuscule subatomic level.

---

* According to twentieth-century physics, quanta are unknowable in the sense that they have an indeterminate nature. For example, one cannot simultaneously know an electron's position and its velocity. So too, for any given particle one cannot simultaneously detect both its wave and particle properties.

** Virtually any Jewish prayer book articulates this in the first blessing of the *Shema*. There one finds a phrase referring to the Creator as the One Who "in His goodness renews daily, continuously, the process of Creation."

John Wheeler, the dean of modern physics, has gone one step further. Wheeler was the originator of the Black Hole concept and has provided leadership to three generations of physicists. Nobel laureates often credit him with inspiring their successes, although he himself is quite humble. In a recent *Reader's Digest* interview, Wheeler extends the results of quantum theory to their logical conclusion. He says that man's recognition of order in nature was foreseen, planned and intentionally sought before the first particle was formed. Physics is teaching us that human comprehension was the goal and reason for creating an orderly universe in the first place.[11]

But beyond this point physics cannot probe, because no science is able to address *why* this appreciation was desired.

Torah can.

For example, when one sees the precisely timed emergence of beautiful colors in autumn leaves, and when one considers all the microscopic and submicroscopic levels and processes that underlie this display, and that all the parts and processes are meticulously organized and integrated, and that no team of scientists could duplicate one iota of any of it... all this adds to the realization of the greatness and power of the One who could create, sustain, and coordinate all those zillions of parts.

Still the complexity is finite. How much greater, then, is the Almighty God, before whom supernovae and atoms are equally minuscule and governed with equal skill and care. This awareness enhances our awe of the Creator; to regard Him with awe is a *mitzvah* (Torah commandment), and through the performance of *mitzvot* we fulfill *our* purpose.[12] Through this we also come to loving God, since we appreciate His kindness in granting us an opportunity to actually participate in a relationship with Him. The appreciation one feels is further enhanced by considering that He does not need a relationship with us, but chooses to engage in one for our benefit.

Modern science and Torah are both letting the individual say, "*Bishvili nivra ha-olam*—for my sake was the universe created."[13] But only Torah takes the next step and explains why *we* were created: To relate to our Creator with well-chosen thoughts, words and deeds, thus providing meaning for both man and the cosmos.

NOTES

1. This narrative is adapted from a United Press Syndicated comic strip by Lynn Johnston, entitled *For Better or for Worse.*
2. G. N. Schlesinger, *Religion and Scientific Method* (Boston: Reidel, 1977).
3. W. Blum, "Science for Humanity's Sake," *Science* 64, Issue 1647 (1926):77-80.
4. K. R. Popper, *Conjectures and Refutations* (New York: Basic Books, 1963); K. R. Popper, *The Logic of Scientific Discovery* (New York: Harper and Row, 1968).
5. C. R. Michael, "Retinal Processing of Visual Images," *Scientific American* 222 (5) (1969).
6. John Eccles, *Facing Reality* (Berlin: Springer-Verlag, 1970), 1, 2, 55.
7. R. M. Augros and G. N. Stanciu, *The New Story of Science*, Second Edition (New York: Bantam, 1986), 15.
8. See the figure taken from S. Haskel and D. Sygoda, *Contemporary Biology* (New York: Amsco Scientific Publications, 1977), 203-204.
9. Dr. Massimo Sivilotti, Computer Science Department, California Institute of Technology, Pasadena, California.
10. P. Davies, "God and the New Physics," *New Scientist* 98 (1983):872-874.
11. J. Boslough, "Inside the Mind of John Wheeler," *Reader's Digest* (March 1987):92-96.
12. E.g., *Deuteronomy* 10:12-11:25.
13. Mishnah *Sanhedrin*, Ch. 4.

Abraham M. Hasofer

Jewish Mysticism and the Intelligibility of Nature

PERHAPS THE MOST striking aspect of modern science is the extraordinary success of the application of mathematics in building models of physical reality. These models enable scientists to predict the course of physical processes with unexpected accuracy.

To comprehend how puzzling this is, one must be aware of the fact that the mathematical concepts which are used by scientists have been devised by mathematicians *without any reference* to the real world. Mathematicians develop profound concepts purely to demonstrate their ingenuity and their sense of *formal beauty*. Such concepts as abstract algebra and analysis, topology, number theory and many others are, by the testimony of the mathematicians themselves, purely creations of the human mind. Mathematics has a

---

ABRAHAM M. HASOFER, after graduating as an electrical engineer in Alexandria, Egypt, took a Ph.D. in mathematical statistics from the University of Tasmania, Australia. Since 1969, he has held the Chair of Statistics at the University of New South Wales, with visiting Professorships including M.I.T. and Princeton. His fifty-odd publications include several dealing with genetics, but his main interest is the application of statistics to civil engineering. He is co-inventor of the Hasofer-Lind Reliability Index, widely used in civil engineering design. He was Foundation President of the Association of Orthodox Jewish Scientists of Australia, and he lectures widely on Jewish topics.

unique *perfection* in its internal consistency: we can string together one thousand arguments without ever getting a contradiction.

Nevertheless, many of these abstract constructions have found a direct application to understanding and predicting phenomena in the real world—for example, electromagnetic theory, quantum mechanics and relativity theory. In the words of E.P. Wigner, "Mathematical formulation of *crude* experiments has led, in an uncanny number of cases, to an amazingly accurate description of a large class of phenomena."[1]

It is worthwhile at this stage to illustrate how this process is actually carried out. One of the most dramatic examples is the discovery of radio waves by Clerk Maxwell and Heinrich Hertz.

In 1861 Clerk Maxwell produced a set of partial differential equations to represent electromagnetic phenomena. These were generalizations from the experimental work of Ampere, Faraday, Oersted and others. However, Maxwell was not satisfied with the equations as they stood. Some say that he felt that they lacked symmetry, while others maintain that he reasoned analogically from hydrodynamics. Whatever the case may be, he simply *added* to the equations a term that did not have any experimental basis—the so-called "displacement current." (This is illustrated in Figure 1.) It then followed from the *modified* equations that there existed electromagnetic waves that propagated with a velocity given by $c_0 = 1/\sqrt{\mu_0 \varepsilon_0}$ in vacuum, where μ_0 is the permeability of vacuum, $\mu_0 = 4\pi \times 10^7$, and ε_0 is the permittivity of vacuum, $\varepsilon_0 = (36\pi \times 10^9)^{-1}$. (These values were obtained from measurements.) It then turned out that $c_0 = 3 \times 10^8$ meters per second. Maxwell was quick to realize that this was exactly the *velocity of light* in vacuum, and concluded that light was a particular form of electromagnetic wave. He further claimed, on the basis of his equations, that other electromagnetic waves, of different frequencies, also existed. It was only *twenty years* later, in 1881, that Heinrich Hertz was able to prove experimentally the existence of these waves. This of course was the starting point of the immense development of radio, television and radar that we have witnessed in our time.

Such stories occur in many areas of modern physics, and have led to expressions of wonder by the scientists concerned. Here are

Figure 1

Maxwell's equations
(in modern notation)

$$\underset{\sim}{D} = \varepsilon_o \underset{\sim}{E}$$

$$\underset{\sim}{H} = \mu_o^{-1} \underset{\sim}{B}$$

$$\nabla . \underset{\sim}{J} + \frac{\partial \rho}{\partial t} = 0$$

$$\nabla \times \underset{\sim}{H} \boxed{- \frac{\partial \underset{\sim}{D}}{\partial t}} = \underset{\sim}{J}$$

added term

$$\nabla \times \underset{\sim}{E} + \frac{\partial \underset{\sim}{B}}{\partial t} = 0$$

$$\nabla . \underset{\sim}{B} = 0$$

$$\nabla . \underset{\sim}{D} = \rho$$

some quotations from prominent scientists, many of whom have personally experienced such successes:

> The universe shows evidence of a design or controlling power that has something in common with our mathematical minds... in any event, it can hardly be disputed that nature and our conscious mathematical minds work according to the same laws.
>
> Sir James Jeans[2]

> What has led me to science... is the not-at-all obvious fact that the laws of our thoughts coincide with the regularity of the flow of impressions which we receive from the external world, [and] that it is therefore possible for man to reach conclusions through pure speculation about these regularities.
>
> Max Planck[3]

> A study of mathematics and its contributions to the sciences exposes a deep question. Mathematics is man-made. The

concepts, the broad ideas, the logical standards and methods of reasoning... were fashioned by human beings. Yet with this product of his fallible mind, man has surveyed spaces too vast for his imagination to encompass; he has predicted and shown how to control radio waves which none of our senses can perceive; and he has discovered particles too small to be seen with the most powerful microscope. Cold symbols and formulas completely at the disposition of man have enabled him to secure a portentous grip on the universe. Some explanation of this marvelous power is called for.

Morris Kline[4]

That mathematics, an emanation of the human mind, should serve so effectively for the description and understanding of the physical world is a challenging fact that has rightly attracted the concern of philosophers.

Richard Courant[5]

The enormous usefulness of mathematics in the natural sciences is something bordering on the mysterious and... there is no rational explanation for it... it is difficult to avoid the impression that a miracle confronts us here.

Eugene Wigner[6]

[Maxwell's equations]... illustrate the marvelous power of pure thought, aiming only at the satisfaction of intellectual desires (e.g., beauty, order, symmetry) to control the external world.

Norman Campbell[7]

One cannot escape the feeling that these mathematical formulas have an independent existence and an intelligence of their own, that they are wiser than we are, wiser even than their discoverers, that we get more out of them than was originally put in them.

Heinrich Hertz[8]

You find it surprising that I think of the comprehensibility of the world... as a miracle or an eternal mystery. But surely, *a priori*, one should expect the world to be chaotic, not to be grasped by thought in any way. One might (indeed one

> should) expect that the world evidenced itself as lawful only so far as we grasp it in an orderly fashion. This would be a sort of order like the alphabetical order of words. On the other hand, the kind of order created, for example, by Newton's gravitational theory is of a very different character. Even if the axioms of the theory are posited by man, the success of such a procedure supposes in the objective world a high degree of order, which we are in no way entitled to expect *a priori*. Therein lies the 'miracle' which becomes more and more evident as our knowledge develops. And here is the weak point of positivists and professional atheists, who feel happy because they think that they have preempted not only the world of the Divine but also of the miraculous.
>
> Albert Einstein[9]

Divine Design

The sentence that follows the last quotation, by Albert Einstein, in his letter to Solovine, leads us directly to the topic of this paper, for Einstein continues: "Curiously, we have to be resigned to recognize the 'miracle,' without having any legitimate way of getting any further."

Certainly Einstein is right to state that within the framework of science there is no explanation for the mystery. However, the moment we allow ourselves to enter the realm of metaphysics, the solution becomes apparent, and has been apparent to believing men for a long time: The mind and the world operate in parallel because they have a common Creator. And, in fact, the "mystery" of the intelligibility of nature is the strongest pointer of Divine design in the universe. It also points to a special lovingkindness on the part of the Creator, who has given man this precious gift.

However, the purpose of this paper is to go further. Rather than dwelling on generalities, some of the teachings of Jewish mysticism, i.e., of Kabbalah, will be examined and shown to throw much light on the reasons for the success of mathematical techniques in the understanding of the universe. The relationship between mysticism and science has already been observed by Fritjof Capra[10] in his book *The Tao of Physics*. Of course Capra discusses only Eastern mysticism, but it is well-known that much of Eastern mysticism actually derives from Kabbalah.* Much of what will be pointed out goes far beyond what Capra has observed.

Jewish Mysticism and Science

One of the fundamental teachings of Jewish mysticism is that the world was created according to the Sefirotic Scheme. This is explicitly stated in *Sefer Yetzirah.*** There we learn that the world was created through thirty-two paths: namely ten *sefirot* and twenty-two letters of the (Hebrew) alphabet. The various creative processes through which God created the world can be represented by the various permutations and combinations of these supernal letters.♦

On the other hand, we are also taught (see, e.g., *Tanya*♦♦) that the same scheme operates in the human soul. Thus, each distinction and grade of the various levels of the soul consists of ten faculties, and these correspond to the Ten *Sefirot*. In fact, they are descended from them. In other words, the structure of the human mind reflects the Sefirotic Scheme, just as the world does. And, moreover, the ten faculties of the soul that correspond to the Ten *Sefirot*

---

* See *I Kings* 5:14 and 10:23. see also Manasseh Ben Israel, *Soul of Life*, Section 4, Chapter 21, where he writes: "And similarly, when he [Abraham] went down to Egypt and lived there, he taught this philosophy, after which he sent the sons of his concubines away from Isaac, while he was yet alive, towards the East to their holy land, India. They also disseminated this faith.... From there, the new belief spread all over India, as is evident from writings of that period."

** Chapter I, *mishnah* 1-3: "With thirty-two mysterious paths of wisdom God... created the world: ten *sefirot*... and twenty-two letters.... The Ten *Sefirot* are analogous to the ten fingers [of the human body].... There are ten *sefirot*, not nine and not eleven. Comprehend this wisdom and understand this knowledge, inquire into it and ponder on it...."

♦ Chapter II, *mishnah* 2: "The twenty-two letters... were appointed and established by God. He combined, weighted and permuted them, and formed from them all beings which are in existence, and all those which will be formed in all time to come."

♦♦ Part I, Chapter 3: "Each distinction and grade of the three [levels of soul]—*nefesh, ruach* and *neshamah*—consists of ten faculties, corresponding to the Ten *Sefirot* from which they descended."

are enclothed in "letters" that correspond to the supernal letters from which the world was created (*Tanya**).

One can already, at this stage, remark on the amazing similarity between the above and the basic building blocks of mathematics, which has been the key to our understanding of the universe.

(1) The word *sefirot,* although having many meanings, has a basic connotation of *number.* And at that point we find the number *ten,* the basis of our number system. It is well-known that the number ten represents perfection. Moreover, all numbers as given in the Torah are written in the decimal system. It is important to remember that there is no *logical* necessity for the basis of the number system to be the number ten. In fact it has been argued that either the number twelve (which has more factors than ten) or a prime number such as eleven would be a better basis from the point of view of mathematical convenience. And it is well-known that computers use the binary system. But in spite of all this, the only system which has gained universal acceptance in the whole of science has been the decimal system! There is undoubtedly a deep mystical reason there, and it is revealed to us in Kabbalah: *ten* denotes perfection.

(2) The second ingredient mentioned in *Sefer Yetzirah* is the Hebrew alphabet and its twenty-two letters, which by their permutations and combinations represent the whole universe. Here again, although there was no logical necessity for it, it is algebraic symbolism based on *letters* which has proved to be the key to the construction of modern mathematics.

Thus we see that the ability to comprehend the universe does not stem from a singular act of Divine Providence, but rather from the fact that the structure of the universe and the structure of the human mind are both images of the Sefirotic Scheme, through which they were created.

One can obtain further insight by examining the detailed struc-

---

* Part I, Chapter 20: "The essence and identity of the soul [is] its ten attributes [i.e., the Ten *Sefirot*]... from which are derived the "letters" of thought that are clothed in speech when it is uttered."

ture of the Ten *Sefirot*. They are called: *Chochmah* (wisdom), *Binah* (understanding), *Da'at* (knowledge), *Chesed* (lovingkindness), *Gevurah* (might), *Tiferet* (harmony, beauty), *Netzach* (victory), *Hod* (majesty), *Yesod* (foundation), and *Malchut* (kingship). They are arranged in triads, as shown in Figure 2,* with another *sefirah*, *Keter* (crown), above the whole scheme.[11]

Chochmah represents the first creative activity of the Creator. And as an image of this, the corresponding soul faculty is the intuitive flash of intellectual illumination, the seminal hypothesis which is at the core of every scientific and mathematical achievement. The next *sefirah*,

Figure 2

The Sefirotic Scheme

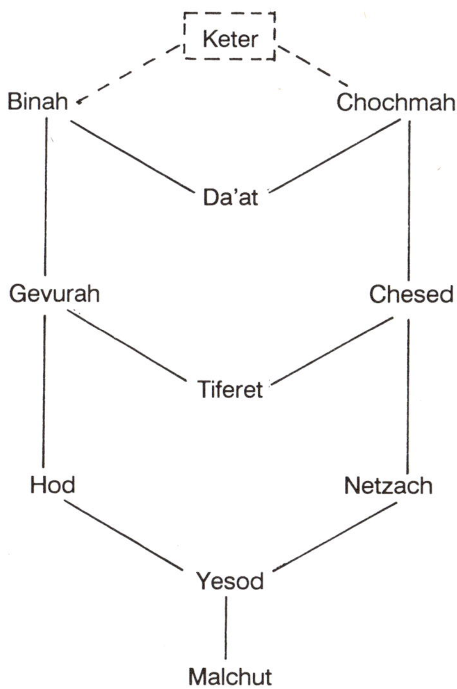

* This is according to the scheme that contains *Da'at* as a *sefirah*. Some other schemes do not count *Da'at*, but count *Keter* instead.

Binah, is the cogitation on the idea, when its details and implications become revealed and manifest in the mind. This is followed by the practical implementation of the informed concept, effected by the faculty of *Da'at.* We see here the two basic aspects of the implementation of the hypothesis: working out its logical implications, and then bringing it to practicality.

The two poles between which the scientific process oscillates are further illustrated by two *sefirot*: *Chesed,* which represents the unbounded outpouring of emotive imagination, and *Gevurah,* which represents structuring within a strict formal framework. The balancing element of the triad at this second level is *Tiferet,* which means harmony or beauty. And this is exactly what the scientists and the mathematicians tell us repeatedly (see quotations above): One of the most important guiding threads in creative thinking is *beauty.* There is *a priori* no reason at all why the universe should be beautiful, in the sense of abstract beauty and harmony. But Kabbalah tells us that beauty is one of the cornerstones of the process of Creation of the universe! And this is why we are successful when we choose *beautiful* theories to understand and predict reality.

Another cornerstone of modern scientific thinking is *symmetry,* and this again is one of the characteristics of the Sefirotic Scheme, which is structured symmetrically between the left and right. Let us note in passing that the Scheme illustrated in Figure 2 reminds us forcefully of a structural formula of chemistry, and in particular of the structure of aromatic compounds.

Torah as the Blueprint of the Universe

Another avenue for understanding the inexplicable success of certain aspects of scientific method is the realization that, as Kabbalah teaches us, the Torah is the blueprint of the universe, as it is stated: "He looked into the Torah and created the world."[12] It follows that methods of study of the world which are parallel to the methods of study of Torah should be successful. Now it is well known that the Torah can be expounded by means of thirteen rules (see, for example, Mindel[13]). Three of these rules have an immediate obvious relevance to scientific study.

The first one is known as *kal va-chomer*, i.e., "deduction from minor to major." A little thought will easily show that this rule is the foundation of the notion of functional relationship, for what the rule says is that if two attributes are positively functionally related, then an increase in one will imply an increase in the other. And in fact, if there were no functional relationships in the world, everything would be totally unpredictable.

The second rule is called *gezerah shavah*, meaning "analogy." And here we encounter again one of the cornerstones of modern science and mathematics, namely, reasoning by analogy. It has already been pointed out above that it is suspected that Maxwell devised his equations by analogy with hydrodynamics. And this is the general experience of researchers.

The third rule is called *binyan av*, meaning "generalization." It teaches that laws derived from one object will apply to other objects having some common characteristic. And this is exactly the path that mathematicians and scientists follow to generate new hypotheses.

Limitations of Science

One must nonetheless remember that in spite of all the resounding successes of modern science, the universe still remains overwhelmingly unknown to man. This is alluded to in the Hebrew name for the world: *olam*, which comes from a root that means "hidden." As previously pointed out, the intelligibility of the universe is a special gift of lovingkindness on the part of the Creator. This is specifically mentioned in the Midrash, where we read: "Originally it arose in God's thought to create the world with the attribute of stern judgment; He saw, however, that the world could not endure, so He combined with it the attribute of mercy."[14] This is interpreted to mean that originally, Divinity was not readily evident in nature. But through the attribute of mercy (i.e., *Chesed*), Divine design became at least partially apparent to a thoughtful person through various avenues, one of them being science.

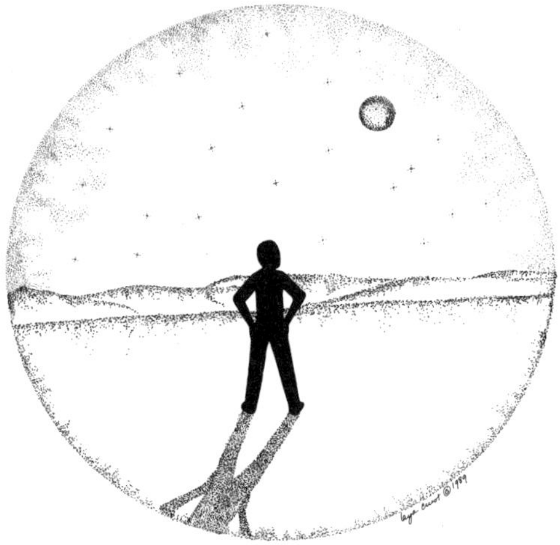

"The intelligibility of the universe is a special gift of lovingkindness on the part of the Creator."

Epilogue

Concerning the Flood, the Bible states (in *Genesis* 7:11): "In the six hundredth year of Noah's life... all the fountains of the great deep burst forth, and the windows of the heavens were opened." On this the *Zohar* commented, some 1,900 years ago: "In the six hundredth year of the sixth millennium the gates of wisdom on high and the fountains of wisdom below will be opened and the world will be brought to *tikkun* (a state of restoration) to be ushered into the seventh millennium."[15] (The date given is 5600 of the Creation, corresponding to 1840 C.E.) The Lubavitcher Rebbe explains that the "wisdom on high" refers to the wisdom of Torah, while the "wisdom below" refers to worldly wisdom, that is, to science.[16]

The Rebbe goes on to explain that the publishing of the works *Torah Or* (1837) and *Likkutei Torah* (1848) heralded the opening of the gates of Torah referred to in the *Zohar*. At the same time tremendous development in science began.[17] He then points out that the Divine purpose in the remarkable development of science since that time is that science should be applied in the service of God and His Torah.[18] This is in accordance with the statement in *Isaiah* 40:5: "And the glory of the Lord shall be revealed, and all flesh shall see together that the mouth of the Lord has spoken."

The above does not mean, of course, that science may not be put to use to advance man's material comforts as well. In fact, the situation here is parallel to that which our Sages describe in relation to gold. They state in the Midrash[19] that gold was created for use in the Tabernacle and in the Temple in Jerusalem, for the world did not merit to use it. But nevertheless we are permitted to use gold for worldly purposes.

The Rebbe discusses two ways in which the development of science has helped in revealing Divinity in the world:

(1) The development of instantaneous worldwide communication gives us a direct analogy of how it is possible for God to know what happens in the whole world.

(2) Modern physics has heavily underscored the essential *unity* of the world, which itself is a reflection of the essential Divine unity.

This paper has demonstrated a third aspect—the development of modern science and the light it sheds on some fundamental teachings of Jewish mysticism. One must emphasize at this point that the development of modern science has not by any means been only in the direction of revealing Divine glory. And this opposite trend had to be expected, in accordance with the well-known precept: "God has created the one in opposition to the other."[20] It has expressed itself in such theories as Darwinism and its present-day version, neo-Darwinism, which have been used to deny the existence of purpose and design in the universe, particularly in the realm of biology, and to attribute the existence of order in the universe to chance.

Conclusion

The insights of Kabbalah enable us to see the great scientific achievements of the last century not as fortunate accidents, but as the realization of a built-in potential: the special gift of lovingkindness, originating in the very structure of the universe and the human mind. And we are taught that the realization of this potential heralds the oncoming of messianic times, when the world will be full of the knowledge of God, may it be speedily, in our days.

Acknowledgment

The author wishes to acknowledge the help of M.M. Groner in the search for Chasidic sources from which the material for this paper was drawn.

NOTES

1. E.P. Wigner, "The Unreasonable Effectiveness of Mathematics in the Natural Sciences," *Communications on Pure and Applied Mathematics* 13 (1960):1-14.
2. *The Mysterious Universe* (New York: MacMillan, 1930).
3. "Wissenschaftliche Selbstbiographie," *Physikalische Abhandlungen* 3 (1948):374.
4. *Mathematics and the Physical World* (New York: Dover, 1980), ix.
5. "Mathematics in the Modern World," *Scientific American* 211 (1964):48-49.
6. *Symmetries and Reflections: Scientific Essays* (Cambridge and London: The M.I.T. Press, 1970), 222.
7. *What is Science?* (New York: Dover, 1952), 71.
8. Cited in E.T. Bell, *Men in Mathematics*, 16.
9. *Lettres à Maurice Solovine* (Paris: Gauthier Villars, 1956), 102.
10. Fritjof Capra, *The Tao of Physics* (Fontana/Collins, 1976).
11. For a detailed description of the Sefirotic Scheme, see in any recent edition of *Tanya* with English translation the Appendix: "Mystical Concepts in Chassidism" by Rabbi Jacob Immanuel Schochet.
12. *Zohar*, Part II, folio 161A.
13. Nissan Mindel, *My Prayer* (Kehot Publication Society, 1972), 97-109.
14. *Bereshit Rabbah* 12:15. Quoted in Rashi on *Genesis* 1:1.
15. *Zohar*, Part I, folio 117A.
16. *Likkutei Sichot*, Vol. 15, 42.
17. Some idea of this development can be gathered from the following brief historical outline, covering only mathematics, physics and chemistry:

(a) *Mathematics*

Prominent figures:

A.L. Cauchy:	1789-1857
K.F. Gauss:	1777-1855

W.R. Hamilton:	1805-1865
G.J. Jacobi:	1804-1851
N.I. Lobachevski:	1793-1856

Topics developed: complex analysis, partial differential equations, differential geometry, non-Euclidean geometry, linear algebra, quaternions, analytical mechanics.

(b) *Physics*

Important dates:

1818	A. Fresnel:	Wave theory of light (diffraction)
1824	S. Carnot:	Thermodynamics
1850	R. Clausius:	
1831	M. Faraday:	Electromagnetic induction
1842	J. Mayer:	Conservation of energy
1847	J. Joule:	
1854	Lord Kelvin:	Absolute scale of temperature
1864	J.C. Maxwell:	Electromagnetic equations

(c) *Chemistry*

Important dates:

1832	J. von Liebig and F. Wohler:	Organic chemistry
1852	E. Frankland:	Theory of valency
1858	A. Kekule:	Molecular structure
1874	van't Hoff and Le Bel:	Stereochemistry

18. *Tanya*, end of Chapter 8, p.26.
19. *Shemot Rabbah*, Chapter 35, A.
20. *Ecclesiastes* 7:14.

Menachem Kovacs

Relativism and Absolutism in Sociology

THE SOCIAL SCIENCES are defined as the scientific study of human behavior, as opposed to the natural sciences which include the study of physical and biological behavior. The social sciences generally include sociology, anthropology, economics, history, political science and psychology. These fields are very interdependent and are all based on major theories and research which have great influence as they are applied to specific concrete problems in fields such as law, public administration, social medicine, social work, education and business administration.

Sociology in particular is the scientific study of human behavior *in groups*. The discipline is rather new, dating from the nineteenth-century industrial revolution in Europe. Major changes and upheavals took place simultaneously. They included the movement of millions of Europeans from rural to urban areas as the economy shifted from an agrarian to an industrial one, and the end of the rule of old monar-

---

MENACHEM KOVACS is a Professor of Sociology and Hillel Director at Montgomery College in Rockville, Maryland. He graduated with honors from Roosevelt University in Chicago (B.A.), the London School of Economics (M.Sc.) and the Union Graduate School (Ph.D.). He studied at the Rabbinical College of America and also earned a certificate in International Relations from the University of Geneva. His areas of special interest include the sociology of science and political sociology.

chies like the French royal family, which had ruled for as long as the French could recall, and their replacement with new dictatorships and sometimes a most peculiar new form of government—democracy. Other major changes included the tremendous erosion of religious beliefs and practices in Europe, due to the rise of modern science based on the theory of evolution, which discredited belief in God and religion in the minds of educated Europeans. Parallel to the transfer of belief from religion to science—from God to doctors and scientists—was a transfer of belief in the existing political structure to a new ideology which gained credibility by its assertion that it was based on *scientific* laws of history. This, of course, is a reference to Marx's communism, which he packaged and sold as "scientific" socialism. Finally, the institution of the family, as the traditional foundation of society, was weakened by the mass migrations of millions of Europeans who left Europe and their roots behind for a new life in North and South America, and also by the decreased value attributed to the family in modern societies.

Modern sociology was forged in nineteenth-century Europe by five great social scientists who studied the profound changes taking place in their societies. These were Auguste Comte, Herbert Spencer, Emile Durkheim, Karl Marx and Max Weber. These sociologists were not merely neutral observers and analysts; they were also advocates of particular views. Their contributions demonstrated that, while sociology from its beginning was indeed a *relativistic* science, leading social scientists nonetheless advocated certain theories with an *absolutistic* certainty that would later be modified. The point here is that sociology—as indeed all the social sciences—represents its major theories as absolute at a certain point in time, even though subsequent study invariably forces the revision of the original absolutism so that it is compromised to the point that its original formulation becomes undone.

For example, the British sociologist Herbert Spencer (1820-1903) built on the contributions of Auguste Comte, who was called the father of sociology. Spencer emphasized the importance of using a change model in studying human societies, but he also contended that human societies inevitably progressed. This was an absolutistic bias which eventually had to be discarded. Moreover, Comte's advocacy of an objective, value-free social science has been challenged in several quarters as being not only impossible but also undesirable. For example, Max Weber's concept of *verstehen* contradicts Comte's approach by specifically advocating subjectivity in certain cases.

Karl Marx is the most famous illustration of an absolutist whose viewpoint has been modified on many counts. The most brilliant of the nineteenth-century sociologists was Max Weber, whose significant contributions in many areas included his studies of bureaucracy, religion and music. Weber argued against the popular Marxist view that swept Europe from the 1840s on. One of his points was that an idealistic philosophy like Marxism, which envisioned a revolution for the sake of economic justice, could in fact become, in the wrong hands, a cover for rule by very inhumane rulers. In short, Weber foresaw, *even before* the first Marxist revolution in Russia in 1917, that Marxism could be a wolf in sheep's clothing—that is, inhumanity in the name of humanity.*

It is appropriate to add here that Weber's criticism of Marx's absolutism was of course vindicated by history. While the Torah's premise is that man is first and foremost a spiritual being, Marx attacked and dismissed religion—which promised a good life in the next world—as simply a diversion used by the capitalists to keep the proletariat from the reality of its exploitation. Weber claimed that Marx's economic determinism was actually a form of economic reductionism, meaning oversimplification. Weber claimed that even if there were some truth in Marx's assertion about religion, it did not address the question of whether there is or is not truth in the basic tenets of West-

---

*Parenthetically, it is interesting to note two major causes of death in the twentieth century. Approximately twenty-four million people were killed in the two world wars: nine million in World War I, and fifteen million in World War II. But the main killer in this century has not been the battlefield; rather it has been the murder by communist governments of their own citizens! According to Professor R.J. Rummell, a political scientist at the University of Hawaii at Manoa, the Soviets under Lenin and Stalin killed forty million of their own people during the years 1918-1953, and Communist China under Mao killed forty-five million during the years 1949-1976. These communist regimes killed, altogether, more people than were killed in both world wars.

ern religion. That would include an evaluation of four major premises: (1) There exists a Creator, (2) Who made this world from nothing, (3) Who puts a special soul into human beings, who are the ultimate purpose of His Creation and (4) Who rewards good acts and punishes bad acts in this world and/or in the next world. These basic tenets of the three Western monotheistic religions—Judaism, Islam, and Christianity—are dismissed rather than confronted and evaluated by Marxian analysis.

In *contemporary* sociology the dominance of relativistic ideas is being seriously challenged and modified by absolutist approaches which are generally consistent with a Torah viewpoint. For example, anthropologists who study other cultures were always taught how essential it was to avoid ethnocentric bias—the belief, either conscious or not, that one's own culture is superior to that of other societies, notably those in the Third World. Historically, anthropologists argued against ethnocentrism, considering it a biased perspective, and advocated what they termed cultural relativism. The great anthropologist Charles Sumner explained cultural relativism by saying that everything in the mores of a time and place must be regarded as justified with regard to that time and place. According to this reasoning, there is no universal standard that can be used to evaluate cultures or norms as being good or bad.

In moderation, cultural relativism can be usefully applied to the study of another culture's folkways, that is, to a study of their customs. For example, there is no more logic in wearing Scottish kilts than in wearing Western pants or Indian saris; there is no more logic in using chopsticks in the Orient than in using silverware in the Occident; there is nothing innately better in rice as a food staple than in bread. Each is functional and logical for a particular culture.

But the application of cultural relativism has not been limited to a strictly functional analysis of folkways. Rather, it has been overextended as a "universal principle" to the point where there are no standards at all by which to evaluate the moral practices and issues in a culture. Thus, the most bizarre acts of cruelty and barbarism are above criticism if one only uses the standard of cultural relativism.

In recent years a new term has been introduced to rectify this problem: moral, or ethical, absolutism. Moral absolutism refers to

issues raised by cultural practices which show disrespect for human life. Examples of practices which would thus be viewed negatively, and not neutrally or sympathetically, would be slavery, cannibalism, female infanticide, racism, ageism and sexism. Most anthropologists still hold to the relativist view, but a growing minority now argue that practices like the Chinese coolie slave-labor system that built the Great Wall of China, and Pharaoh's bondage of the Jews are more properly understood with the criterion of moral absolutism.*

---

* It is interesting to note that for many Western anthropologists the danger is not they that will succumb to ethnocentrism, cultural relativism, or moral absolutism, but rather that they will become sentimentalists, and will be intentionally or subtly biased *in favor* of the Third World culture they are studying, and biased *against* Western, and particularly American, culture. This bias is sometimes called "the Peace Corps syndrome," or the "noble savage syndrome."

Another area of contemporary sociology in which absolutism is challenging the historic dominance of relativism is sociolinguistics, the study of the relationship between language and culture. A major theory in cultural analysis in sociolinguistics has been radical empiricism, which argues, with the relativistic viewpoint, that all languages are simply different ways of expressing fundamentally the same ideas and *weltanschauung* (world view). In contrast, the hypothesis of the linguists Sapir and Whorf has gained wide respect by asserting (with much cross-cultural evidence) that language differences reflect fundamental and deep cultural differences.[1] This means, for example, not only that the Hebrew, Chinese and American language differences reflect different symbols of communication, but that these different symbols (and even the varied *directions* of their scripts) reflect basic differences in thought and world view. This latter, absolutist theory is consistent with the Torah view that Hebrew is the Holy Tongue and no other language possesses this holiness.

The third area of sociology to illustrate the growing challenge to relativism by absolutism is the study of deviance and criminology. The relativist view of deviance has been very dominant and is expressed in labeling theory, the view that deviance is simply a label which those in power put on an unpopular minority group. Again, in limited usage, this is a good theoretical framework to use in explaining deviance. For example, a deviant label was put on Japanese-Americans who were imprisoned by the Roosevelt administration during World War II and on Jews by the Nazis. The problem is that labeling theory has been applied so broadly that it allows no standard or justification for ever labeling a person as deviant, even when fundamental human rights are transgressed. According to labeling theory, deviance has a changing definition based on time and place.

In recent years, however, this view has been challenged by an absolutist definition of deviance, that is, an unchanging definition of deviance based on one or both of two criteria: (1) The medical model, which says that the best medical opinion of the day, rather than statistical factors or relativistic considerations, is a primary determinant of deviance. Thus, according to the medical model, smoking tobacco is labeled deviant because of the medical evidence that it is unhealthy. (2) Biblical morality (Western religious values) uses the criterion of whether a practice is moral according to the Bible. Using the example of homosexuality, the relativist labeling theory will contend that it is simply deviance attributed (unfairly) by those in power to an unpopular minority group; but to the absolutists using both the medical and the Biblical models, homosexuality is deviant because it is unequivocally correlated with a dramatically higher fatality rate, and because God defines this behavior as immoral in the Bible.

A field within sociology, the sociology of science, can help us better appreciate how science works and how compatible the absolutism of Torah is with a scientific approach. In 1942, the prominent sociologist Robert Merton identified four norms or rules which he said should govern all science.[2] The first rule is *universalism*, which means that scientific research should be evaluated only for its scientific value, without regard to non-scientific factors like the social backgrounds of particular scientists. Not following a norm like universalism is called a violation of the norm. Violations of the norm of universalism include Hitler's discrimination against scientists who were Jews, Stalin's favoritism toward the biologist Lysenko, and discrimination by white Northern scientists against the black Southern scientist George Washington Carver in the last century.

The second norm is *communalism*, which means that scientific research is to be shared with other scientists and the general public. A good example would be current multi-national efforts to control greenhouse-effect gases. Violations of this norm include technology which is patented and classified for exclusive military or commercial use.

The third norm is *detachment*, the maintenance of professional honesty in research, whereby a scientist separates his personal biases from his professional work. One violation of this norm is fraud, in which the over-ambitious scientist may be tempted to falsify his research in order to enhance his prestige. A second example of a violation of this norm would be unintentional bias.

The fourth and last norm is *skepticism*, the belief that no theory in science is sacred and stands above criticism, even if political, religious, or social dogma supports it. One of many violations of this norm occurred when leading scientists the world over initially refused to listen to Einstein's assertion of relativity because they were content with their own views based on the Newtonian view as *the* valid paradigm.

We can usefully apply these four norms to contemporary science and charge that there are major violations of the norms being committed. Especially with regard to following the norms of detachment and skepticism, many prominent evolutionists are biased and partisan secularists. One of the most prominent evolutionists today, Stephen Jay Gould of Harvard, made it very clear in a speech at the University of Chicago that he *knows* that there is no Creator (God forbid)! His own personal views had overridden his professional obligation to adhere to the scientific norms of his profession.

The views of Karl Popper, an influential British philosopher of science, are also relevant here.[3] Popper wrote in 1935 that from a logical point of view, science does not attempt to prove theories, but rather to disprove existing theories. The implication of Popper's view is that there are theoretical reasons to expect that scientific theories will continue to come and go through the revolving door of progress. In contrast, the Torah offers an absolutist standard unlike any other paradigm, in that it is unscathed even while acknowledging the arguments and observations of the scientific method.

Thomas Kuhn, a Harvard physicist and historian of science, has made very useful contributions to the sociology of science which are relevant here.[4] Kuhn distinguishes between normal science, which he defines as fitting new facts into an existing and useful theory, and what he calls scientific revolution, a situation in which fundamental anomalies (or contradictions) develop in the current scientific model (or paradigm) which create such a crisis that a new paradigm is required. The implication of these two states of science in a discipline is relevant to the role which the Torah can play as an alternative paradigm, as popular scientific models continue to be discredited.

From Kuhn's analysis, we see the potential advantages of a relativistic approach in that it allows one the flexibility to drop or pick up ideas as necessary. To the outsider, Torah may appear too rigid and static to effectively address new information and theories; but this is completely untrue. Although Torah, being of Divine origin, is absolute, it is not absolute in a way that excludes relative viewpoints. On the contrary, any system which excludes a phenomenon cannot be truly absolute since *de facto* it lacks something. The concept of relativism is a basic aspect of the Torah and is found both in the *niglah,* the revealed parts of the Torah like the Bible and Jewish Law, and in the *nistar,* the more hidden or mystical aspects of the Torah like Kabbalah. The Talmudic saying, "This view *and* that view are *both* the words of the living God," is a clear statement that there exists great validity in different—and indeed opposing—viewpoints. In fact the Talmud, which has been compared to the sea for its breadth and depth, reflects this approach numerous times by citing various legitimate, logical (and holy) views which contradict each other (at one level, as will be explained shortly).

A further example of the importance of relativism according to the Torah is the story of the great Sage, Rav Zeyra, who fasted seventy times in order to forget the Babylonian Talmud in preparation for learning the more elevated Jerusalem Talmud. A parallel concept is found in *Chasidut.* For a soul to move from a lower spiritual world (the lower Garden of Eden) to a higher spiritual world (the upper Garden of Eden), it must first forget its existence at the lower level. It must, so to speak, adopt a totally different outlook and approach to be able to enter and exist in the higher world. A further illustration of relativism according to Chasidic thought is the Ba'al Shem Tov's explanation that a particular answer in the Torah may be correct only at a particular spiritual level or world; at a higher level a different answer is correct. This demonstrates the relativistic viewpoint in a most profound way. Clearly there is merit in retaining the flexibility of relative viewpoints within an absolute framework that remains true to its criteria and values.

Dr. Gershon Kranzler, a respected Torah scholar and sociologist, has proposed incorporating a clearly defined element into sociology (and indeed into all major disciplines). He calls this approach *metasociology.*[5] It is based on the premise of the reality of God, Who is both active in human affairs and permits humans moral freedom.

In conclusion, in various branches of sociology today an absolutist analysis (which parallels the Torah approach in general) has emerged to challenge long-dominant relativism. This absolutism is most fully developed in the metasociological approach which explicitly acknowledges the fact of the Creator who has given moral guidelines to the humans He has created. The metasociological approach gives us a unique opportunity to study human behavior in a much more profound way by acknowledging the larger spiritual context in which human behavior occurs.

NOTES

1. Caroline Pernell, *Understanding Society*, Second Edition (New York: Harper and Row), 85-87.
2. Merton's norms of science are summarized in Pernell, *Understanding Society*, 431-32. Merton uses the term *norms* to mean *rules*. Elsewhere, sociologists generally define norms as values.
3. Popper's position is more fully explained in Pernell, *Understanding Society*, 433-34.
4. Ibid., 432-33.
5. Dr. Kranzler's explanation of metasociology is outlined in *B'Or Ha-Torah*, No. 2 (Summer 1982). As he explains it there, metasociology "proposes the systematic study of society within a framework that accepts: (1) the presence and continuous function of a Creator; (2) the existence of a universe in which man and his world are a functional part in accordance with the original purpose and will of the Creator and His Divine Providence; and (3) a Divinely-ordained framework of basic values that are not subject to the vagaries and limitations of man's ever-changing culture and its relative norms."

   Among the many important ideas in Dr. Kranzler's approach are the premises that we must always take into account the active teleological presence of God in human affairs, and that He has given us moral criteria with which to evaluate human behavior. Thus life on earth can be measured by Heavenly standards, which are the means to the perfection and completion of God's plans for life on earth.

   Even a minimal elaboration of metasociology's basic ideas constitutes a forceful attack on the logic of Marxism and other relativist, secular and reductionist approaches. For example, a sociological concept as basic as alienation now needs to be challenged and reassessed as a result of the penetrating logic of the metasociological approach.

Zalman I. Posner

Adolescents Face Modernity

ETHICS DON'T belong exclusively to ethicists. Even scientists, who diligently try to avoid making value judgments, must take stands in their professional capacities. A physician who deals with adolescents, for example, may be dealing with issues of ethics, with moral right and wrong, more than with physical disease. For that matter, adults who display disabling symptoms may never be cured unless some subterranean moral issues are resolved. For challenges such as these, which all professionals encounter daily, scientific resources may be inadequate, while Torah can provide crucial guidance. Ethics are not just grist for the ethicist's mill, not some "specialty" with new arcane wisdom, but rather a field relevant to other scientists and to other human beings generally.

This essay discusses an aspect of the transmission of values—

ZALMAN I. POSNER, ordained by the Lubavitcher Yeshiva in New York, has been Rabbi of Congregation Sherith Israel in Nashville, Tennessee, since 1949. He is founder and head of the Akiva Hebrew Day School, and has served as military chaplain and Nashville Human Rights Commissioner. Rabbi Posner has authored many books and articles relating Torah to contemporary life, including the book Think Jewish, *which is now in its third printing. He has also translated numerous scholarly works, including the classic Chasidic text,* Tanya. *Rabbi Posner has lectured before professional, scholarly and lay audiences in twenty-two states as well as in Europe, Asia, Africa and Australia.*

whether from parent to child, teacher to pupil, or therapist to patient. That aspect is the validation of the code.

It is conventional for the older generation to bewail the dire condition of the younger, and like most conventions it is not taken too seriously. We have a faith of sorts in the cyclical nature of human experiences, in repetitions, pendulums swinging way over and inevitably swinging back; this pattern keeps repeating itself with reassuring regularity. Things will work out eventually, and wild oats will be sown but not harvested. No real harm done.

We open the newspaper and find that candidates for the Supreme Court and aspirants for the White House, no less, are suddenly reminded of what they did decades ago, and their dreams end with ignominy. But their foolish youthful errors were not condemned at the time, certainly not by public opinion, although the letter of the law may have prohibited them. The aftereffects are there, however. Some may bear scars or wounds beyond remediation—irreversible drug damage, for example. Not everyone outgrew the counterculture days. Sentimental reminiscences about those glorious days sometimes note that contemporaries are still, and will remain, in mental institutions. The same holds true for current adolescent behaviors which may also result in greatly delayed, yet no less catastrophic, consequences.

And so the question of adolescents and values is not a weary rehash or an overworked conventional concern. It has fresh life today, and yesterday's confidence may not be warranted. We cannot look to cycles and pendulum swings to bring us solace. Too many people are hurt too deeply in the process to justify a fatalistic acceptance of it. There can be intervention even if we do not find panaceas. But we must first examine the problems carefully, and see what solutions are open to us.

There are two great differences between the ethical problems of the past and those of today. One is the sheer complexity of today's issues—in medical ethics, for example, the range of options is enormous, the swiftness of developments is stunning, and the conflicts are very complicated. Another difference is that yesterday's certainty hardly exists today. It is this point that I wish to address.

Transmitting a moral code—principles, ethics, values—is the primary function of education, and the first and most important teachers are the parents. I suggest that concern is usually centered on the transmission of one element—the code proper—to the virtual exclusion of the second element—the roots of the code, its validation, its authority. It is not terribly difficult to devise a moral code with lofty principles, but these are ethereal, insubstantial, arbitrary, until we articulate the roots of the code, its validation, its claim on man. The longevity of the code is contingent on the longevity of its validation.

There are three stages in the transmission of a code and its validation. This concept is found in a wise and seminal book, and quoting from it will not disqualify me from the Presidency of the United States on grounds of plagiarism—you see, I wrote the book. To illustrate the three stages, we might consider the American experience.

Stage 1

The moral code of America—not by total commitment but by effective agreement—included simple and straightforward principles like *Thou shalt not kill* and *Thou shalt not steal.* These were preached from the pulpit, taught in the classroom and inculcated into children at home. If a curious and challenging child asked, "Who said so?" the answer was obvious: "The Bible." "Who wrote the Bible?" "God." It was really quite simple. The code and its roots, validation, authority and origin went together. I agree that this may be an oversimplification, and that the world did not lack scoundrels and outlaws, but it is nevertheless a fair representation of the first stage.

Stage 2

As time passed, people began to challenge the roots and validation of the code. Not all the Founding Fathers were religious, even during stage one, but the nineteenth century brought massive changes. Examples include Darwin and the *H.M.S. Beagle* and the inferences he drew from his observations; Marx's new and radical view of man's history and destiny without religion, the opiate of the people; and increased awareness of the existence of other societies, each with its distinctive moral system. The anthropologists concluded that moral systems are designed by societies in response to their circumstances and needs, and these systems are thus subject to obsolescence, irrelevance, and are ultimately devoid of any moral claim higher than practicality. With these changes came what was possibly the most powerful force of all—science, with its promise of resolving all human problems without recourse to any wisdom or power beyond man's. Still, the moral code remained basically intact, a bedrock of self-evident morality, including basics like prohibitions of murder and robbery.

The humanists—or, if you please, the secular humanists of the day—were decent folk, honest, considerate, generous, humane. But one should remember that their moral code was not their own creation, but their inheritance. In this second stage, people drew from the reservoir of stage one, but were not replenishing the reservoir. The world is full of wise and witty people who amusingly ridicule stodgy moralisms but have no idea of what their young listeners are inferring. The young often fail to hear the moral principles that their second-stage elders profess, but they do get the clear message that there are no absolute statements to be made, that what is wrong for A may be right for B. I have had intelligent and decent graduate students thoughtfully propose that the fellow in the tower in Texas, taking potshots at passersby and killing over twenty people at random, was not doing anything "immoral," because, and I quote, "It may be all right for him."

When ethics and morals are solely the product of man, the almost inevitable result is a dramatic twist in the function of the code. Instead of governing and directing human behavior, they merely reflect and justify it. It is not a human failing but a human characteristic that man cannot rise above his level by his own resources. Fluid morality is roughly analogous to water—it goes downhill. Man's self-concerns, his ego, demand preservation and gratification. He may have a choice, but he will choose the option that serves him best, however he defines "best." Man cannot elevate himself by pulling his hair upward. There can be no self-control, no denial of breathless pleasures, unless the demand comes from a source higher than himself.

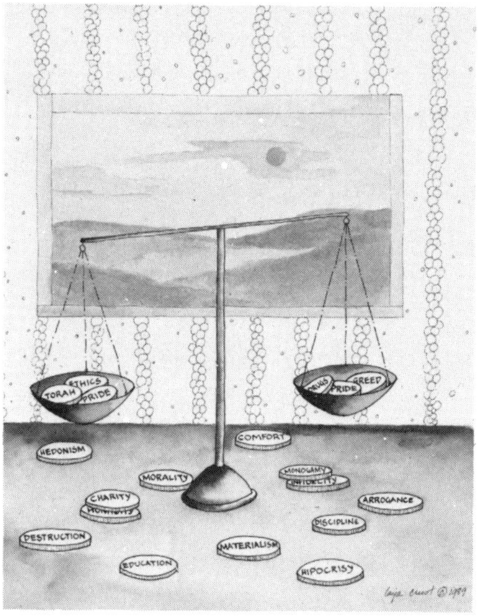

"There can be no self-control, no denial of breathless pleasures, unless the demand comes from a source higher than oneself."

Stage 3

Stage two leads inexorably to stage three: no roots—no code. The good people of stage two did reject the foundation of the code. To their thinking, it was not a revelation of God's will, but the product of man's mind, developed to enable humans to live together without tearing each other up alive. They had a beautiful vision. Poverty was to be eliminated, illiteracy erased, the arts would flourish unimpeded by man's crassness. Enduring peace was at hand as the centuries changed from nineteenth to twentieth, the elimination of disease well on its way, utopia in man's grasp. This was the second stage. The code without roots, a beautiful flower in a lovely vase.

Challenges to moral principles were not as readily answered as they were in stage one. "Who said you shall not steal?" "It's obvious," or, "Man (or society or a committee or whoever) says so."

That's not a very compelling answer. No wonder people don't eagerly accept its guidance. Of course there are other factors, like laws and police and the IRS and social pressures that deeply affect behavior, but these have no necessary contact with ethics or morality. Society's guidance is feeble. There are hundreds, thousands of societies at any given time, each exerting influence on people's behavior. This group which is meeting here today is a society; Western civilization is a society; so is the Ku Klux Klan, and the Union of South Africa and the Civil Liberties Union and the Temperance Union and Planned Parenthood and Right-to-Life. You pays your money and picks your choice.

In stage three the goal is not the validation but the code. In the *New York Times* story of the murder of a boy by the Klan, the words of the Klansmen were revealing. They acted explicitly as members of their society, the Klan, a society that advocates murder. Are the credentials of that society invalid? Who says so? And for that matter, what did Eichmann do that was immoral? He and the Klan acted in accordance with the values of their respective societies.

We must confront the implications of a fluid moral system. Probably ninety percent of the problems and dilemmas of today's world are expressions of fluid morality. As a very contemporary example, twenty years ago the best and brightest indulged in smoking pot; but now their acceptability for nomination to the Supreme Court and the Presidency is sharply questioned. The taste-makers and trend-setters popularized recreational drugs as harmless and chic who are directly responsible for many of the drug problems among young people today as well.

Perhaps what we are confronting now, or trying not to confront, because it may involve too much reexamination, is that the issue is not this particular moral code or that one, but whether there can be a moral code at all. The more realistic choice is between having moral individuals in a moral society and amoral individuals in an amoral society.

If ethics and morals in a given situation depend on personal, subjective, variable definitions, then we are dealing with taste and preference—Rice Krispies vs. Cornflakes, rather than right vs. wrong or good vs. evil, for the distinction between these has been eliminated. Society, the creator and arbiter of ethics, has erased the line between

Gandhi and Hitler, between Schweitzer and Stalin, between the Klansman and Mother Teresa. Are we prepared to declare that these six are moral equals, because each had the right to determine what is right for himself as an individual, or that they are equals because each had a society that enthusiastically supported what he did?

We must accept them as equals unless we have an objective yardstick by which to measure them—one that applies equally in their various circumstances. Hitler and Stalin are not aberrations. They are ineluctable conclusions, the symbols of the twentieth century's unique moral stature. This should give us reason for caution even when we seek moral guidance. Today we have ethicists, experts on moral and ethical issues. In some cases I get the troubling feeling that their proposed *solutions* are in fact the *first* step, the response to the problem at hand, and the second step is an *ex post facto* justification, rationalization, an underpinning that is rigged up to support the solution. Let me be specific instead of being coy. I refer to issues like care and responsibility for babies born with birth defects. The responses I read were drawn from preferences of the society, a hazardous venture considering what civilized societies in Central Europe in the middle of the twentieth century were able to do within a framework of their own laws and ethics.

Age: 13-19

The Wannsee Conference that determined Hitler's Final Solution comprised fourteen participants, eight of them Ph.D.'s. Our problem is not with the dregs of society but with its elite. And now we come, finally, to the subject I was asked to address: Adolescents and Ethics. Under the most favorable of circumstances, adolescence is the legendary time of rebellion, challenge and experimentation. Directed to society for guidance in choosing life styles and values, many teenagers find a society that approves, encourages, even insists upon alcohol, drugs and licentiousness as criteria for acceptance. "It's against the law!"—"Then change the law." "Society disapproves."—"But my society approves."

A human life is priceless? "Nonsense," is the retort of the adolescent, verbalized or implicit. "You are important if you are rich or famous or successful, but not if you are me. If you are poor and unknown and failing everything and ugly and unpopular—how important are you?"

And if they do turn to society for guidance, what do they get? Looking at the newspapers—and I'm not talking about sleaze media—we find that the *New York Times* deplores the rise of teenage pregnancy on page 1, and applauds an unmarried, pregnant, popular high school teacher on page 47, without realizing the magnificent hypocrisy. Maybe the reporters and editors don't read the *Times*—I don't know. The mixed messages reaching the young are not really confusing to them; they are perfectly aware of what phoniness is and what the papers are really preaching.

Ah, but the *Times* is a national institution, not "down home." So let us look at the *Tennessean*, which on page 1 touts a tennis-playing lout who is the father of a starlet's unborn child, and quotes his exuberant boast, "I am proud of it." At the same time, the *Tennessean* devotes endless and impassioned editorials to the crying necessity for sex education, in order to reduce the number of teenage pregnancies. Our teenagers don't lack sex education. They get it all the time; it's all around them. That, I humbly suggest, is an example of the problem of Adolescents and Ethics.

We are told that this is a tiny planet, a global village; that we are one family. I suggest that this is the case not simply because of the photographs that astronauts took from space, nor because of the threat of a nuclear holocaust, nor because of the possibility of plagues like AIDS decimating or destroying mankind. We are one family because there was one Creator who made us all. We are unique in all the universe, not because of our size or number, for we are physically infinitesimal. We are unique because we are human, and a human being is not only a speaking, tool-using biped, nor a programmed, predictable automaton. A human being is a creature who can *make moral decisions*. Murder and robbery and deceitfulness are evil not only because they destroy the fabric of society, though that is reason enough, but because these activities corrupt man's soul. Soul? What is a soul? I cannot define it. Nor can you define a quark. Every adolescent, and obviously I choose that term because we are speaking about them at the moment, is priceless, not because he is an

A-student or a good athlete or popular, but because he has a function in life that is unique to him and shared by no other human being. If he fulfills his potential he enriches the world in a way that no other person can. Man is not a quantity, not subject to statistics. Every act of every person is crucial, and has cosmic importance, whether it is a hand raised to strike or a hand raised to help, a thought to deceive or a thought to improve, a word to bring comfort or a word of falsehood. So that in effective terms, we can no more hope to give our young people a moral sense without a foundation than we can give them beautiful cut flowers and expect the blossoms to endure, as in stage two.

Of course, in my calling it is acceptable to have biases, to make value judgments, to be moralistic. (I haven't quite figured out the difference between moralistic and moral, since a moral person will presumably articulate his moral principles.) We have a very special view of man, one which says that man determines the quality of his life by the choices he makes. We teach our children ה' נצב עליו: that God stands with you because He loves you and watches over you, to help you serve Him and live in the best way you can.

Maimonides declares that there is no power in Heaven or earth that compels any person to be righteous or wicked. We may infer that every person, even an adolescent, has both potentials, both capacities in himself. This is man created in God's image, a free being who cannot be dominated by any power. This is God's perspective of man, and man's perspective of himself, if he is to be fully and truly human.

Avi Rabinowitz
Herman Branover

The Role of the Observer in Halachah and Quantum Physics

ACCORDING TO THE PHILOSOPHY of quantum physics, actual physical reality can exist (in the scientific meaning of the term "existence") only as a result of observation. When not being observed, the universe is in a quasi-real state amenable to description only in terms of probabilities and not facts. Some eminent physicists argue that observation (or measurement) must be performed by a conscious entity. According to this view, it is only observation

---

AVI RABINOWITZ, since obtaining his Ph.D. in quantum physics at New York University, has been teaching and researching physics and Judaism at various colleges and universities in New York and Israel. His published works include several B'Or HaTorah *articles on topics spanning prayer, free will, and geocentrism.*

HERMAN BRANOVER is Editor-in-Chief and founder of B'Or HaTorah. *He obtained his Ph.D. at the Moscow Aviation Institute and D.Sc. at the Leningrad Polytechnical Institute, and was appointed a Senior Research Fellow of the Latvian Academy of Sciences. In 1972 he emigrated from the Soviet Union to Israel, where he created the Center for Magnetohydrodynamic Studies at Ben-Gurion University, which has pioneered the development of low temperature liquid metal magnetohydrodynamic power generation systems.*

performed by a conscious being which can bring the universe into full reality.

The idea to write an article exploring the parallels between quantum physics and *Halachah* was inspired by a discourse of the Lubavitcher Rebbe, *shlita,* on Shabbat *parashat Shemini,* 5746, in which the dependence of physical reality on testimony of witnesses was discussed. The second author of this paper was present for the above discourse and the parallels between the ideas discussed by the Rebbe and the views of quantum physics struck him. He shared his impressions with the first author and that is how work on this article began.

This paper explores various fundamental perspectives in Jewish philosophy and *Halachah* which reveal parallels to this quantum world view. These parallels pertain to ontology, which addresses the essence of existence, as well as to epistemology, which deals with criteria for knowledge. In the first section, we present a very brief summary of the relevant aspects of quantum theory. In the second section we discuss some relevant aspects of Jewish philosophy and *Halachah.* These include the Jewish view of the Creation of the universe; the relation between the Creation, man's purpose and man's unique characteristics; and finally the halachic methodology for the establishment of fact. All of these are related by the common theme of determination of reality via observation performed by a consciousness.

Duality

For many years there was a debate among scientists regarding the nature of light. Certain phenomena seemed to indicate that light is a wave, while others pointed to its having a particle-like nature. The debate was stilled early this century when it was realized that all entities can be considered to be both waves and particles—some physical conditions cause a manifestation of the wave-like properties of these entities, and some cause a manifestation of their particle-like properties. This duality became one of the fundamental concepts of the newly developed quantum physics.

The duality concept arises as follows. If one were to eject an electron from an electron gun and run it through a slit of some sort, one would expect that since an electron is a particle, it would continue straight in a flat trajectory and reach a screen or a detector directly opposite to where it emerged. On the other hand, if one has a wave—for example, light coming out of a light bulb—one is not terribly surprised to find out that the light waves, as they pass through the slit, might bend in some way and form strange diffraction patterns on the screen.

The surprising fact was the discovery that electrons and indeed all particles also show wave properties, and when injected through a slit, produce a diffraction effect. This led to the understanding that all entities in the universe are both waves and particles.

Probabilistic Determinism

Prior to the advent of quantum physics, science believed that every event in the universe occurred as an inevitable and necessary result of previous events. The state of the universe at any one instant was believed to be totally determined by the states of the universe in the past, and in turn the present state totally determined what all future states of the universe would be.

Quantum physics, introduced at the beginning of the century, brought with it a drastic change in this viewpoint. Each event was now understood to be able to occur in a number of ways, with the actual way that it does occur left to 'chance.' Despite the fact that chance 'ruled' each individual event, however, when numerous similar events occurred, the pattern which emerged resembled the results one would have expected using pre-quantum physics.

That is, each individual event, though occurring 'at random,' nevertheless contributes somehow to a pattern, in the aggregate, which can be determined beforehand. This combination of random and determined behavior is called here *probabilistic determinism* or *probabilistically determined randomness.*

Physicists were troubled, however, for this 'random' aspect seemed to be contrary to the 'spirit of physics.' Much inquiry was directed to the question of whether the chance aspect was only apparent—i.e., due to our lack of sufficient scientific knowledge and adequate instrumentation—or if it was an actual physical requirement. With the accumulation of more experimental evidence it was shown that indeed the nature of the physical universe appears to be such that intrinsically, at the most fundamental level, events are probabilistic and not deterministic.

Reality and Measurement

Most surprisingly, it has been found that the act of measurement does not *reveal* what state a thing is in. Rather, what one measures actually *determines* a thing's state; it brings that condition into being. A taste of the experimental physics behind this bizarre statement may render the idea more intellectually palatable (although no less odd).

One of the important experiments in quantum physics is the one-slit experiment mentioned above. Other studies involve projection of a particle or a wave toward two slits. Now, we may either construct the experiment to tell us which slit the photon (or electron or whatever) did go through, or we may construct that same experiment in such a way as to show a diffraction pattern, which indicates that it went through both slits. It should be impossible for us to determine both which slit the electron went through—which implies that it went through only one—and at the same time to receive a diffraction pattern, which implies that it went through both.

Indeed if one constructs an experiment which tries to do both, one finds that it's impossible, theoretically as well as practically. The new result achieved by Wheeler was to show that this decisive measurement may be done even *after* the (electron or photon or whatever) entity passes through the slit, and even then one can change the experiment in such a way as to determine one or the other—in other words, either which one it went through, or if it went through both.

Prior to its measurement, an event can occur in a number of ways, and actually does so in some sense. Without measuring the state of a particle, we cannot say, "It is in some particular state, which is however as yet unknown to us." It is *not* in some particular state. Instead, it is (in some sense) simultaneously in *all* the possible states in which it can be! Indeed, even after measurement is made, and the particle is found to be in a particular state, we cannot then say that the particle was in that state all the time—no! It had no definite state until one measured it. Our measurement forces the universe to assume one definite state from among all the possibility-states it is in prior to the measurement! This is usually called "the collapse of the wave function into reality."

This surprising, even bewildering, property can be interpreted as saying that the universe can emerge into reality only as a result of its measurement! In a way this is trite and in a way it's radical. It is trite in the sense that for at least two centuries philosophers such as Berkeley and the positivists have explored the idea that reality is only set by our consciousness of it, because we can perceive things through the senses. It is radical, however, in that this result has now been achieved by physics. Therefore, what is true in the realm of words and ideas has been shown by physics to be true of physical reality as well: the actual thing itself is not set until it is measured.

Summary

From the preceding discussion, we can make the following summary: All entities in the universe have a dual nature, one material and localized (particulate) and one non-material and non-localized (wave-like). The universe, or any subsystem of it, is capable of being in two (or more) mutually contradictory states simultaneously. Saying that the universe is in one state is just as valid (or invalid) as saying that it is in the other state. However, a decision can be made between the two by having a measurement made of the situation. Both views are correct, but only until the measurement is made. After that, only one becomes correct. However, this does not imply that it was always the correct one; there *was* no 'correct' state until the measurement was made.

The Role of Consciousness

What is the active factor in a measurement which causes this emergence into reality? According to some leading physicists, this factor is the human consciousness. The great mathematician, John Von Neumann, who provided a rigorous mathematical foundation for quantum mechanics, believed that only a *human* consciousness can collapse the wave function.[1,2]

The eminent Nobel prize-winning physicist Eugene Wigner writes:

> ... It follows that the quantum description of objects is influenced by impressions entering my consciousness.... It follows that the being with a consciousness must have a different role in quantum mechanics than the inanimate measuring device.[3]

The famous physicist John Wheeler has taken this one step further. According to him the entire universe can emerge into true physical existence only via the observation of a consciousness!

> ... [perhaps] no universe at all could come into being unless it were guaranteed to produce life, consciousness and observership somewhere and for some little length of time in its history-to-be?...
> ... the observer is as essential to the creation of the universe as the universe is to the creation of the observer...
> ... the universe would be nothing without observership, as surely as a motor would be dead without electricity...
> ... is observership the 'electricity' that powers genesis?...
> ... 'observership' allows and enforces a transcendence of the usual order in time...[4]

Thus, according to "quantum metaphysics,"[5] a consciousness is indispensable to the universe if it is to emerge into reality. Physical reality can be said to exist only as a result of our presence within it, or, more precisely, as a result of our perception of it.[6]

Wheeler has constructed a fascinating diagram to illustrate

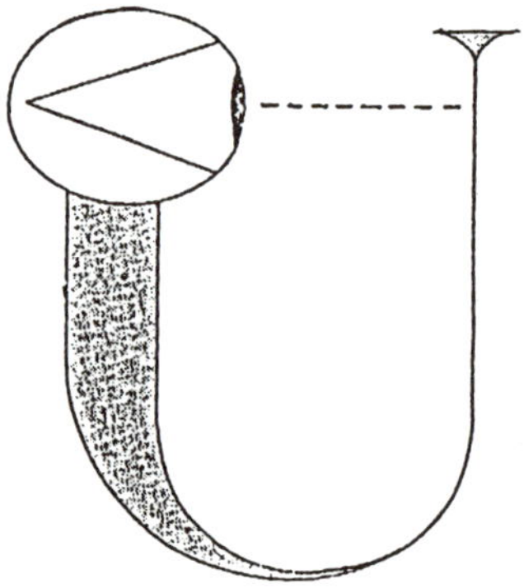

this concept. Explaining this diagram, he writes: "Beginning with the big bang, the universe expands and cools. After eons of dynamic deelopment it gives rise to observership. Acts of observer-participancy in turn give tangible 'reality' to the universe not only now but back to the beginning."[7]

Free Will, Quantum Physics and the Collapse of the Wave Function

A free-willed decision, in order to be truly free, has to be unconstrained by the laws of nature and not determined by any physical phenomena. Hence free will must be neither the result of deterministic processes nor the result of random processes occurring in accordance with the natural order of phenomena. Hence if the universe contains a free will, this free will must operate via interactions which transcend both the determinism of classical physics and the randomness of quantum physics. Free will is then unique in this respect.

If some entity exists which can collapse the quantum wave function, then it is reasonable to postulate that this entity has to be free will, since, as we just discussed, only free will transcends quantum randomness, as it transcends nature in general.

Since a consciousness can affect the universe only if it has a free will, and a free will is by definition unthinkable without a consciousness, we will assume in the course of further discussion that free will subsumes within itself the concept of consciousness.[8]

Existence of the Universe and the Role of Free-Willed Conscious Beings

We will try now to apply the conclusions we reached above to the question of the existence of the universe. As we saw, according to quantum metaphysics, the universe can emerge into reality only when it is observed by a consciousness. This consciousness possibly must function in a non-quantum fashion in order to "collapse the wave function." The only such non-quantum factor in the universe is free will! Thus, we postulate that it is the presence of a free-willed, conscious being which enables the universe to emerge into reality!

Meaning and Reality—the Torah Viewpoint

According to Jewish thought, the true reality is the spiritual realm,the physical cosmos being God's precision-crafted instrument for achieving spiritual goals. Indeed, the physical universe is a shadow of the spiritual world, the illusion perceived by limited beings who are in contact with the spiritual cosmos but can directly sense and perceive only its shadow. According to Kabbalistic and Chasidic terminology, the physical universe is an emanation of God.

Thus, since the true reality of the universe is the spiritually meaningful aspect, it should not be surprising that the emergence of the universe into reality is so intimately bound up with the emergence of those beings who endow physicality with meaning. Furthermore, once this connection is understood, it is most appropriate that the very characteristics of man which allow the emergence of the universe into reality (i.e., his free-willed consciousness) are the very same characteristics which endow it with meaning. We can thus see the fundamental interrelationship between meaning, purpose, free will, consciousness and the very nature of reality (and how this is reflected in Creation).

Summary

We have seen that according to quantum (meta)physics, reality is established via the observation of a (free-willed) consciousness. In addition, we have shown that according to Jewish thought, free-willed choice gives the universe meaning, and is thus the "motivation" for the very existence of the universe. We will now explore how the nature of everyday Jewish law is correlated with this radical conception of the reality of the universe.

Man, Torah and Reality

According to Jewish tradition, the Torah is the "blueprint" which was used by God in creating the universe.[9] Moreover, God is continually renewing Creation—recreating the universe every moment—by interpreting the blueprint for the recreation of the universe at that instant. These statements pertain to a more abstract form of Torah, to a Torah that exists spiritually in the form of "black fire on white fire."[10] However, once this Torah was translated into human terms and given over to man at Sinai, the prerogative of its interpretation and application rested solely with man—it is man's responsibility and his alone. And through involvement with Torah, man actually becomes a partner in the continuous renewal of the cosmos.

In our universe, the operative concepts are "free-willed conscious choice," not "nature, i.e., objective scientific fact." It is the former which provides the motivation for the existence of the latter (the purpose of the universe is free-willed choice), and it is the former which causes the latter to emerge into existence (collapse of a probability wave). Thus, it will not come as a surprise that, in Jewish law, free-willed conscious moral choice rules over the "laws of nature," rather than vice versa.

The true reality is the spiritual one. The physical is in existence only to serve the spiritual. The entire physical universe is an artifact created by God. Man is a precisely crafted instrument designed to interact with the physical universe in ways which have the potential to achieve spiritual goals unattainable without the vehicle of the physical. Thus the physical is of central importance, but only as a means: It can have sublime beauty and dignity, but only by virtue of its ability to achieve in the spiritual realm. Thus the human body, rather than being a hindrance to spirituality, is a potentially holy physical tool which can control the spiritual.[11]

Indeed, every action/thought/word affects the spiritual cosmos, and the Jewish way of life as prescribed by the Torah is designed to resonate with the spiritual and to correctly utilize the physical in order to elicit the fusion of ultimate spirituality with the physical. God is the Creator of the universe and of man. He has designed the universe, man and the way to complete each other, to complement one another, in a self-consistent optimum system. He communicated the method to man in the form of the Torah (Written and Oral) and He, the Designer and Creator of this system, has promised us that we are superbly qualified to successfully perform our role and attain our goal. More than this, we are told that since we are designed to be the best instrument to achieve this goal within

the context of a physical universe, when we perform at optimum, we can determine the nature of the physical/spiritual interaction.

Halachah and the Determination of Reality

There are three ways by which man determines halachic reality: by determining which one of several rabbinic opinions shall be authorized for implementation; by determining which of several scenarios (having halachic relevance) is the factually correct one; and by determining the reality itself, i.e., forcing the reality to conform with the halachic opinion.

Halachah and Reality

A) Halachic Decisions: Normally, one would assume that of two conflicting viewpoints regarding legal matters in a Divinely mandated code of life, one must be incorrect. However, the power of man to determine spiritual reality is reflected very clearly in halachic philosophy, and in *Halachah* itself. According to the Talmud, when two qualified rabbis arrive at conflicting and mutually exclusive conclusions, if both have researched the matter as required, and both are sincere and interested only in the truth, then both are right. This attitude is recorded in the Talmud and is given here in rough translation: "For two-and-a-half years the schools of Rabbi Hillel and Rabbi Shammai were in dispute regarding a certain ruling. Finally, a voice came from Heaven and declared: 'Verily, both views are the words of the living God, but the ruling is according to Rabbi Hillel.' "[12]

Since the spiritual reality is determined by *man,* there is no paradox involved in two mutually contradictory results being both right, as long as they represent two human opinions arrived at through religiously legitimate means. The Torah also gives us rules for deciding the actual path to take when we are presented with two or more valid opinions, for example, the principle of decision by majority.[13] Once one of the paths has been accepted by rabbinical authority, it alone becomes the *only* viable path of action. Even though the other path is still theoretically correct, it becomes absolutely unacceptable as an actual path as soon as the religious reality is decided in favor of the other.

For example,[14] the dates for Jewish holidays were set according to rabbinical ruling based on observation of the moon and on calculations. One year the date for *Yom Kippur* (the holiest day of the year) calculated by Rabbi Yehoshua differed by one day from the date arrived at by Rabban Gamliel. Since Rabban Gamliel was the *Nasi* (Chief Justice), the ruling followed his view. In order to prevent anarchy, he then ordered Rabbi Yehoshua to come to see him on the day that Rabbi Yehoshua considered to be *Yom Kippur*—and to do so in a manner forbidden on *Yom Kippur*. This would prove that there was only one authoritative ruling. Rabbi Yehoshua came, violating what he considered to be the holiest day of the year, in deference to Rabban Gamliel's view. Rabban Gamliel then told him that he considered Rabbi Yehoshua to be his superior in wisdom and learning, but that as *Nasi* his word was nevertheless law. Thus, even though Rabbi Yehoshua's view was possibly more logically valid than that of Rabban Gamliel, as soon as the decision was made in favor of the other view, his own ruling became totally unacceptable as religious law, and the day he considered the holiest ceased to be so.

We have just seen that two conflicting opinions can both be considered valid, yet that only the majority opinion is accepted as normative. This is an example of the simplest level at which man determines the halachic reality, i.e., that of determining which of several opinions shall be accepted as normative *Halachah*. We will now present examples of the other two levels on which this is true: disclosure of factual reality and causation of factual reality.

B) Disclosure of Factual Reality: In the same *mishnah* discussed above, Rabbi Akiva brought proof from the Torah that even if the court set a festival on the incorrect day through its own error, the declaration was religiously valid. The following *mishnah* relates that even if all the people of Israel, including all the court justices, saw the new moon and/or received the testimony of the witnesses, if the court did not *declare* it as the new moon (by the day's end), the new moon was considered to begin the next day.

Even when *Halachah* seemingly depends on objective physical reality, such as the temporal sanctification at the time of the new moon, what actually determines the *Halachah* is the decision/measurement made by man (in this case the court ruling), even though the physical facts seem to present a contradiction. Neither nature nor supernatural events can usurp the prerogative of man in deciding *Halachah*, and thus the spiritual reality. This can be seen graphically in the account presented in the following narrative from the Talmud.[15]

> Rabbi Yehoshua and Rabbi Eliezer were arguing a point of religious law. Rabbi Eliezer was unable to convince Rabbi Yehoshua of his point, and so he then tried to convince him by using miracles. He said: "If I am right, let the stream run uphill." And it did so. This however did not convince Rabbi Yehoshua. "If I am right, let the wall bend," declared Rabbi Eliezer, and the wall indeed bent. Rabbi Yehoshua, however, remained unconvinced! So Rabbi Eliezer called upon Heaven itself to decide the matter. He said, "If I am right, let Heaven prove it." Indeed, a voice came from Heaven and declared, "What do you want from Rabbi Eliezer? The ruling is always in accordance with his views."

> At this point, Rabbi Yehoshua arose and quoted the Torah saying, "It (the Torah) is not in Heaven."[16]

By this he meant that it is *man*—not physical law or even Heaven—who decides spiritual reality. That is, he did not dispute the fact that Heaven had decided in favor of Rabbi Eliezer (and that probably this meant that "nature" favored him as well); rather he claimed that Heaven had already delegated the authority in such matters to man alone!

The most far-reaching example of such a philosophy can again be found in the Talmud.[17] There we are shown quite clearly that neither the inhabitants of the spiritual realm, nor God Himself, define *Halachah*—only man can do so. A debate about a religious ruling was taking place between the members of the "Heavenly College" (the souls of deceased saintly rabbinical scholars) and God Himself: God held to one view and the members of the College to another. The College then decided that in order to reach an authoritative ruling neither God nor Moshe *Rabbenu* could decide, but rather that the living rabbinical authority (Rabbi Bar Nachmani) must decide.

The Talmud also tells us what God's view of all this is: At the end of the case with Rabbi Yehoshua and Rabbi Eliezer described previously, Elijah the Prophet is quoted as reporting that God was immensely pleased with man's understanding of his role in determining religious reality, and that God even laughed with joy, saying: "My sons have bested me, my sons have bested me." Thus on questions of *Halachah* and spiritual reality, the world, the Heavens, and God Himself, all defer to man, though he be incomplete and limited.

C) Halachah and the Causation of Reality: Since the Torah is the blueprint of Creation, man's interpretation of it can have cosmic effect; halachic ruling causes physical reality to emerge and even change so as to conform with the blueprint from which it was created. Thus an extremely potent level on which man can determine physical reality is that of halachic decision. This astonishing concept is referred to in a famous passage in the Jerusalem Talmud.[18] In order to understand the passage, one must be familiar with the concept of the leap year in the Jewish calendar.

A Jewish leap year involves the addition of a 13th month to the

12-lunar-month year, in order to correlate it with the solar year. If a child is born in the middle of the last month of a non-leap year, then the month of birth is both "the 12th" and "the last" month of the year. During leap years, when the 12th month is not the last month, it is not obvious which month is the child's birth month: the last (13th) month, or the 12th (second to last) month. The Talmudic ruling is that the birthday is on the last (13th) month.

The passage in the Jerusalem Talmud which we mentioned above concerns physical changes in the body of a child involving a lessened ability of the body to regenerate certain tissues; this change is determined as occurring at the conclusion of the third year of life. Thus, if the child's birthday is, for example, on the fifth day of the last month, then in his third year, on the fifth of the last month, the physical change occurs. However, if at the end of the month, *after the change has taken place,* it is decided by the court that a 13th month will be added to the year, his third birthday according to *Halachah* has not yet occurred (it will occur only on the fifth day of this newly added 13th month), and thus the physical change should not yet have occurred. According to this Talmudic source, the physical change will, in this circumstance, actually reverse itself in conformance with the halachic decision! (If an observation is made already, the reality is "frozen" and cannot be changed retroactively by a later observation; it can however be changed if no observation is made.)

For another instance, the famous Rogatchover *Gaon* once indicated a similar philosophy regarding the ability of *Halachah* to determine physical reality. A woman once came to him with a defective slaughtered chicken, to ask whether or not it was *terefah* (an animal with a terminal disease or fatal defect that renders it not kosher). The chicken seemed to be a clear-cut case of *terefah,* yet the Rogatchover's students noticed that their Rabbi spent hours checking it, consulting books, thinking and so on, rather than spending the usual few minutes. They were astounded that this great genius would waste his time on such a trivial matter instead of simply buying the chicken from the woman and throwing it out. In the end, the Rogatchover was able to find a way to reach the halachic decision that the chicken was not a *terefah,* i.e., that its disease was not fatal according to the halachic definition of "fatal." The students were stupefied at the exertion of such genius over such triviality.

The next day, a woman came to the Rogatchover wailing and sobbing. Her husband was deathly ill, she cried, asking the Rabbi for help. The Rogatchover asked the woman what was wrong with her husband. She described precisely the disease which afflicted her husband. The Rogatchover then answered thus: "Don't worry—only yesterday I examined a chicken with the identical disease and I ruled that it was not a *terefah*—your husband is therefore not deathly ill, and will recover!"

The Biblical sources given for this far-reaching concept are passages in *Psalms* and *Isaiah*, whose hidden meanings had been passed down along with the text from generation to generation. For example, in *Isaiah* 44:24-26, we read: "I am the Lord that makes all things; that stretches the heavens, alone; that spreads abroad the earth by Myself; that frustrates the omens of impostors, and makes diviners mad; that turns wise men backward, and makes their knowledge foolish; that confirms the word of His servant, and performs the counsel of His messengers."

God created the universe *ex nihilo*, but has left to man the fashioning of this raw material, as indicated in the traditional interpretation of the passage: "For then He rested from His work, which He created to be fashioned" (*Genesis* 2:3).

The Sages interpreted the apparently superfluous term לעשות ("to be fashioned") as indicating: "All that was created in the six days of Creation requires 'fashioning' (by man)" (*Bereshit Rabbah* 11:7).

Quantum *Halachah*

We can now compare the halachic view of reality with that of quantum physics. According to the Talmud, two, or many, logically valid halachic rulings may be consistent with the available facts. Indeed, two independent valid viewpoints can be diametrically opposed and mutually contradictory. *Halachah* allows either one to determine the reality in principle, but will accept only one of the possibilities in actuality.

The analogy between this conception and the idea of the multiple possibilities for reality prior to a "measurement" in quantum physics is now obvious. Although both are the (living) words/realities of (the living) God, only one can determine reality. Also, even though all entities can be measured to produce the characteristics of either waves or particles—both are living reality—only one aspect by itself can be seen "statistically" as the result of an actual measurement.

Furthermore, just as according to quantum physics (or metaphysics) nature has delegated to man the ability to determine the nature of physical reality within the limitations of natural law, similarly, according to Torah God, the Creator of nature, has delegated to man alone the ability to determine the nature of spiritual reality, within the limitations of *Halachah*; and the spiritual, in turn, influences the physical. Of the two levels, the physical is merely the means to the spiritual end. Thus the determination by man of spiritual reality is even more fundamental than his determination of physical reality. So too it is man's spiritual qualities (free-willed consciousness) which are more fundamental than these physical qualities.

As illustrated in the previously cited instances, it is up to man to use his own limited sense of right and wrong, guided by Torah criteria, to determine the *Halachah*, and thus to determine reality. *Halachah* is the guideline for the Torah way of life, the way to achieve one's purpose—and it is this purpose which also gives meaning to the universe. Since it is man's consciousness and free will which invest his choices with the possibility of meaning, it is therefore only free-willed consciousness which has the possibility of conducting reality-determining observation and measurement.

Nature by itself is powerless even to achieve self-realization; man is required to bring both himself and the universe into reality. Thus nature cannot determine *Halachah*. Similarly, God Himself does not decide *Halachah*—it is man's prerogative and sole responsibility. Man, alive and physical and yet spiritual as well, albeit limited and fallible—or perhaps *because* he is limited and fallible—is uniquely qualified, by virtue of his possessing a free-willed consciousness, to determine the nature of physical and spiritual reality.

Some Epistemological Consequences of Quantum Metaphysics

As we have seen, quantum physics connects ontology (being) with epistemology (knowing), and quantum metaphysics postulates that the universe can emerge into true physical existence only when there are (free-willed) conscious beings in it. According to this scenario, man is not a random product of the universe, but is rather a necessary condition for the very existence of the universe. In addition, since the universe can emerge into existence only when free-willed conscious man is present within it, there is no true physical reality to any time prior to the emergence of the first free-willed conscious man. According to the Torah, this man was Adam.[19]

The conclusion that reality is established only as a result of direct observation by a free-willed consciousness has very far-reaching consequences in relation to the epistemological meaning and value of a number of theories. For one, every attempt to describe or explain events which supposedly took place prior to man's existence appears to be fundamentally impossible. Therefore all the well-known arguments about the validity of theories of evolution, assessments of the age of the universe, etc., become merely useless, since according to the approach of quantum mechanics, reality simply did not exist (in the rational or "scientific" meaning) at the time under consideration because the necessary free-willed observer did not exist. On the other hand it also becomes clear that the only possible source of knowledge about events and things which preceded the existence of man is Torah, the word of God Who wanted to reveal to us knowledge which is inaccessible through scientific inquiry. Whether one accepts or rejects this source is obviously again a free-willed decision.

NOTES

1. J. Von Neumann, *Mathematical Foundations of Quantum Mechanics* (Princeton University Press, 1955), esp. notes 207 and 238. Translated from *Mathematische Grundlagen der Quantenmechenic* (Berlin: Springer, 1932, and New York: Dover, 1943).

2. M. Tammer, *The Conceptual Development of Quantum Mechanics* (McGraw-Hill, 1966), esp. 370-373.
3. E. Wigner, "Remarks on the Mind-Body Question," *Scientist Speculates,* I. J. Good, ed. (New York: Basic Books, 1962), 284-302.

   That an observation performed by a consciousness is also a "measurement" is not disputed. What is noted here is the postulate that *only* a measurement by a consciousness (i.e., an observation) can "collapse" the wave function.
4. J.A. Wheeler, *Genesis and Observership.*
5. That the wave function is collapsed by measurement is fact, and thus it is part of physics. What it is that causes this collapse is not yet known—various mechanisms are possible. Thus, speculations in this direction are more properly labeled "quantum metaphysics" than quantum physics.
6. One very important comment is in place here. In all of the above, when we say "physical reality" we mean reality with respect to man and his perception. Thus the statement that reality does not exist prior to observation (measurement) means that it does not exist in respect to man, and human, rational knowledge. However, from the Torah perspective it exists, since God reveals to us through His Torah the whole story of Creation. Moreover, God of course knows the exact state of the universe, any part of it, and any entity in it prior to and independent of any human observation, as Maimonides writes in his *Mishneh Torah* [Moses Hyamson, ed., *The Book of Knowledge* (Jerusalem and New York: Feldheim Publishers, 1981), 36a-36b]:

   "All beings, except the Creator, from the highest angelic form to the tiniest insect that is in the interior of the earth, exist by the power of God's essential existence. And as He has self-knowledge, and realizes His greatness, glory and truth, He knows all, and nought is hidden from Him.

   "The Holy One, blessed be He, realizes His true being, and knows it as it is, not with a knowledge external to himself, as is our knowledge. For our knowledge and ourselves are separate. But as for the Creator, blessed be He, His knowledge and His life are One, in all aspects, from every point of view, and however we conceive Unity. If the Creator lived as other living creatures live, and His knowledge were external to Himself, there would be a plurality of deities, namely; He himself, His life, and His knowledge. This however is not so. He is One in every aspect, from every angle, and in all ways in which Unity is conceived. Hence the conclusion that God is the One who knows, is known, and is the knowledge (of Himself)—all these being One. This is beyond the power of speech to express, beyond the capacity of the ear to hear, and of the human mind to apprehend clearly. Scripture, accordingly, says "By the life of Pharaoh" and "By the life of thy soul" but not "By the life of the Eternal." The phrase employed is "As God Liveth"; because the Creator and His life are not dual, as is the case with the life of living bodies or of angels. Hence too, God does not apprehend creatures and know them because of them, as we know them, but He knows them because of Himself. Knowing Himself, He knows everything, for everything is attached to Him, in His Being."

7. J.A. Wheeler, "Beyond the Black Hole," in *Some Strangeness in the Proportion: A Centennial Symposium to Celebrate the Achievements of Albert Einstein*, H. Woolf, ed. (Massachusetts: Addison Wesley, 1980).
8. A. Rabinowitz, "Free Will," *B'Or HaTorah* 6 (1987):141-158.
9. *Midrash Bereshit Rabbah* 1:1; *Zohar, Parashat Terumah*, p. 161b.
10. Jerusalem Talmud, *Shekalim*, 1: end of *halachah* 1.
11. M.C. Luzatto, *Derech Hashem*.
12. *Eruvin* 13b.
13. *Exodus* 23:2.
14. Mishnah *Rosh Hashanah* 2:9; Talmud *Rosh Hashanah* 25a.
15. *Bava Metzia* 59b.
16. *Deuteronomy* 30:12.
17. *Bava Metzia* 86a.
18. Jerusalem Talmud, *Ketuvot*, 1:2.
19. A. Rabinowitz, *Let There Have Been a Big Bang*, in press. This work contains a more comprehensive discussion of the connection between Genesis, evolution theory, the Big Bang, and quantum mechanics.

Paul C. Rosenbloom

What's in a Name?

A CENTRAL CONCEPT in Kabbalah is that the essence and life-force of a created being is contained in its Hebrew name.[1] One of the clearest and most explicit statements of this very old doctrine (and the best reference in English) is found in the *Tanya*.

> The Holy One, blessed be He, however, contracted the light and life-force in order that it should be able to diffuse from the 'Breath of His Mouth' and invested it in the combinations of the letters of the Ten Utterances and their combinations of combinations, by substitutions and transpositions of the letters themselves and their numerical values and equivalents. For each substitution and transposition indicates the descent of the light and life-force degree by degree, so that it will be able to create and give life to creatures whose quality and significance is lower than the quality and significance of the creatures created from the letters and words of

---

PAUL C. ROSENBLOOM is Professor of Mathematics and Mathematics Education at Columbia University and its Teacher's College. After earning his Doctorate at Stanford University in 1944, he taught at Brown, Syracuse, and the University of Minnesota. He has authored six books and some fifty research papers, and has been honored with the Frechot Prize, and memberships in the Institute for Advanced Studies and the National Science Foundation's Advisory Panel for Mathematics. Together with his wife, he is involved with FREE (Friends of Refugees from Eastern Europe), aiding Jewish immigrants from the Soviet Union.

> the Ten Utterances themselves, in which the Holy One, blessed be He, in His Glory and Essence, is clothed, for the Ten Utterances are His attributes. And the numerical value indicates the progressive diminution of the light and life-force until there remains from it only the final level which is that of the sum and number of kinds of powers and grades contained in the light and life-force in a particular combination of a particular word.[2]

The classical interpretation of the process of Creation through Divine speech is derived from the verse, ... הוא אמר ויהי—"For He spoke and it was."[3] Thus, for example, when the Creator says, ... יהי אור—"Let there be light,"[4] the word אור contains the essence of the thing created by that Divine Utterance.

What can this doctrine mean? How can one interpret it in terms of modern science? The aim of this paper is to suggest a possible interpretation in the sense of indicating what kind of name the Hebrew name might be.*

First, we must understand the special character of names in the Torah. Maimonides, in his *Guide for the Perplexed,*[5] says that "the Almighty commenced the Holy Writings with the description of the Creation,

---

* We only make a beginning here. A fuller explanation would require extensive research into the Divine Names, their permutations, combinations and substitutions, among other topics, which are far beyond the scope of this article, and for which others are more qualified. However, we hope, with His help, to write a future article on the concept of Creation by means of Divine Utterances.

that is, with physical science... our means of comprehending these problems being limited. He described those profound truths, which His Divine Wisdom found it necessary to communicate to us in allegorical, figurative, and metaphorical language.... It has been treated in metaphors in order that the uneducated may comprehend it according to the measure of their faculties..., while educated persons may take it in a different sense." Thus, the words of Torah have one meaning to us, who need to know its precepts and how to observe them, another meaning to those who have the background and ability to analyze them more deeply, and probably still another meaning to the Almighty who used Torah as a blueprint for Creation. According to the commentators, during the revelation of the Torah at Sinai, each person received it to the measure of his capacity.

(The fact that names can have different meanings to different people is illustrated by the word *relativity* in the very title of this conference. In physics, that word means that each observer may describe events from his own point of view, with his own clock, frame of reference, and measuring sticks. The only things in such descriptions which have *physical meaning* are those which are left unchanged, passing from one observer to another. The Lubavitcher Rebbe, in his introductory letter to the conference, refers to Einstein's fundamental postulate that the velocity of light is one such absolute. Thus the emphasis is on the search for *invariants*, those things which are independent of the observer. In the social sciences, the word *relativity* also refers to the dependence of the description of events on the observer, but most social scientists emphasize the absence of absolutes.)*

Second, we must understand that there are many different kinds of names. This essay will include a discussion of conventional names, compositional names, structural names of various kinds including two- and three-dimensional ones, names written in languages whose letters are molecules, and names in mathematical language. Familiarity with

---

* However, see the article by M. Kovacs in this volume for a discussion of the pervasive trend in the humanities toward invariant criteria and standards.

the concepts involved will be helpful in understanding what kind of name the word אור might be.

The English number names (one, two, three,... twelve, thirteen... twenty-one...) illustrate two different categories of names. The number names from one to twelve are purely *conventional*. There is no relation between the name and its meaning. The names from thirteen to nineteen have a *structure*—first they indicate the number of units, and then the number of tens. Thus the structure of each of these names is intimately related to the meaning of the name. The names from twenty to ninety-nine have a different structure—first they indicate the number of tens, and then the number of units. More generally, English number names are based on the names for the powers of ten: ten, hundred, thousand, ten thousand.... Each name begins with the number of the largest power of ten, then the number of the next largest power of ten, and so on until one reaches the units: one thousand, nine hundred, eighty-eight.

The number names in Hebrew are analogous, except that the structural names begin with eleven (אחד עשר) instead of thirteen.*

The Hindu-Arabic numerals begin with conventional names** for zero, one, two, three,... nine, but from there on we have systematic names whose structure completely describes what the name

---

* The word אחד (one) has a structure related to its *cosmic* meaning, which is interpreted in rabbinical writings. Moreover each letter has a structure with a very ramified interpretation. Similarly for the other Hebrew number names up to עשר (ten). (In fact, Ibn Ezra writes of the special properties of each of the numbers from one to ten.) However, the relation between structure and numerical meaning from the number עשר אחד (eleven) on is more obvious. The structures discussed in the rabbinical literature, on the other hand, emphasize the unique aspects of each number rather than its relation to other numbers as part of a numeric system.

** We are writing here on the level of the simple meaning. It is conjectured that the numerals 1, 2, and 3 were originally the tally marks (= ≡) which evolved into the present forms when people began to write cursively. Any relation between the structures of the other digits and their meanings is now lost in the distant past.

means. Thus the name 1988 means: one thousand, nine hundreds, eight tens and eight units.

The Hebrew alphabetical numerals *l'havdil,* also have a systematic structure* beginning with י (*yod*) for ten, but there is no numeric symbol for zero (although there are linguistic terms). The names for the numbers of tens are conventional. Consider this comparison between the two types of numerals:

א	1	י	10	ק	100
ב	2	כ	20	ר	200
ג	3	ל	30	ש	300
ד	4	מ	40	ת	400
ה	5	נ	50		
ו	6	ס	60		
ז	7	ע	70		
ח	8	פ	80		
ט	9	צ	90		

The Hindu-Arabic numerals show clearly the relation between three-plus-five and thirty-plus-fifty, but this is not obvious with the Hebrew numerals. Furthermore, the Hebrew numerals for the numbers of hundreds have a still different structure since the Hebrew alphabet ends with ת (*tav*), for four hundred. Thus we have:

תק	500
תר	600
תש	700
תת	800
תתק	900

Interestingly, the use of the Hebrew letters leads to connotations which the Hindu-Arabic numerals lack. For example, the Hebrew date for the year 5748 is written: תשמ"ח, which spells out a Hebrew word meaning "you shall rejoice."

---

* Our discussion here is on the level of the simple meanings. For further reference, see the *Sefer Ha-Arachim Chabad,* which has 89 pages of analysis of the letter א (*alef*), including its structure as a written symbol and some of the subtleties of its numerical meaning.

The ancient tradition of numerology, *gematria,* uses the numerical total of the letters in a word to interpret its meaning.* One of the names of God, אלוקים,** and the word for nature, הטבע, have the same total, 86; this relation is used to interpret this Name as one which reveals God in his capacity as the source of order and lawfulness in the universe, be it natural law or man-made law.

We have seen that there are purely conventional names and also structural names. When we examine names of substances, we find that there are actually several kinds of structural names. The names: salt, alcohol, ether, and sugar, for certain well-known substances, are purely conventional names. The names: sodium chloride, ethyl alcohol, and dimethyl ether, on the other hand, have structures which impart information about the constitution of the substances they name. The molecular formulas NaCl, C_2H_6O and C_2H_6O, respectively, are structured names which give information about the total composition of these substances. The name NaCl for salt tells us that each molecule is composed of one atom of sodium and one atom of chlorine. This is quite adequate for salt. But the name C_2H_6O, for a substance whose molecules are composed of two atoms of carbon, six of hydrogen and one of oxygen, does not distinguish between the alcohol and the ether. These substances, called *isomers,* have the same composition, but the atoms in their molecules are arranged differently. To distinguish them we may use *structural formulas* such as C_2H_5OH and $(CH_3)_2O$ to show better how the atoms are grouped in these substances.♦

These are very different substances: ethyl alcohol is a liquid at ordinary temperatures with a boiling point of 78°C, whereas dimethyl ether is a gas with a boiling point of -23.6°C. The Kekulé-Couper graphic formulas:

---

* It should be noted that according to *Halachah,* one may only use numeric interpretations that one has learned from his teacher. Thus there is recognition that *gematria* must be used with caution.

** We have, as usual, written the Divine Name here with a ק instead of a ה (whose numerical value is 5) to avoid transgressing the Third Commandment, not to take His name in vain.

♦ Thus, the molecular formula of a compound is analogous, in a way, to the *gematria* of a Hebrew word.

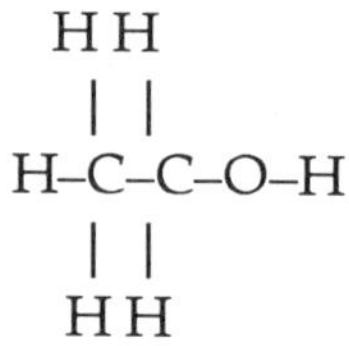

ethyl alcohol

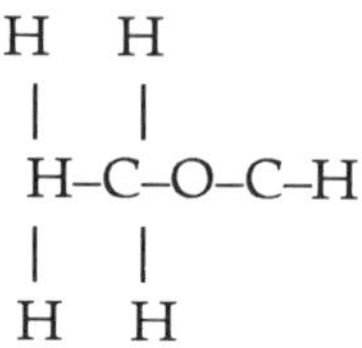

dimethyl ether

show even more clearly how the hydrogen, oxygen, and carbon atoms are linked in these molecules. These two-dimensional names reveal a good deal about the properties of these substances. But two-dimensional names are not adequate to distinguish between glucose and levulose, both sugars with the molecular formula $C_6H_{12}O_6$. To describe them properly we need three-dimensional names!

Since the development of the Rutherford model of the atom, and further research on elementary particles, it has seemed feasible to replace the conventional names of the elements such as carbon, iron, tin, etc., by names describing the constituents of their nuclei. This leads to questions about what electrons, protons, neutrons, etc., really are. For instance, are they particles, and if so, of what material? Or are they waves, and if so, in what medium?

Dirac, a Nobel laureate in physics and one of the founders of quantum mechanics, said that such questions are meaningless, that, for example, all we can know[6] about an electron is that its behavior can be described by a certain system of equations. Thus Dirac's equations for the electron can be considered as a name for the electron, a name whose structure tells us all the physical knowledge attainable by men about what an electron is. (Of course, the information a given person can extract from this name depends on his ability.)

Similarly, Maxwell's equations can be considered as a structured name for an electromagnetic field. If we supplement these equations with an inequality stating that the wavelength is between that of violet and that of red light, they can be considered as a name for (visible) light. Our usual way of writing such equations and inequalities in mathematical language is, then, one particular way of encoding these names.*

So far, we have exemplified human-generated names. Following is an example of a real linguistic entity which is not man-made—

DNA. Complete with a most precise spelling, vocabulary, grammar and countless major tomes, this genetic language was carved into biochemistry millennia before Watson and Crick "cracked" the code. The DNA of any living organism (whether plant, animal, or otherwise) is an encoded set of instructions for producing vital proteins and transferring hereditary information. The instructions are written in a four-letter chemical alphabet, the letters being certain nucleotides.** Thus the DNA molecule is really a three-dimensional name of the organism which tells how the organism is made up and what it passes on to its offspring. This name is so precise and individual to that organism that it is now being used to settle paternity suits.

The Torah attaches great importance to names. When God changes Abram's name to Abraham, He interprets the new name—father of nations.[8] The Torah also shows us the significant differences in

---

* There are many ways of encoding names or other messages, each with its specific characteristics. For example, if we encode the Latin alphabet A, B, C,... Z, by means of pairs of digits 01, 02, 03,... 26, then the name "Adam" would be encoded as 01040113. Words in English, or even better, in a phonetic language like Hebrew or (*l'havdil*) Italian, are phonograms, symbols indicating the sounds of words. Names in the mathematical language of Maxwell's equations are ideograms, symbols indicating their meanings. The rules of this language tell how to use the sentences which constitute Maxwell's equations to derive others which describe further properties of the things (electromagnetic fields) which satisfy Maxwell's equations. In this sense, such names are also functional.

Tangentially, there are some logical difficulties with names. The English phrase, "The smallest positive whole number not nameable in English in less than fifty words," is itself a 14-word name for a certain number. This paradox, known as Richard's Paradox, shows that there are inherent limitations in what can be named in any language with a precise syntax.[7]

** Actually these letters form a DNA vocabulary of about 60 words, each word being a different 3-nucleotide sequence of chemicals. Several hundred of these words strung together form a gene, which is a chemical paragraph that serves as a blueprint for the manufacture of a protein. With many thousands of genes, the DNA is really a microscopic yet voluminous textbook of hereditary information.

Jacob's two names: Jacob (יעקב) and Israel (ישראל). Jacob was born "with his hand holding Esau's heel (עקב)"[9] and was called Israel because "you have striven (שרית) with God and men and prevailed."[10]

The Alter Rebbe[11] gives Chasidic interpretations of these names: Jacob is the Jew as servant of God, while Israel is the Jew as son of God, or prince. The first meaning is derived from *Isaiah* 46:1, 2, and the second from *Exodus* 4:22. Similarly, the changes from Sarai to Sarah[12] and from Hosea to Joshua[13] have special significance, as Rashi explains.

If the Hebrew name of a person describes, in some way, his essence, then one would expect people with the same name to have some common characteristics. But the Torah does not explicitly tell us enough about the two Enochs,[14] the two Lamechs,[15] and the two Sauls[16] to give us any idea of what these common features might be. The same is true of the seven (or nine)[17] Rabbi Simeons mentioned in the Talmud.

The Talmud[18] says of one of the Sages: "His name was not R. Me'ir but R. Nehorai. Why was he called R. Me'ir? Because he enlightened (*me'ir* in Hebrew) the eyes of the Sages in the Law." But elsewhere[19] we read that "R. Me'ir said: Let a man always have his son taught a decent and easy trade. R. Nehorai said: I have put aside every occupation in the world, and I teach my son nothing but the Law." How can we reconcile these apparently contradictory statements?

One explanation has been given by the Chiddushei HaRYM, the first Gerer Rebbe,[20] who said that as R. Nehorai he tells us of his own personal practice, which is too difficult for most people to follow, while as R. Me'ir he tells us the law as it applies to the general public. Thus the two names refer to two aspects of the same person.

On the opening page of the Talmudic tractate *Pesachim*, there is a fascinating discussion of the meaning of the word אור (*or*). The *mishnah* there states that the search for leaven before Passover should take place "at אור of the fourteenth of the month of Nisan." The problem discussed in the Gemara is this: אור usually means "light," but everybody knows that one searches for leaven in the evening of the fourteenth of Nisan. How then can אור mean "evening"?

The Sages quote *Genesis* 1:5: "And God called the אור day, and the חושך (darkness) He called night." They interpret thus: "The Merciful One summoned the אור and appointed it for duty by day, and He summoned the חושך and appointed it for duty by night." Thus אור is not the actual physical light, but it is some emanation which usually, but not necessarily, occurs by day.

This interpretation is reinforced by the fact that the sun, moon, and stars were not created until the fourth day. We read in *Genesis* 1:14-18: "to separate the day from the night, and let them be signs, ...the greater light [illuminator] to rule the day and the lesser light [illuminator] to rule the night." Thus it seems that the physical light emanated by the sun and the stars is a signal by means of which human beings can know when it is day, when אור is on duty, or night, when חושך is functioning. We need this information in order to carry out properly the precepts of the Torah, such as those of the Sabbath.*

The *Tanya* does not give a complete analysis of any particular name. It does, however, begin[21] a study of the word אבן—"stone," which gives some idea of how much there is in a Hebrew name. The source of this name is in the Divine Name ב"ן, whose numerical total is 52, "with an א as one, added to it for a reason known to its Creator." Much further investigation is needed, since the Rebbe does not discuss how these Divine Names are related to the nature of the being denoted by אבן. In *Sefer Yetzirah*[22] the word אבן is used to mean "letter," and combinations of letters are called בתים—"houses." This suggests the possibility that the real meaning of אבן is its meaning in a higher, spiritual world, and that the Rebbe's analysis pertains directly to this, whereas its meaning down here in the material world is actually a figurative one.

Our preceding discussion suggests a possible approach to the

---

* Thus to understand what being was created by the apparently simple Utterance יהי אור, requires a subtle analysis with many ramifications. Nevertheless the simple meaning is usually sufficient for practical, everyday use by ordinary people.

Incidentally we learn that any translation of the Torah is also an interpretation and must be taken with skepticism.

doctrine in the *Tanya*. The Hebrew name is some kind of a code which, like Dirac's equations, implies the defining properties of the thing named. Just as all physical knowledge that we can obtain about an electron can be derived from Dirac's equations, so *all* that can be known about a creature is somehow implied by its Hebrew name. The structures both of Dirac's equations for the electron and (*l'havdil*) of the Hebrew name of a created being are deeply related to the meanings of the names. What we can understand from such names depends on our knowledge and ability to extract implications from the name. Any good name is probably, like Dirac's equations, inexhaustible.

However, a name like Dirac's equations, which tells how an electron behaves, cannot by itself capture the whole essence of the object named. After we learn that Dirac's equations *describe* the behavior of an electron, we are still totally uninformed about the *purpose* of such a creature. Why should God choose just such a particle, behaving in just such a manner, as one of the basic kinds of matter from which He shaped* our universe? Why should the mass and charge of the electron, and the velocity of light have just the values which appear in these equations?**

Is the essence of the Sage mentioned above contained in his genetic constitution as encoded and spelled out in his DNA, or in the names Nehorai, which describes the private person, and Me'ir, which describes the public figure?

The most recent physical theories relate the first fractions of a second after the Creation to the forces between the smallest elementary particles as well as to the present distribution of the most distant stars. And Torah law relates the definition of "night," e.g., in specifying the end of the Sabbath, to our perception of light from distant stars as well as to the precepts governing our behavior here on earth.

Our Sages tell us that God created this universe—in which all

---

* See Nachmanides' comment on *Genesis* 1:1.

** One of the attempts to find a rationale for the values of the fundamental physical constants was made by A.S. Eddington in his *Fundamental Theory* (Cambridge University Press, 1946). See also Schlesinger's article in this volume.

things near and distant, both in space and time, are interrelated—by consulting the Torah as a blueprint, and enunciating the Ten Utterances. This suggests that the essence of a creature involves not only its constitution and behavior, but also its purpose—what it is good for in God's sense of good,[23] its place in the cosmos,[24] and its role in Torah law.

NOTES

1. *Sefer Yetzirah,* 1:1, 1:2; *Zohar,* 15a-17a (Ashleg ed., 10-49; Soncino ed., trans. M. Simon, 64-68). *Tikkunei Ha-Zohar,* 16a-16b. See also writings of R. Haim Vital, based on lectures of R. Yitzchak Luria, such as *Sha'ar Ha-Mitzvot, Sha'ar Ha-Gilgulim, Sha'ar Ha-Pesukkim,* as well as R. Moshe Kordevero, *Sefer Ha-Pardes,* Sha'ar 2, chaps. 3-6, and Sha'ar 27. For an encyclopedic account of the analysis of the letters, see *Sefer Ha'Arachim Chabad,* Vol. *Othioth* (New York: Kehot Publications). For a more popular account in English see R.M.L. Munk, *The Wisdom in the Hebrew Alphabet,* Artscroll Mesorah Series (New York: Mesorah Publications, 1983).
2. Rabbi Schneur Zalman of Liady, *Likkutei Amarim—Tanya,* Bilingual Edition, trans. Rabbi N. Mangel *et al.* (New York: Kehot Publication Society, 1981), Part 2, chap. 7, 319.
3. *Psalms* 33:9.
4. *Genesis* 1:3.
5. Maimonides, *Guide for the Perplexed,* trans. M. Friedlander (New York: Routledge, 1904).
6. For a more extended discussion of the scientific significance of limitations on human knowledge, see my paper "What We Cannot Know," *B'Or HaTorah,* No. 3 (Winter-Spring 1983).
7. For further information about logical paradoxes, see the author's *Elements of Mathematical Logic* (New York: Dover, 1950).
8. *Genesis* 17:5.
9. *Genesis* 25:26.
10. *Genesis* 32:28.
11. Rabbi S. Z. Baruchovich (The Alter Rebbe), *Likkutei Torah, Parashat Balak,* 19th Edition (New York: Kehot Publications).
12. *Genesis* 17:15.
13. *Numbers* 13:16.
14. *Genesis* 4:17 and 5:18.
15. Ibid., 4:18 and 5:25.

16. Ibid., 36:37, and *I Samuel*, 9:2.
17. Rabbis Ben Zoma and Ben Azzai are almost never referred to by their given name, Simeon.
18. Babylonian Talmud, *Eruvin* 13b.
19. Babylonian Talmud, *Kiddushin* 82b.
20. B. Yoashzohn, *Fun Unser Alten Oitzar*, Volume 2 (New York: Shengold Publishers, 1956), 221.
21. Rabbi Schneur Zalman, *Tanya.*
22. *Sefer Yetzirah*, Chapter 4, *mishnah* 2.
23. *Genesis* 1:4.
24. *Ethics of the Fathers* (*Pirkei Avot*), Chapter 4, paragraph 3.

Zvi Victor Saks

Applications of Mathematical Infinity in Jewish Philosophy

THE DESCRIPTION of the Creation of the world by God as given in Jewish philosophy is very abstract and complex, with many references to infinity. I feel that the mathematics of infinity can help us to understand and visualize some of the processes through which God Almighty created the world. This should not be surprising. One of the basic tenets of this conference is that not only can there be no conceivable contradiction between true science and Torah, but that science can be helpful in understanding Torah. True science is an investigation into the world, which is the creation of God. Torah is the blue-

---

ZVI VICTOR SAKS is developing his second career, the application of artificial intelligence in manufacturing. His projects include a master scheduling program for an aircraft plant, and an automated system for industrial fault diagnosis.

Prior to this he served as Professor of Mathematics at the University of Costa Rica and at Daemen College, Amherst, New York. He received his postgraduate degrees in mathematics and computer sciences at the University of Massachusetts (M.A.), Wesleyan University (Ph.D.) and the State University of New York at Buffalo (M.Sc.). An internationally reputed topologist, his area of specialty is abstract infinite space, a field which prepared him well for learning and teaching the challenging concepts found in Kabbalah and Chasidic philosophy.

print that God used for Creation, meaning that He looked into the Torah (which preceded the world) and created the world according to the Torah.[1] With that view, we see that science can help us reveal the Creation and thus help us understand Torah. Since God used infinite processes when He created the world, as will be discussed at length, it is logical that the science of infinite processes, namely mathematics of infinity, should be useful to help us understand those portions of the Torah which deal with the Creation.

Some of the insights that I will be describing in this paper are quite personal. As Professor Hasofer discussed in his paper presented at this conference, a mathematician develops an intimate relationship with his mathematical work and with the mathematical objects with which he works. Thus, although the concepts discussed are quite abstract, to me they are very real. The personal context for this paper is that I am a *ba'al teshuvah,* a Jew who was not raised in a Torah-observant home but made a personal decision as an adult to observe Torah and *mitzvot* (commandments). At that time I was already a mature professional mathematician. My field of expertise is topology, and the best way that I have of describing my work is to say that I did research into abstract infinite space. In fact, I used to say that my doctoral thesis and the research that followed it had no known relationship with the physical world. Many people used to ask me to speculate on what possible application there might be for this work, and I had no meaningful answer. Thus it came as a great surprise to me when I began to study Torah, and in particular Chasidic philosophy, and specifically the description of the Creation of the world by God, that I felt that this was indeed the actual application of the mathematical work which I had done.

I use the term "application" in the following sense: Mathematics is perhaps the purest and most rigorous science and the closest to real truth. The propositions that one is assuming must be clearly specified. In addition, the acceptable methods for constructing new objects and proving new propositions are clearly defined. Thus mathematics is as objective as any science can be. Nonetheless, the truth of any mathematical system depends on the truth of its assumptions, and hence is relative. When I began to study Torah, the great difference between the relative truth of mathematics and the absolute truth of Torah, which puts us in contact with God Who is the Ultimate Truth, became very clear to me. My view of the relationship between mathematics and Torah is that mathematics allows us to construct abstract models which can be useful in helping us to understand and visualize some of the processes through which God Almighty created the world. Thus the mathematical model is pure and abstract and its real actual application is the Creation of the world by God.

I feel that I must emphasize the profound love and respect that I have for mathematics. My mathematical work was and is tremendously important to me. I have certainly learned a great deal from mathematics, and genuinely appreciate its beauty. It's just that compared to Torah, it becomes much less significant.

Although, as I have said, the mathematical objects that I work with are quite abstract, over many years I developed an intimate, personal relationship with them. In a very natural way, I came to look at their world from *their* perspective. Being able to do this can be very helpful and useful, for when studying incredibly complex and abstract mathematical objects, one is often at a loss as to how to grasp them and make progress toward discovering their properties. I feel completely comfortable and natural doing this and ask the reader to join me in trying to see the world from the perspective of these objects.

Creation *Ex Nihilo*

The first example to be discussed is the concept of creation *ex nihilo*, creation of something from nothing. The primary example of creation *ex nihilo* is the creation of the physical from the spiritual. When God created the physical world, He did it putting a spiritual life-force into each created being. This spiritual life-force is the source of the existence of that being and is the force which not only created the being but also continues to keep it in existence. In other words, everything that was created has some aspect of Godliness in it.

I would like to develop the following question. Creation *ex nihilo* is commonly called the creation of something from nothing. Actually it should be called the creation of "nothing from something," with the "something" being Godliness and the "nothing" being the physical world. This makes sense because Godliness is the true existence and the physical world is a secondary existence which depends on Godliness for its existence. So why is creation *ex nihilo* called "something from nothing"? There are surely many answers to this question, and I will focus on one, which is that the "something" *thinks that it is a true something*. The physical world, and most people generally, are unaware of their true source, which is the Godliness that created them and keeps them in existence, and therefore are unaware of their dependence on God for their existence. So the "something" thinks that its source is a "nothing." Actually the "something" is usually totally unaware that it has a source, or that it even needs a source, and hence thinks of itself as a completely independent being.

This is the critical condition for creation *ex nihilo* that I am focusing on here: that the created being cannot trace itself back to its source, that it is unaware of its dependence on the source for its existence, and perhaps even unaware that it has a source which is outside of itself. Note that this is strongly contrasted with the concept of creation of "something from something," like a work of art or a building. A building is made from an architect's plans with physical materials. No matter how complex the building may be, we can (at least in principle) trace the construction back to the raw materials that were used and the plans that were followed.

Mathematical Infinity

A mathematical construction which embodies an idea similar to creation *ex nihilo* is the notion of a limit point of an infinite sequence. Of course I need to explain that and first will discuss the concept of mathematical infinity.

Let's begin by considering the sequence of positive integers 1, 2, 3, ... This sequence is generated by starting with the number

1, and to each number that we get up to, we add 1, to generate the next number. Thus each number, say, n, has an immediate successor which is $n + 1$. Each number n (except 1) has an immediate predecessor $n - 1$. We will denote this sequence by **N**. **N** is mathematically infinite. The modern theory of mathematical infinity was formulated by Georg Cantor in the 1870s. Perhaps the single main contribution of Cantor was that infinite sets and sequences are seen not just as infinite in potential but as real objects which are actually infinite. The fact that these objects are infinite gives them many strange properties, but the point I want to make is that they are seen as truly existing objects and hence can be dealt with as single entities. In fact one of Cantor's first main results was that there are different sizes of mathematical infinities. Mathematically infinite objects can be bounded and extended, as will be discussed shortly.

Before giving our first main mathematical example, I will give a simpler example of an infinite sequence with a limit point: 1/2, 1/3, 1/4, . . . , 0. The sequence 1/2, 1/3, 1/4, . . . is infinite and yet it converges to the number 0. In fact, if one were to watch a computer simulation of this sequence, even on a screen with a very fine graphic picture, eventually no difference would be seen between the numbers of the sequence and 0.

Now let's do something considerably more complex, to put something at the end of the sequence **N** as a limit point. Cantor called this limit point $\aleph_0$ and it is the smallest infinite number. Thus our sequence now looks like 1, 2, 3, . . ., $\aleph_0$.

In a numerical sense, $\aleph_0$ is the *number* of elements in the sequence **N**. However, recall that I am interested in abstract space and so I am looking at our example in terms of its *spatial* structure. An abstract space is defined by specifying the elements (or objects) of the space, together with the structure of the space. The structure may be thought of as a description of the structural relationships that hold between the elements. These structural relationships can be given by specifying which sequences converge to which elements. In our current example, the elements of the space are 1, 2, 3, . . ., $\aleph_0$ and the structure can be defined by specifying that the sequence 1, 2, 3, . . . converges to $\aleph_0$. Thus it is in an *abstract spatial* sense that $\aleph_0$ is a limit point of **N**.

What is the relationship between the sequence 1, 2, 3, . . . and the limit point $\aleph_0$? In what way does the existence of $\aleph_0$ depend on the sequence? $\aleph_0$ is generated by the whole sequence. On the other hand, for each individual member, *n*, of the sequence, *n* is not the source for $\aleph_0$, since it is the source for $n + 1$. It's really the case that the whole sequence is the source, and not any individual member. Looking at $\aleph_0$'s relationship with the sequence 1, 2, 3, . . . *from the perspective of* $\aleph_0$, this means that if $\aleph_0$ looks back and tries to see where it came from, it is going to have a very hard time realizing that there is an infinite sequence which comes into it and generates it. Thus $\aleph_0$ cannot trace itself back to its source.

Now this was precisely the critical condition for creation *ex nihilo*, that the created being could not trace itself back to its source. The relationship that $\aleph_0$ has with the mathematically infinite sequence 1, 2, 3, . . . is a model for the relationship that a created being has with the Infinite Godliness that created it. It certainly is the case that $\aleph_0$ has a powerful and complex relationship with the sequence **N**, but I can clearly visualize that *from the perspective of* $\aleph_0$, it can be totally unaware of that relationship, and therefore $\aleph_0$ could easily (yet erroneously) see itself as an independent being. Even if we are talking about conscious human life, where intellectual abstraction is most pronounced, and daily life revolves around abstract realities, a person may still not recognize the complex spiritual structure through which his life is created and guided.

An important question which I am asked quite frequently is: If the sequence **N** is really infinite, how can it be limited and bounded? The answer is that it depends on what we mean by "really infinite." **N** is only mathematically infinite. It's not finite, because for any number *n*, **N** has more elements than *n*, since it contains all the numbers from 1 through $n + 1$. On the other hand, **N** is not a True Absolute Infinity and that is what allows it to be bounded by its limit point $\aleph_0$. Thus mathematical infinity is a limited form of infinity which can be seen as a bridge between God's True Infinity and the finite. Much of this paper is in fact devoted to showing that it's a useful bridge. We finite human beings naturally have difficulty in relating to a Truly Infinite God, and in this paper I will be trying to show you how mathematical infinity can help us to conceptualize God's Infinity. (While attending the conference, my colleague Avi Rabinowitz suggested that I read *Infinity and the Mind*[2] by Rudy Rucker. I did so, and must admit that I was surprised to discover that the view of mathematical infinity as a bridge was also Cantor's.[3] I am grateful to Avi for recommending the book to me and heartily recommend it to anyone who enjoys mathematics.)

It is implicit in the view that mathematical infinity is limited, that since God is Truly Infinite, He is outside of the realm of mathematical infinity. This can in fact be proven. Let's refer to everything that exists as the Totality. I will prove that the Totality is above mathematical infinity. One of the basic axioms (assumptions) of mathematical set theory is that for any set, there exists a set called the power set, which is the set of all subsets of the original set.* It can be proven that the number of elements in the power set is distinctly greater** than the number of elements in the original set. However, since the Totality already includes everything that exists, it cannot be that there is a bigger set. In other words, if the Totality could have a number associated with it, that would have to be the biggest number. But it can be proven that there is no biggest number, since if n is the biggest number, 2^n is greater than n. Thus the Totality cannot be subjected to the confines of mathematics, and neither can God, Who is, of course, much greater than the totality of everything that exists.

The Creation

The following discussion is based♦ on part of the Introduction by Rabbi Nisen Mangel to Part 2 of the *Tanya*.[4] The *Tanya* was writ-

---

* For example, let's consider a set X with elements a and b. We will write $X = \{a, b\}$. The power set of X consists of the empty set, the set consisting of just a, the set consisting of just b, and the set consisting of a and b. More succinctly, the power set of X = {the empty set, $\{a\}$, $\{b\}$, $\{a, b\}$}. As an exercise, the reader might try to show that if $Y = \{a, b, c\}$, then there are 8 subsets of Y so the power set of Y has 8 elements.

** More precisely, it can be proven that if X has n elements, then the power set has 2^n elements, and that 2^n is always greater than n.

♦ Some sections are copied exactly, while others are pruned to concentrate on the points to be developed here.

ten by Rabbi Schneur Zalman who founded the Chabad movement, the intellectual branch of Chasidism.

How the Creation Was Performed

Jewish philosophic and Kabbalistic thought has been deeply concerned with the seeming contradiction between the Divine attribute of omnipresence and the existence of the universe. Since God is omnipresent and nothing can exist outside of Him, where was there place for the universe to materialize at Creation? How could the finite world emerge from God the Infinite? How could the world's dependence on God for its existence be kept hidden from the world?

To solve these problems, Rabbi Yitzchak Luria, one of the most famous and influential Kabbalists of the sixteenth century, advanced the doctrine of *Tzimtzum,* the withdrawal and contraction of the Infinite. He explained that before Creation, God filled all space* and there was no room (possibility) for the existence of the universe. However, when it arose in His Will to create the universe, He withdrew His Infinite Light and concealed it within Himself, allowing the revelation of His finite power and light, and thereby creating the possibility of a finite world and making room for the emergence of finite existence. Actually there are two kinds of Divine emanations: a boundless and completely unlimited light, called in Kabbalah *Or En Sof,* the Infinite Light, and a light of finite order which can give rise to and be confined in finite existence. But even this finite power, the source of all Creation, which was revealed as a result of the concealment of the Infinite Light, is itself too abundant and powerful to give rise to finite beings. It is only after innumerable *Tzimtzumim* (condensations), which progressively condense and conceal the creative power, that it is possible for finite and physical matter to exist. Unlike the initial *Tzimtzum* which is a complete concealment of the Infinite Light, each of the subsequent *Tzimtzumim* is but a gradual diminution of this concealed Light and

---

* The term "space" is used here in a figurative sense since space itself is a creation *ex nihilo.*

an adaptation of its creative force to the capacity of the endurance of created beings. Via this screening and diminished expression of the power by which all things exist, the world appears to enjoy an independent existence, as if it were apart from God. But truly, "The whole earth is full of His Glory," for all things exist only by virtue of the Divine creative power immanent in them and endure only because it is screened from their view. Were permission granted to the eye to see beyond the external physical form, declares Rabbi Schneur Zalman, then we would perceive only the Divine power that pervades and animates every created thing and is its true essence and reality.

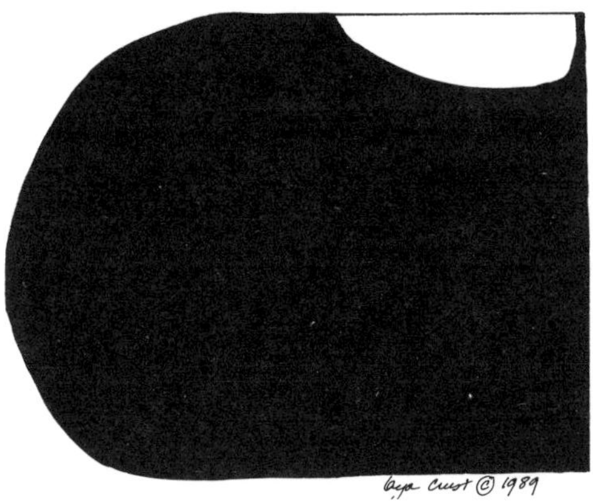

What We Will Try to Model Mathematically

The process of progressive dimming and condensation of God's Infinite Light brought about an infinite progression of spiritual worlds, each one lower than the previous ones, meaning that the Godliness in that world is less revealed and more concealed. The culmination of the progression is our physical universe. The first model that I will propose for this progression is the sequence **N** together with its limit point $\aleph_0$. This model is an infinite sequence and we can think of each integer as representing a spiritual world, with $\aleph_0$ representing the physical world. As was discussed before, $\aleph_0$ is created *ex nihilo* from the sequence **N** and the physical universe is created *ex nihilo* from the progression of spiritual worlds, so the model looks good so far. However, if we look further at the Creation we see that it is an inadequate model. I will consider two properties of the Creation and expand our mathematical model to incorporate these properties.

The first reason for the inadequacy of our model is that it is too uniform. All of the positive integers are qualitatively the same. Moreover there is only a gap of one between any of the adjacent numbers. The Creation is more complicated than that. There are major steps along the way, for example,[5] the four worlds of *Atzilut* (emanation), *Briah* (creation), *Yetzirah* (formation), and *Asiyah* (action). *Atzilut* is infinite[6] and is infinitely higher than *Briah.*[7] There are worlds which are more sublime than *Atzilut* but are so elevated that only the four worlds are spoken of and referred to.[8] Thus we need to expand our model to include the concept of major, even infinite, distinctions in level. The simplest way to expand our model is to look at $\aleph_0$, not only as the limit point of the sequence **N**, but as the beginning of a new sequence. This involves the concept of *ordinal numbers*, and since there was an involved discussion about these ideas after my talk at the conference, I will discuss them at some length now.

Ordinal Numbers as a Model

Mathematically there are (at least) two different ways of looking at numbers: as cardinal numbers or as ordinal numbers. Cardinal numbers express quantity; ordinal numbers also express quantity but the quantity is ordered. Thus, for example, if we speak of six people, *six* is a cardinal number. On the other hand, if we speak of the sixth person, *sixth* is an ordinal number and there are implicitly five other people to whom this one is the sixth. For finite numbers, the distinction is not so critical because there is really only one essential way to order linearly any collection of objects. For example, if you want to place an ordering on a group of six people, then you know that what you will end up with is a first person, a second person, and so on until the sixth person.

For infinite sets, cardinality is very different from ordinality. This is because for a given infinite set, there are very many different ways of ordering it that are essentially different.

Let's give an example of this by adding 1 to $\aleph_0$ and getting $\aleph_0 + 1$. For infinite numbers like $\aleph_0$, the operation of adding 1 *does not change the cardinality* of the number, but it does change the ordinality.* Thus given an ordinal number, one can always add 1 to it and generate the ordinal successor of the original number. One usually thinks of the ordinality of a number as being (identified with) the sequence of numbers which precede it. Let's look at the sequence of numbers up to $\aleph_0 + 1$: $1, 2, 3, \ldots, \aleph_0$. $\aleph_0$ is now identified with the sequence $1, 2, 3, \ldots$, while $\aleph_0 + 1$ is identified with the sequence $1, 2, 3, \ldots, \aleph_0$. These two sequences are essentially different from an ordinal point of view. The first is an infinite sequence with no limit points and the second is an infinite sequence together with a limit point.

Now that we have begun to extend our mathematical model, let's extend it a good deal more, all the way out to $\aleph_1$, which is the first ordinal number which is *cardinally* (quantitatively) bigger than $\aleph_0$:

$$1, 2, 3, \ldots, \aleph_0, \aleph_0 + 1, \aleph_0 + 2, \ldots, 2\aleph_0,$$
$$2\aleph_0 + 1, \ldots, 3\aleph_0, \ldots, 4\aleph_0, \ldots, \aleph_0 \cdot \aleph_0, \ldots, \aleph_1.$$

Let me explain how we get to $2\aleph_0$. Starting from $\aleph_0$, we generate a new infinite sequence called S which looks like

$$\aleph_0, \aleph_0 + 1, \aleph_0 + 2, \ldots, \aleph_0 + n, \ldots, \aleph_0 + \aleph_0 = 2\aleph_0.$$

Since $\aleph_0$ is the limit point of the sequence **N**, the sequence S has the limit point of $\aleph_0 + \aleph_0$, or $2\aleph_0$. Continuing in this way, we generate $3\aleph_0$, $4\aleph_0$ and so on. Now the sequence of the coefficients $1, 2, 3, \ldots$ converges to $\aleph_0$, and so the sequence $\aleph_0, 2\aleph_0, 3\aleph_0, \ldots$ has the limit point $\aleph_0 \cdot \aleph_0$. The main idea of this construction is that from any given ordinal number, we can go one step further, and whenever we have an infinite sequence, we can put a limit point at the end. Mathematically we can continue this process until reaching $\aleph_1$, which, again, is the first ordinal number which is *quantitatively* bigger than $\aleph_0$.

---

* See Rucker, *Infinity and the Mind*, p. 80, for a discussion with a diagram of why $\aleph_0$ and $\aleph_0 + 1$ have the same cardinality.

This Is a Better Model

Recall our earlier objection to sequence 1, 2, 3, . . ., $\aleph_0$ as a model for the Creation. The objection was that, according to Torah, the progression of spiritual worlds which culminates in this world is not uniform. It has major reference points along the way that are identifiable as such and which have infinite gaps between them. $\aleph_1$ is a better model because it has these properties. In particular, there are infinitely many ordinal numbers between $\aleph_0$ and $2\aleph_0$, and then infinitely more to get to $3\aleph_0$. $\aleph_0 \cdot \aleph_0$ is in some sense qualitatively different from any number smaller than it, but not quantitatively bigger. Thus the model incorporates the notion of infinite gaps. Actually we can expand even this model and go out to $\aleph_2$ or even beyond.[9]

Infinitely Many Forms at Each Level

A wonderful discussion of the Infinity of God and the Creation is given by the previous Lubavitcher Rebbe in one of his final written discourses.[10] (I would like to express my gratitude to Rabbi Yisroel Rosenfeld for suggesting that I study this discourse, as well as related discourses by the present Lubavitcher Rebbe.)

The second reason for the inadequacy of our original model, and our current model as well, is given by the previous Lubavitcher Rebbe,[11] who said that the Godly Light, the life-energy that gives life to the Creation, is infinite in nature; therefore it descends in an infinite amount of different forms. The present Lubavitcher Rebbe[12] emphasizes that the descent of God's Infinite Light is manifested in an infinite variety of forms even at the lowest levels, and that the Light is in a state of revelation.

The current model that we have only generates one entity at each level. We need to expand it to generate infinitely many entities at each level, which in our current model means to generate infinitely many limit points at each level. What I will show, with some detail, is how to generate infinitely many limit points for the sequence **N**.

Generating Infinitely Many Limit Points

Before presenting a method for generating infinitely many limit points (at the same level), let's consider a method for generating two limit points for the sequence **N**. The main idea is to break up the sequence **N** into two separate subsequences. The most natural way to do this is to think of the even numbers and the odd numbers. Just as we could put a limit point at the end of **N**, we can put limit points at the end of each of the two subsequences of the evens and the odds. So the sequence of the even numbers is: 2, 4, 6, . . . and let's put the limit point $\aleph_{\text{even}}$ at the end of it. The sequence of odd numbers is: 1, 3, 5, . . . and let's put the limit point $\aleph_{\text{odd}}$ at the end of it. The critical insight is that the two limit points $\aleph_{\text{even}}$ and $\aleph_{\text{odd}}$ are *different*. They are different because the two subsequences of the even numbers and the odd numbers have no numbers in common, and this allows us to construct distinct limit points for these subsequences. Thus our construction looks like:

$$\begin{array}{l} 1, 3, 5, \ldots, \aleph_{\text{odd}} \\ 2, 4, 6, \ldots, \aleph_{\text{even}}. \end{array}$$

Now both $\aleph_{\text{even}}$ and $\aleph_{\text{odd}}$ are limit points of the original sequence **N**; so let's redraw our construction as follows:

$$1,2,3, \ldots, \begin{array}{l} \aleph_{\text{odd}} \\ \\ \aleph_{\text{even}}. \end{array}$$

We can use the same idea with a little mathematical finesse to generate infinitely many limit points. The trick is to break up the sequence **N** into infinitely many separate subsequences. This can be accomplished by use of a diagonalized construction as follows. Write a 1 in the upper left-hand corner. Then we will proceed to write diagonals of numbers in order, starting from the top and going down the left diagonal until reaching the leftmost column (the column with the 1 at the top). Thus after putting in 2, we put the 3 down one row and one space to the left. The 3 is under the 1, so we start a new diagonal with 4, the 5 goes in one row down and one space to the left, and so on:

1, 2, 4, 7, 11, 16, . . .
3, 5, 8, 12, 17, . . .
6, 9, 13, 18, . . .
10, 14, 19, . . .
15, 20, . . .
21, ...

Since each of these subsequences has no element in common with any other subsequence, the limit point that each subsequence generates is different from the limit point that any other subsequence generates. Since there are infinitely many subsequences, the number of limit points generated is infinite. Let's put these limit points into our picture. First we have to call them something, so let's call the limit points $\aleph'$, $\aleph''$, $\aleph'''$ and so on. So now our sequences look like:

1, 2, 4, 7, 11, 16, . . ., $\aleph'$
3, 5, 8, 12, 17, . . ., $\aleph''$
6, 9, 13, 18, . . ., $\aleph'''$
10, 14, 19, . . ., $\aleph''''$
15, 20, . . ., $\aleph'''''$
21, . . ., $\aleph''''''$.

Thus we can have an infinite number of limit points for **N**, and this is what **N** might look like together with some of these limit points:

$\aleph'$
$\aleph''$
1, 2, 3, . . ., $\aleph'''$
$\aleph''''$
$\aleph'''''$
$\aleph''''''$.

Now try to conceptualize joining together the processes that have been described. Our construction begins with the sequence **N** and proceeds in steps. At the first step, we construct infinitely many limit points of **N**, which we called א′, א″, א‴, and so on. Now continue this process so that at each step, we construct infinitely many limit points of this sequence just as we did for the sequence **N**. There, for each integer n, we have inductively defined the nth step. Now try to think of constructing the αth step, for each ordinal number $\alpha < \aleph_1$, in which we construct infinitely many limit points of the previous sequence. (There are technical details involved here which are beyond the scope of this paper.) This is surely very complex, but I think that it is a fairly good model of the Creation as discussed in Jewish philosophy and *Chasidut*.

Ultrafilters

All of the mathematics that I have presented so far is standard and well-known to virtually all professional mathematicians. I would now like to describe briefly my own mathematical research and discuss how it fits in to our perspective of providing mathematical models of the Creation. My research provided a method of classifying all of the basic ways in which infinite sequences can have limit points. The basic notion is convergence with respect to an ultrafilter. Convergence with respect to an ultrafilter was defined independently by several mathematicians. (In particular, I defined it in a somewhat cumbersome form in my doctoral thesis.[13] See a later article[14] for my discussion of some other equivalent formulations.) It was first defined elegantly using the concept of **D**-limit by A. Bernstein.[15] John Ginsburg and I developed the **D**-limit concept further.[16] Then I generalized the concept and showed that it was deeper and had a much wider range of use than we had first realized.[17]

In order to understand convergence with respect to an ultrafilter, let's try to think about a normal filter. Conceptually a filter can be viewed as a process that can be performed on a stream (say, of water) to extract previously unrecognizable elements from the stream. Somewhat similarly an ultrafilter is applied to the sequence **N** to generate new limit points. Actually there are many ways, besides ultrafilters, of generating new limit points for sequences. Ultrafilters, however, give significant control over what kinds of limit points are generated. Moreover, once the limit points have been constructed using whatever mechanism, ultrafilters can be used to describe the relationship between the limit points and the original sequence. This relationship is described in the next section.

In our last example, where we generated infinitely many limit points for **N**, **D**-limits could be used to describe the particular relationship that each of $\aleph', \aleph'', \aleph''', \ldots$ has with **N**. More generally, for any sequence and any limit point of the sequence, **D**-limits provide a way of describing the relationship between the limit point and the sequence. In fact it was my own need to find a way to describe the relationship of a limit point with respect to a sequence that led me to originally define (something equivalent to) **D**-limits.

Convergence with Respect to an Ultrafilter

This section is written for the mathematically trained reader.

Although it is not really necessary, let's assume that all topological spaces are Hausdorff. To simplify the exposition, X will always be a space, $x \in X$, and $(x_n: n \in \mathbf{N})$ a sequence in X and similarly for Y. Recall that x is a cluster point of $(x_n: n \in \mathbf{N})$ if for every open set O containing x, $\{n: x_n \in O\}$ is infinite. In this case, we write $x \in (x_n: n \in \mathbf{N})'$.

To show the elegance of the **D**-limit concept, let's pose the following problem: Let X and Y be spaces, and suppose that $x \in (x_n: n \in \mathbf{N})'$ and $y \in (y_n: n \in \mathbf{N})'$. Give a non-trivial condition guaranteeing that in $X \times Y$, $(x,y) \in ((x_n,y_n): n \in \mathbf{N})'$. Even better, make the condition necessary and sufficient. If either sequence converges, that is a sufficient condition but not terribly interesting in a general topological setting.

To solve this problem, let's first define an ultrafilter: A family of sets $\mathbf{F} = \{X_i: i \in I\}$ has the *finite intersection property* provided that for each finite $J \subseteq I$, $\bigcap_{i \in J} X_i \neq \emptyset$. An *ultrafilter* on a set Z is a family **U** of subsets of Z with the finite intersection property and which is maximal. An ultrafilter **U** is *fixed* if $\bigcap_{U \in \mathbf{U}} U \neq \emptyset$. Note that in this case, the intersection will be exactly one element. If the intersection is $\emptyset$, then **U** is said to be *free*.

Using Zorn's Lemma, or any other maximality principle, it is straightforward to show that any family of sets with the finite intersection property is contained in an ultrafilter. In particular, if our family **F** with the finite intersection property has empty intersection, then any ultrafilter extending **F** will be free. For example: Let $F_n = \{i \in \mathbf{N}: i > n\}$. Then the family $\mathbf{F}=\{F_n: n \in \mathbf{N}\}$ **has the finite intersection property but** $\bigcap_{n\in\mathbf{N}} F_n = \emptyset$.

Now let's define **D**-limits.[18] Let **D** be a free ultrafilter on N. A point x is said to be a **D**-*limit point* of the sequence $(x_n: n \in \mathbf{N})$ if, for every open set O containing x, $\{n: x_n \in O\} \in \mathbf{D}$. **D**-limits, when they exist, are unique, and we shall express the fact that x is the **D**-limit of $(x_n: n \in \mathbf{N})$ by writing $x = \mathbf{D}\text{-lim } x_n$.

If $x \in (x_n: n \in \mathbf{N})'$, then there exists a free ultrafilter **D** on **N** such that $x = \mathbf{D}\text{-lim } x_n$.[19] It is easy to show that **D**-limits are productive.[20] Then we have the following theorem as an answer to our earlier problem:

THEOREM. *Let* $x \in (x_n: n \in \mathbf{N})'$ and $y \in (y_n: n \in \mathbf{N})'$. *Then* $(x,y) \in ((x_n, y_n): n \in \mathbf{N})'$ *if and only if there exists a free ultrafilter* **D** *on* **N** *such that* $x = \mathbf{D}\text{-lim } x_n$ *and* $y = \mathbf{D}\text{-lim } y_n$.

Let me now give one application of the **D**-limit concept. My favorite topological property is countable compactness. Recall that a space X is *countably compact* provided that every infinite sequence in X has a cluster point in X. More specifically, I have always been interested in products of countably compact spaces. **D**-limits are very useful for proving theorems and constructing counterexamples for questions involving products of countably compact spaces. This is so because they give some insight on the ways in which a cluster point of a sequence *is* a cluster point. My original discovery of the **D**-limit concept arose from a desire to construct non-compact spaces all of whose powers are countably compact. To do this, we need the concept of **D**-compactness. Let **D** be a free ultrafilter on **N**. A space X is **D**-*compact* provided that every sequence $(x_n: n \in \mathbf{N})$ has a **D**-limit in X.

The key to our example is the following theorem:

THEOREM:[21] *A space X has all of its powers countably compact if and only if it is* **D**-*compact for some free ultrafilter* **D** *on* **N**.

Thus we now need to construct a **D**-compact space X which is not compact. We will work inside of the space $\beta\mathbf{N}$, the Stone-Čech compactification of **N**.[22] The main idea of the construction is as follows: Let $N_0 = \mathbf{N}$. For each ordinal α such that $0 < \alpha < \aleph_1$, let

$$N_\alpha = \cup_{\beta<\alpha} N_\beta \cup \{x \in \beta\mathbf{N}: x = \mathbf{D}\text{-lim } x_n \text{ where each } x_n \in \cup_{\beta<\alpha} N_\beta\},$$

and let $X = \cup_{\alpha<\aleph_0} N_\alpha$. Then we have the following:

1. $N_\alpha \subseteq N_\beta$ for $\alpha < \beta$.
2. card(N_α)=**c**. Let's sketch a proof. Since $N_0=\mathbf{N}$, card(N_0)=$\aleph_0$. Then card(N_1)=$\aleph_0^{\aleph_0} = \mathbf{c}$, so for each α, $\mathbf{c} \leq \text{card}(N_\alpha) \leq \aleph_1 \cdot \mathbf{c}^{\aleph_0} = \mathbf{c}$.
3. Therefore card(X)=$\mathbf{c} \cdot \aleph_1 = \mathbf{c}$.
4. Since card($\beta\mathbf{N}$)=$2^{\mathbf{c}}$, $X \subset \beta\mathbf{N}$.
5. Since **N** is dense in X, X is not compact.
6. X is **D**-compact. For, let $(x_n: n \in \mathbf{N})$ be a sequence in X. Then, for each n, there is a $\beta_n < \aleph_1$ such that $x_n \in N_{\beta_n}$. Pick $\alpha < \aleph_1$ so that $\beta_n < \alpha$ for all n. Then for $x \in \beta\mathbf{N}$ with $x = \mathbf{D}\text{-lim } x_n$, $x \in N_\alpha \subset X$.

For some more details and a more general construction, see articles by Bernstein, and Ginsburg and Saks.[23]

Conclusions

In this paper I have described mathematical constructions involving generating limit points for infinite sequences, performed successively over a large number of iterations. There might be as many as $\aleph_1$ stages of construction, or even more. The limit points might be added using different techniques, although adding limit points via ultrafilters can be particularly useful. These were mathematical processes that I had a deep feeling for and understanding of. This mathematics is extremely pure and abstract, and while I was developing it, I would often tell people that my mathematics research had no actual application whatsoever. Then when I became a Torah-practicing Jew and started to learn *Chasidut*, I sat in classes where rabbis and texts were discussing infinite descents of worlds, a vast panorama of condensations of worlds producing lower worlds, culminating in a major condensation to produce this scents of worlds, a vast panorama of condensations of worlds producing lower worlds, culminating in a major condensation to produce this physical world. I had the overwhelming feeling that this Reality was the actual application of my mathematical work. Subsequent meticulous analysis of both the mathematics and the Torah validated this feeling. This was truly awesome and inspiring!

Relationship with God

The previous Lubavitcher Rebbe has written the following:[24] The basic premise of *Chasidut* is that the mission of Man (and the purpose of the descent of the soul into the body) is the attainment of perfection, through Divine service, in love and awe of God, and through proper conduct in social intercourse. The goal is to be achieved through meditation on and understanding of "How manifold are Your Creations, O God" (*Psalms* 104:24) and "How great are Thy works" (92:6).

I truly hope that reading this paper will bring the reader to a greater appreciation of the Greatness of God and His Creation, and will thus motivate a more enthusiastic service of the Absolutely Infinite God in the activities of daily life.

Acknowledgments

The ideas discussed in this paper are the result of many years of thought and effort. I owe thanks to many people who have helped me and taught me along the way. There are too many to list them all individually but I would like to thank the following old friends: Yerachmiel Tilles, my oldest friend; Eric Eigen, who encouraged me to write a paper integrating mathematics and reality many years ago; and Wis Comfort, my mathematics teacher.

NOTES

1. *Bereshit Rabbah* 1:20.
2. Rudy Rucker, *Infinity and the Mind* (Bantam, 1983).
3. Ibid., 10.

5. Ibid; Rabbi Zalman Posner, *On the Teachings of Chassidus* (Kehot, 1959), 14.
6. Rabbi Joseph Isaac Schneerson, *Sefer Ma'amorim* (Hebrew) (Kehot, 5710), 133.
7. Posner, *On the Teachings of Chassidus.*
8. Rabbi Dr. Jacob Immanuel Schochet, "Mystical Concepts in Chassidism," in *Tanya*, Rabbi Schneur Zalman, 861-62.
9. Rucker, *Infinity and the Mind*, 82.
10. Schneerson, *Sefer Ma'amorim*, 132-37; Schneerson, *Bosi L'Gani—5710* (English) (Sichos in English, 1980), 54-67.
11. Ibid; Ibid, 63.
12. Rabbi Menachem Mendel Schneerson, *Sefer Ma'amorim—Bosi L'Gani* (Hebrew) (Kehot 1977), 164.
13. Victor Saks, *Countably compact groups*, Ph.D. thesis (Wesleyan University, 1972).
14. Victor Saks, "Ultrafilter invariants in topological spaces," *Trans. Amer. Math. Soc.* 241 (1978):79.
15. A. R. Bernstein, "A new kind of compactness for topological spaces," *Fund. Math.* 66 (1970):185-193.
16. John Ginsburg and Victor Saks, "Some applications of ultrafilters in topology," *Pacific J. of Math.* 57 (1975):404.
17. Saks, "Ultrafilter invariants," 80.
18. Bernstein, "A new kind of compactness"; Ginsburg and Saks, "Some applications of ultrafilters"; Saks, "Ultrafilter invariants," 80.
19. Ginsburg and Saks, "Some applications of ultrafilters."
20. See note 18 above.
21. Ginsburg and Saks, "Some applications of ultrafilters," 405.
22. L. Gillman and M. Jerison, *Rings of Continuous Functions* (Van Nostrand, 1960).
23. Bernstein, "A new kind of compactness," ex. 4; Ginsburg and Saks, "Some applications of ultrafilters," 407.
24. Rabbi Joseph Isaac Schneerson, *Kuntres Torat Ha-Chasidut* (Hebrew) (Otzar Ha-Chasidim Lubavitch, 1957), 8; Posner, *On the Teachings of Chassidus*, 20.

G. Natan Schlesinger

The Stars Are Singing as They Shine: "The Hand that Made Us Is Divine"

MANY A PIOUS person insists nowadays that belief is literally only that, and is achieved by a leap of faith. According to this view attempts to settle the issue of God's existence through empirical evidence, proofs, arguments, deductive or inductive logic are not only doomed to failure, but manifest a sad inadequacy and a deplorably distrusting heart.

Such was not the attitude of the saintly Rabbi Akiva, however, who asserted: "As a house implies a builder, a dress a weaver, a door a carpenter, so the world proclaims God, its Creator."[1] Nor was it the attitude of the great medieval thinkers who followed in the footsteps of Rabbi Akiva and produced a variety of detailed versions of his Argument from Design.

I believe, therefore, that Judaism's authentic spokesmen of yesteryear would have been gratified by many of the recent findings of scientists, in particular those of contemporary astrophysi-

---

G. NATAN SCHLESINGER, after studying at London University (B.A.) and at Melbourne (M.A., Ph.D.), took up a post at the University of North Carolina, Chapel Hill, where he continues to serve as Professor of Philosophy. Much of his research focuses on epistemological questions, which are dealt with in his nine books and numerous articles. His latest book is New Perspectives on Old Time Religion, *published in 1988 by the Oxford University Press.*

cists. I shall attempt to explain why, after offering some preliminary clarifications.

Ordinary and Extraordinary Events

One of the most fundamental principles of empirical confirmation is to demonstrate that what seemed at first extraordinary is in fact ordinary and indeed had to occur. Empirical confirmation does away with mysteries by demonstrating that what appeared astonishing was—assuming the truth of certain hypotheses—bound to take place. It turns the seemingly inexplicable into the inevitable. Thus an event or a series of events, which we find surprising, prompts us to look for a reasonable explanatory hypothesis, the adoption of which would remove the grounds for puzzlement by showing that what happened was predestined to happen.

The crucial question to pose in this context is: What precisely constitutes a surprise? It is obvious that just because a certain event is highly improbable, it does not necessarily follow that it is genuinely surprising. Suppose Reuben buys one ticket in a lottery in which there are a billion participants—and wins the main prize. Surely, although his win was exceedingly improbable, it is not a surprising event in the sense that it urgently requires an explanation. It would be absurd, for example, to suggest that the police conduct an inquiry on how Reuben, who had no more than a one-in-a-billion chance, managed to win the main prize. From the beginning it was an absolute certainty that one or another ticket was going to win. Thus while the *particular* event of *Reuben's* winning had a very small probability of occurring, the *kind* of event (i.e., that one of the ticket-holders would win) was unquestionably certain from the beginning.

Consider now the case of Simeon, who buys one ticket in three different lotteries, each one of which has one thousand participants, and wins the main prize in all three of them. We would find this highly astonishing. Why? After all, the probability of Simeon's triple win is one in a billion, which is precisely the probability of Reuben's single win; why then is the one a surprising event and the other not? I believe that the reasonable answer is that in the case of Simeon, not only the specific event but also the *kind* of event that took place was highly improbable; for the mere probability that *any* one among the ticket-holders should win three lotteries in succession was also quite remote—more than one in a million. In this case we are witnessing an unusual *sort* of occurrence, and should thus be legitimately puzzled by it. There would be good grounds for further investigation to see whether anyone tampered with the process of drawing.

The relatively simple point made so far may be put in general terms as follows: Suppose E1, E2,... E*n*, is a set of events and it is certain (or highly probable) that one member of the set is going to occur. If *n* is very large then the probability of any particular event, E1, is very small. Nevertheless, its occurrence will not constitute a surprise. E1 should not astonish us, since we know that if it did not take place, then some other, equally improbable event was bound (or was at least very likely) to materialize. On the other hand, when it is highly *im*probable that even one event of the set is going to occur, then if *any* of these events happens, it is an occasion for surprise, calling for an explanatory hypothesis.

What has just been said may reasonably be claimed to express the very essence of surprise. Since it is the core of a surprising event that it catches one unawares, it makes no sense to say: Under current circumstances it is certain or highly probable that such and such a surprise is about to take place. If a *kind* of event is predictable, then obviously its occurrence will not be surprising.

Let us consider another brief example. Suppose I pull a banknote out of my pocket and observe its serial number to be: B20586291M. The prior probability of such an observation was less than one in a billion, yet it would occasion no surprise. Suppose, however, that following this event I call upon a student across the hall to name a serial number that comes to mind and he says: B20586291M. I should regard this as something remarkable, even mysterious. But why? Surely the probability of his naming the number on the bill I looked at was precisely the same as that of finding that number on the bill in the first place!

The answer is that in the first situation the event of my bill's having the particular number we observe it to have was of course a highly improbable event; nevertheless it was not in the least extraordinary, since some instance of its kind was bound to happen. Every banknote has some serial number of two letters and eight digits, and one of the combinations of ten characters is bound to be printed on the bill in front of me. On the other hand, the student's naming the number he did name was a very special and extraordinary occurrence: He named the number identical with the one on my bill. That something of this sort should occur was of course by no means inevitable; in fact the prior probability of this *kind* of event taking place was less than one in a billion.* It is therefore rational in the second case to seek an explanation for the genuine, extraordinary event we have witnessed.

Will the holder of winning ticket #XP1782 please identify him or herself?

---

* I might add that the set of event-pairs in which a printed number observed, and at the same time a number uttered by someone, are identical, is justifiably viewed as forming a naturally connected class. There is very often a causal connection between members of such pairs; for example, frequently a number appearing in print is the cause of someone, who has knowledge of it, mentioning it.

Confirmation as Explaining Away the Extraordinary and the Surprising

An appreciation of the vital distinction between the two kinds of improbable events is indispensable for a correct understanding of the process of confirmation in the empirical sciences. Any scientist worth the name recognizes at once that a given event belongs to one or the other category without necessarily ever having articulated the difference as I have tried here. I believe it will be helpful if I cite some examples to illustrate my point.

Inertial and Gravitational Masses

In the sixteenth century the mathematician Stevinus dropped objects of unequal weight from the same height, demonstrating that they hit the ground at approximately the same time. Ever since Galileo, who formalized these results, scientists have observed that a large lump of lead and a light feather accelerate at an equal rate when, in the absence of air resistance, they are subjected to the same force. Now of course the pull of gravity on the heavy lead is many times greater than on the light feather, but against this the feather has the advantage that it offers appropriately less inertial resistance to acceleration than the massive lead.

Observations like the above led to the belief that bodies have two independent attributes which somehow balance out: inertial mass and gravitational mass. Any object's gravitational mass relates to the force of motion that it exerts on another object. Its inertial mass relates to its own resistance to being moved. These aspects of an object are so seemingly different that it was a most surprising coincidence that their combined effect should be to equalize the acceleration rates of all falling bodies.

After these lead-and-feather experiments, Newton experimented with different pendulums of the same length, made of different material, observing that they had equal periods. Thus he established the principle of the equivalence of inertial and gravitational masses to an accuracy of one part in a thousand. In 1827, Friedrich Bessel continued the experiments with pendulums and showed that inertial and gravitational masses are equal to within one part in fifty thousand. In 1890, these results were vastly improved by Roland von Eötvös who, with the aid of a torsion balance, determined the validity of the principle to within a few parts in ten billion, and with further refinements physicists later succeeded in achieving an accuracy within a few parts in 10^{13}, or ten trillion.[2]

Neither Newton nor his followers had an explanation of why the two types of masses, the gravitational and the inertial, should be precisely equal. They had to reconcile themselves to the idea that the equivalence between these two different features of a physical body is certainly to be marveled at, but may possibly be an unaccountable coincidence. Eventually Einstein developed his revolutionary general theory of relativity, which led to a notable amount of simplification and unification in physics. Among that theory's great achievements was the provision of a compelling reason why the two masses coincide in magnitude. Gravity and inertia have been reduced to one and the same phenomenon. As Einstein said, the grounds for puzzlement at the "coincidence" disappear through "explaining the numerical equality of inertia and gravitation by the unity of their nature."

Let us consider now a somewhat different situation and imagine that Galileo, Newton and others had discovered that gravitational and inertial masses were not equivalent but that the first was, for the sake of the argument, precisely 3.17 times greater than the other. I believe it is safe to assert that, in that case, few scientists would have had any sense of stupefaction at seeing that the ratio assumed the infinitely improbable number 3.17. It is unlikely that much energy and time would have been spent by physicists like Bessel and Eötvös to attain results confirming with accuracies of the order of one in a billion or one in a trillion that the ratio between the two types of masses was neither more nor less than 3.17.

Nor is it likely that many would have felt an irresistible urge to search for a theory that would have explained why the incredibly rare number 3.17 had to represent the ratio between the two masses. However, since the ratio equals 1, the issue was a source of acute concern and the subject of intense investigation. As is known, Einstein worked for many years with great tenacity to develop general relativity, driven on by a profound conviction that such a theory—the outlines of which he had conceived at an early stage—must be true, and that he would eventually be able to iron out its remaining wrinkles. The main factor sustaining him in his efforts was his firm belief that it simply could not be a coincidence that the values of the two masses were exactly the same.

We might ask once more: If the number 3.17 is no less rare, among the values that a ratio between two physical quantities may have, than the number 1, why then is it that the discovery of the former to be the correct value would have most likely left everyone, including Einstein, indifferent? Why is it that one number may play a major role in initiating one of the important revolutions in science, while another may perhaps merely be recorded and then practically forgotten?

The explanation may be that while the probability of the ratio being 3.17 is infinitesimal, finding it to be precisely that value would be a rather commonplace and "uninteresting" result. The value was bound to be *some* number. The number 1 is, however, not just some number; it is out of the ordinary, with a special significance in the context of measuring the ratio between physical quantities. For example, the ratio between the number of animals that are featherless bipeds and the number of those that are sentient beings is 1. It turns out that the set of featherless bipeds is identical with the set of sentient beings. It often happens that when the ratio between two magnitudes is 1, we find that we are not really measuring two distinct things, but rather the manifestations of one and the same thing. Thus it was reasonable for many physicists of the last two centuries to regard the observed value of the ratio of the masses as extraordinary enough either to require an explanation or to be shown not accurate, and it was reasonable for Einstein to suspect right from the beginning that he was confronted with the manifestations of what is ultimately a single property.

The Orbit of the Planets

My second and last example refers to the physics of four hundred years ago. Around the year 1600, different physicists gave different reasons why unsupported bodies near the earth's surface drop to the ground (instead of moving upward, or horizontally, or at this-or-that angle to the horizontal, or just staying put), and why planets move in long, looping paths. Conservative scientists held that all terrestrial bodies have a propensity to reach the center of the earth, which is their innately preferred place. On the other hand, they explained the movement of celestial bodies by assuming them to be embedded in rotating crystal spheres. Others, like Kepler, maintained that the force of gravity between material bodies is what explains both types of movements. Terrestrial objects are subject to the earth's gravity and therefore fall toward it. The movement of planets, on the other hand, is a compromise result between their initial velocity away from the sun and the attractive force exerted on them by the sun.

Even though Kepler did not have much of an idea about the nature of gravity, not knowing how, or with what, its magnitude varied, it is readily conceded that his position was superior to the position of the Aristotelian scientists. The reason is fairly simple. The Aristotelians were not attempting to explain something truly surprising; there is nothing extraordinary in finding one group of bodies moving in a particular way and a second group in another, even though each particular way had an exceedingly small prior probability to be chosen as the path to be traversed by any set of physical objects. After all, whatever moves is bound to move along *some* path or other. Kepler, however, was confronted with the surprising coincidence of the modes of motion of two different classes of objects: terrestrial and celestial bodies, both of which are pulled toward the most massive body in the vicinity. Thus Kepler's hypothesis was designed to explain what could otherwise legitimately be regarded as a puzzling phenomenon. It was therefore thought to be better confirmed by the data than that of Aristotle's followers.

Is the Universe a Put-Up Job?

We are now in the position to consider a variant on the most famous and most frequently misunderstood argument for the existence of the Creator: the Argument from Design. This version emerges from several very recent results in physics and astronomy. In the last few decades a tantalizingly great number of very rare coincidences, vital for the existence of a minimally stable universe without which no form of life could exist, have been discovered. One of the felicitous coincidences discussed by the physicist Brandon Carter concerns a seemingly trivial fact. Carter notes that the speed of light, multiplied by Planck's constant, and divided by the square of the electron's charge, roughly equals 137. Carter argues that if this ratio were ever so slightly more than it is, then all stars would be blue giants and there would be no planets at all, let alone living creatures; if it were somewhat smaller, all stars would be red dwarfs and thus the planets orbiting them far too cold to sustain any kind of organism. It seemed natural to some to regard such a startlingly fortunate fact as indicative of a supernatural and powerful being with a special interest in the emergence and survival of human-like creatures.

Paul Davies, whose masterful expositions of the latest results in physics and cosmology are a joy to read, discusses our point at great length in several of his books. In his *Superforce* he says, among other things:

> ... there is an unbelievable delicacy in the balance between gravity and electromagnetism within a star. Calculations show that changes in the strength of either force by only one part in 10^{40} would spell catastrophe for stars like the sun.... The sheer improbability that [such] felicitous concurrences could be the result of a series of exceptionally lucky accidents has prompted many scientists to agree with Hoyle that "the universe is a put-up job".... Had the universe been created with slightly different laws, not only would we (or anybody else) not be here to see it, but it is doubtful if there would be any complex structures at all.

The theist has thus been given an unprecedented opportunity to make substantial capital out of the newly-wrought ideas of astrophysics. He now has at his disposal a whole array of thoroughly investigated conditions which support the so-called "anthropic principle," which states that the universe is precisely the way it is in order to make human life possible.

Many have fiercely resisted the suggestion that the cosmos is a "put-up job" for man's sake. It is not that anyone wishes to deny that the universe does exhibit many minutely attuned vital features. Rather the attacks have been directed against the way some, like Hoyle, felt entitled to draw inferences from the recent findings, and not against the findings themselves. These inferences, according to non-believers, are not merely dubious but downright preposterous. They are preposterous, because they were supposedly made on the witless assumption that a highly improbable phenomenon always calls for an explanation. Faced only with the fact that something immensely improbable did indeed take place, they feel there is no room for explanatory hypotheses, let alone for supernatural ones. The famous Jacques Monod, for instance, writes in his *Chance and Necessity*:

> Among all the events possible in the Universe, the *a priori* probability of any particular one of them occurring is next to zero. Yet the Universe exists: particular events must exist in it, the probability of which before was infinitesimal.... Destiny is written as and while, not before, it happens.

A science writer, Michael Lemonick, is one of many who makes essentially the same point. He does not deny the existence of all those infinitesimally improbable, favorable conditions. However, to infer from all this that someone is likely to have planned and willed those conditions is, to Lemonick, "not at all compelling":

> We can always, after the fact, find examples of highly improbable events that happened anyway. If you close your eyes and throw a dart, for instance, it will stick *somewhere* in the wall. Before you throw, chances are overwhelmingly against hitting that particular point. You hit it anyway, but so what?[3]

Ralph Estling, in a widely discussed essay that appeared in the *New Scientist*, adopts a similar line. He explains in some detail why the theistic argument based on the fine tuning manifested by the universe is unacceptable. The core of his charge is that the believer's reasoning is based on the discredited practice of using the concepts of probability and randomness on an *a posteriori* basis. It is silly to be enraptured with finding the universe to be precisely the way it is, he says, when inevitably the universe has to be precisely the way it is. He reminds us that "every human being (and everything else) has truly enormous odds against his being precisely him, and nobody else, but once he is he and nobody else, the matter rests, and no seeking retrospectively over fantastic odds is called for." (It is worth noting that John Updike puts precisely the same argument into the mouth of the protagonist in his remarkable novel *Roger's Version.*) Estling's paper is instructive, lucid and fun to read, but his reasoning is unfalteringly fallacious.

The central, elementary error of Estling, as well as of Monod and many others, is the failure to make the vital distinction between genuinely surprising and non-surprising improbable events. Earlier I have conceded that scientists are perfectly surefooted when required to make this distinction. It seems, however, that this is only so when they are engaged in their scientific work. When they venture into theology or philosophy, however, they often put on a different kind of thinking-cap.

Monod is, of course, absolutely right that given any one of infinitely many universes, some conjunction or other of physical magnitudes will have to obtain. However, the prevailing conjunction is not merely one of indefinitely many; it is also an instance of a virtually infinitesimally rare *kind* of universe: the kind capable of sustaining life. The hypothesis that it was produced by a Being interested in sentient organic systems adequately explains this otherwise inexplicably astonishing fact.

A somewhat wary reader might be wondering whether it is reasonable to answer "this otherwise inexplicably astonishing fact," by invoking Divine planning for man's sake. Do we find in any other area of inquiry, he might demand to know, an instance of an explanatory hypothesis that resembles even remotely the theistic hypothesis? Does the believer not thus flagrantly violate the spirit of rationality by introducing such an unheard-of type of hypothesis?

Against this I submit that, while one and the same logic, deductive and inductive, applies to every conceivable domain of investigation, not all questions need to have similar kinds of answers. In fact it is absurd to expect similar kinds of answers to typical scientific questions about *what* nature is like, as well as to the radically different question: *Why* is nature the way it is? A supernatural agent may have no particular place within natural science, but it is just the sort of Being one should anticipate meeting outside its confines.

Obviously someone who wishes to resist this latest version of the Argument from Design will be able to do so by devising any number of objections to it. There is simply no chance of anyone's producing an argument for the existence of a Divine Being in which someone, trying hard enough, will not be able to find something to dispute. Let us not forget that there exist many thousands of people all over the world who place their confidence in the horoscopes printed in daily newspapers, even though arguments that these horoscopes are pure fabrication seem impeccable. Or on a somewhat more serious level: Hundreds of leading intellectuals for many years maintained their firm conviction that Stalin was the selfless savior of the oppressed, even though the evidence to the contrary was overwhelming.

But as William James explained in his famous *The Will to Believe*, our convictions are largely shaped by our desires. We are selective in attending to evidence, avoiding certain influences on the one hand, and subjecting ourselves to the impact of different ones, on the other. In general, when one has invested a great deal of emotional capital in a cherished belief, then with a modicum of ingenuity it is possible to evade the implications of any reasoning that would force one to adopt an uncomfortable position.

Still, arguments based on logic and scientific method are not entirely pointless. On the contrary, to a person in a receptive frame of mind, they may serve as a means to clarify for himself the most ultimate problems of human existence.

The Question of Divine Fairness

In the minds of some, an entirely different kind of question may arise, namely: Is it in principle conceivable that, in the middle of the twentieth century, astrophysicists should make discoveries on which novel arguments can be based in support of *emunah* (faith in the Creator)? Is it compatible with Divine fairness that He permit some people, i.e., those of the present and later generations, to have access to proofs that were inaccessible to those who lived before the recent scientific advances were made? If we are to suppose that the argument from the recently discovered fine tuning in the universe is valid, would not a non-believer who was never granted the chance to hear about it be entitled to complain that he was denied equal opportunity to acquire *emunah*?

To reply to this fundamental objection one may wish to point out that it is incorrect to state that the argument we have been discussing was unavailable in previous generations. For example, the early eighteenth-century essayist and poet Joseph Addison proclaimed in his famous *Ode*:

> The spacious firmament on high, With all the blue ethereal sky,
>
> ... publishes to every land, The work of an almighty hand.

Referring to the burning stars, he concludes:

> In reason's ear they all rejoice, And utter forth a glorious voice,
>
> For ever singing, as they shine, "The hand that made us is Divine."

And of course in Addison's time no one had any inkling of all the cosmic coincidences required by a stable universe.

This is not an entirely satisfactory answer. While it is true that the Argument from Design has always been with us, the more recent results of astrophysics furnish substantial material that was not available in the past, and provide it with considerably greater power than it ever had before. Hence one may still wonder why it is not a violation of Divine fairness that so many people were denied access to the more vigorous version of the Argument from Design.

It may not be unreasonable to reply that, as a matter of fact, Divine fairness demands that novel ways to the acquisition of *emunah* be available for the first time to us in our time. The amount of evidence that may reasonably be expected to be sufficient to convince a man of good will of the existence of a Divine designer, sustainer and supervisor depends greatly on the general climate of opinion in which he finds himself. In a generation in which basic presuppositions made by everybody in earlier times are no longer taken for granted, much more weighty evidence may be required for what was easily assented to in the past. Thus the different availability of proofs for theism at different stages in history (or to different people at any given time) need not be interpreted as a sign of discrimination; on the contrary, it may be indispensable for maintaining even-handedness. The different types of social conditioning in which different generations have been steeped demand that the Almighty reveal His design behind the universe to different degrees at different times.

NOTES

1. *Midrash Temurah*, chapter 3.
2. E.R. Harrison, *Cosmology* (Cambridge, 1981), 164.
3. Michael Lemonick, *Science Digest* (August 1986).

Jacob Immanuel Schochet

Society's Legal Codes: Pragmatism or Morality? A Jewish View of Natural Law

PEOPLE HAVE A SAYING: Either companionship or death.[1] This ancient proverb succinctly expresses the old philosophical principle that man is by nature a social or political being, that it is his nature to form communities in order to live in society.

The need for companionship is not merely psychological. It is a practical necessity as well. It is close to impossible for man to live in solitude. He needs clothing for protection against the elements, as well as proper food suitable to his temperament. For practically all of us it is impossible to obtain all the necessities of life except by the aggregation and association of many individuals who assist one another: one sews; one weaves; one manufactures the necessary tools; and so forth, with all other acts and labors, so that by the aggregation of all, each one is able to obtain the food, clothing and

---

JACOB IMMANUEL SCHOCHET is Rabbi of the Kielcer Congregation in Toronto, Canada, and Professor of Philosophy at Humber College. He has received numerous degrees (B.A., M.A., M. Phil., D.D., Ph.D.) and has authored over fifteen books (including the famous texts Mystical Concepts in Chassidism *and* Who is a Jew?*) and numerous articles. An acknowledged authority on Jewish philosophy, mysticism and ethics, Rabbi Schochet is a popular lecturer throughout North America and Europe.*

shelter needed for his support and sustenance.[2]

"Thus taught Ben Zoma: What labors did Adam have to carry out before he obtained bread to eat? He ploughed and he sowed; he reaped and he bound the sheaves; he threshed and he winnowed; he selected the ears and ground them, sifted the flour, kneaded and baked; and after all that, he ate! I, on the other hand, rise early and find all these prepared before me. How many labors did Adam have to carry out before he obtained a garment to wear! He had to shear, wash the wool and comb it, spin it and weave it, and after that he had a garment to wear? I, on the other hand, rise early and find all these prepared before me."[3]

Interdependence makes it necessary for people to live in a communal setup allowing for the interaction of helping one another. The benefit of that social aggregation of people, however, also creates problems. For just as people differ in shape, size and color, so they differ in mental, emotional and moral dispositions.[4] Unlike the case with other species, people may be so different from one another that they appear to belong to more than one distinct species! For example, one can find individuals so compassionate that they cannot bring themselves to hurt or kill an insect, while others may be so cruel as to be liable to kill their own children in anger.[5]

The variety of people in a society, each one set in his or her own ways, must be a continuous irritant leading to disagreements and conflict. The very need to flock together, in order to help and complement one another, also harbors the seeds that lead men to harm one another. There is only one way that self-destruction can be avoided: Members of society must arrive at a consensus, at some agreement on rules and regulations to govern interrelationships.

There is need for a social contract that will set norms of behavior, guidelines of mutual obligations in terms of what the members of that society must do or must refrain from doing.[6] This social contract thus becomes a legal code for the community—regulating relationships and establishing a system of enforcing these regulations. It establishes a governor or government "to gauge the actions of the individuals, perfecting that which is deficient and reducing that which is excessive, prescribing actions and moral habits that all of them must always practice in the same way, so that natural diversity is counterbalanced through the uniformity of legislation and so that the community becomes well-ordered."[7]

The rules and measures of the social contract, inducing man to act one way and restraining him from acting another way, are in effect self-imposed restrictions upon the unlimited freedom he seems to enjoy in his aboriginal state of nature prior to entering a state of society. Assuming, for argument's sake, that the very first humans did not receive a Divine code of behavior, they were as free as the animals in the fields and jungles: nothing was right or wrong. Guided only by their instinctive desires, they could roam about at random, taking and devouring the lives, limbs and possessions of all other creatures at will. "Might makes right," and this means survival of the fittest. Thus to avoid this intolerable chaos of jungle life in that "state of nature," man pays the price of surrendering his unlimited freedom by entering into a social contract with others.

The foundation of this contract is straightforward: Refrain from doing unto others those things which you do not wish to be done to yourself. The initial terms, therefore, are quite simple: laws against violating the life, property and liberty of individuals, with suitable penalties for those who break these laws. Thus are born the legal prohibitions against murder, robbery, and so forth.

One thing is clear, though: The fact that certain actions are now *illegal* does not mean that they are *immoral*. The laws of the social contract are essentially self-serving, practical directives, adopted by consensus of the members of the newly formed association or community. Whatever everyone agrees upon is incorporated in this code for purely utilitarian or pragmatic reasons. There is no recourse to any moral principles, for such principles, in effect, do not exist for simple lack of any frame of reference.

At this point we must keep in mind the basic distinction between legality and morality. These two terms are not synonymous. Something may be legal yet immoral, or moral yet beyond the law. The Nuremberg Laws of Nazi Germany, for example, were enshrined in the constitutional or legal code of that country, but this fact did not render them morally acceptable. Whether laws are imposed by a dictatorship or by a democratic process has no bearing at all on their moral standing. The dictator—or the majority—simply imposes measures which he feels to be to his benefit.

To be sure, more often than not the moral consciousness and convictions of the legislator (or of those exercising the democratic voting process) are determining causes for introducing legislative measures. By the same token, however, as convictions and consciousness change from time to time, and from place to place, so do the laws. What may have been regarded as immoral a century ago, and thus may have been declared illegal, may be unimportant or even moral today to the majority—bringing about a change in the law, and vice versa. We see this with so many decisions—for example, with the laws about slavery, abortion, capital punishment, censorship, and so forth. The law, therefore, is at best a reflection of public opinion or feeling, continuously swinging back and forth.

Those who believe in situational ethics will thus claim that the law is a reflection of moral principles. In terms of the strict definition of morality, in which ethical judgments are in essence no different than logical or scientific judgments—based on the principles of identity (everything is that which it is, and not something else), contradiction (one cannot simultaneously affirm and deny one and the same thing), and excluded middle (a statement is either true or false)—

"The law...is at best a reflection of public opinion."

the relativity of so-called situational ethics strips it of any moral pretense: If something is good, right and just, it remains so regardless of time, place or personal feeling (of one, many, or all).

A change in conditions may affect *practical* decisions and specific procedures, but not the underlying principles and rules. The concept of ethics or morality has meaning and content only in absolute terms. Popular feelings or acceptance are irrelevant. It was not that long ago that well over 90 percent of people believed that the earth is flat, while today at least as many believe that the earth is round. The fact of reality, of course, has nothing to do with either belief. It is absurd to say that both beliefs were or are correct in their own times. To say that the earth is round, is to say that our predecessors who believed otherwise were altogether wrong—regardless of the popularity of their belief. It is likewise with moral judgments: If, for example, it is wrong and immoral to capriciously deprive someone of his life, liberty or property, this remains wrong and immoral regardless of the time, place, cultural background, or whatever circumstances.

Legal rules are conventions which are subject to discussion, change or modification without notice. Moral principles, however, are and remain beyond human manipulation.

The distinction between legality and morality, and between relative (or situational) ethics and absolute ethics, is crucial. In this context, the social contract discussed above is no more than a legal or social agreement, the prototype for legal codes, based on and grounded exclusively in public opinion and emotive aspirations.

This is not to say that the content of the social contract or legal codes is purely emotional, as opposed to rational. On the contrary: The articles enshrined in a code generally make very good sense. They are the result of logical thinking and intelligent decisions. It makes very good sense to prohibit murder, robbery, etc., and to set up instruments to enforce these prohibitions—even if it means surrendering part of our natural freedom to do so. It makes good sense to introduce forced taxation to support the mechanism of government, a judicial system, and public works for the benefit of the members of society. Unbridled freedom for everyone to act as he or she pleases means anarchy. Anarchy may provide short-term gains, but ultimately these will prove counter-productive and self-defeating. Any possible benefits are outweighed by the unavoidable losses, thus rendering a system of free-for-all, which is stupid and irrational.

In summary, it is clear that man is essentially in need of association with fellow beings to obtain what he needs for his life and sustenance. It is equally clear that an aggregate of people residing in a town, city, district or region, or—on the larger scale—all the human beings in the world as a whole, should have some order to follow in their conduct,

> maintaining justice in general and suppressing wrong, so as to keep men from quarreling in their transactions and business relations with one another. Such order would include protection against murder, theft, robbery and the like, and in general all those measures which are calculated to maintain the political group and enable the people to live in welfare. This order the wise men call *dat tivit*—natural law, meaning that it is necessary for man by his nature, whether the order emanates from a wise man or a prophet.[8]

The natural law by itself, however, is not yet sufficient to order the needs of people, their lives and interrelationships. For natural law deals essentially with general rules and concepts. Within the parameter of the general context of natural law there is need for specific rules, laws and guidelines to deal with specific circumstances, conditions, situations and details as they occur in day-to-day life. These specific rules are to enhance all the social and commercial relations and transactions of the people. Rules or laws of this order are called *dat nimusit*—conventional law.[9]

The basic differences between natural and conventional law are: (a) Natural law is general, dealing with general principles, or first principles. For example, the natural law establishes that one is not to harm another, or that wrongdoing must be punished. This still begs the questions: What is called harm? What is proper or appropriate punishment? Would these rules apply unqualified, under all and any circumstances? How is one to decide in the case of a conflict of interests, e.g., self-defense or where one harm would preclude worse harm? And so forth. Conventional law would then provide rulings for these specific cases. (b) Natural law is essentially universal, with principles that rational people recognize and accept—self-evident rational principles. Conventional law is more parochial, where different cultures and systems may define and apply things altogether differently. (c) Natural law, reflecting essentially self-evident rational principles, can be recognized, acknowledged and applied by all normal human beings of average intelligence without the need for discussion, agreement or a regulatory agency. Conventional law, on the other hand, is subjective and individual, dependent on time, place and the nature of the people enacting it. Conventional law, therefore, is dependent on discussion, agreement or social contract, and needs the regulatory agency of a ruler or judge compelling the people to repress wrong and to observe the law so as to secure the welfare of the group. The establishment of a government is thus almost imperative for the continuance of the human species, as stated by Rabbi Chanina so long ago: "Pray for the welfare of the government, for were it not for the fear of it—people would swallow one another alive."[10]

In general terms, then, we can summarize that the purpose of natural law is to repress wrong *per se* and to promote right *per se*, in order that man refrain from murder, robbery and so forth, with the ensuing benefits that man may live safe from wrongdoer and oppressor. The purpose of conventional law is to suppress the unbecoming and to promote the becoming, so that man may keep away from that which society assumes to be indecent. In this context there is an advantage to the (subjective) conventional law over the (more objective) natural law: It serves to control the whole range of human conduct, arranging human affairs with a view to the improvement of human society as a whole.[11]

Even so, conventional law—or the compound of natural and conventional law—suffers from certain deficiencies:[12]

(1) Conventional law controls human conduct in order to maintain a good political society. Thus it deals only with the *socially* becoming and unbecoming, but it does not and cannot impart knowledge of the truth which provides for the moral perfection of man or his soul.

(2) Even in the matter of the socially becoming and unbecom-

ing, conventional law cannot always provide adequate guidelines. Something may very well *seem* to us to be becoming or unbecoming without being so in reality. Any code devised by human beings will reflect human imperfection. As human intelligence and insight are limited, so are their findings and conclusions.

(3) As man realizes these self-evident limitations of human law, he recognizes its relativity: The rules he follows are merely *ad hoc* conveniences and not truth. With human law one can never know whether the procedures followed are truly just, or merely appear to be so. Man cannot, therefore, find the inner peace of mind and sense of satisfaction normally achieved when knowingly following the right path toward the ultimate ends of life.

(4) Human law is not, and never can be, complete. It is situational ethics. As the situation changes in whatever detail, so will the law. It remains in a continuous flux, ever changing and adapting to time, place and conditions, failing to provide clear definitions of right and wrong. In other words, it will make general statements about given situations, but cannot define particular acts. For example, it may establish rules like "A virtuous act consists of doing the proper thing at the proper time and in the proper place," or "The proper measure must be maintained in every act." It cannot, however, define in clear-cut terms the precise meanings of "proper measure," "proper time," or "proper place."

(5) Human law tries to instill a moral sense toward the becoming and unbecoming. The reality of continuous change, however, renders this moral sense an elusive pursuit. For example, the incestuous relationship between a brother and sister was acceptable in the early days of mankind but condemned thereafter. The more modern roller-coaster changes in attitude and legislation about abortion and capital punishment are other examples. The commitment to the becoming and the aversion to the unbecoming, normally acquired through conventional law, do not last forever but change along with the times and mood-swings of the legislators and their subjects.

(6) Human law cannot devise adequate retribution—to recompense every man suitably in accordance with his conduct, or to mete out punishment properly to make it fit every crime.

(7) Human law can deal only with external (empirically perceived)

acts. It cannot deal with internal acts or motives.

And so forth.

In short, natural and conventional law do have an inherent rationale and utilitarian effects. Nonetheless, something basic is missing. These laws are purely political. Their sole object is to establish the good order of the state and its affairs, to free it from mischief and oppression. They do not, however, deal with speculative matters; no heed is given to perfecting our rational faculty, nor is there concern about sound and unsound opinions. Their object is strictly to arrange, under all circumstances, the relations of men to each other, and to secure their well-being, in accordance with the personal views or ideas of the legislator.[13] Thus they are pragmatic and useful, but offer no certainty in terms of truth and ultimate values. They are practical for the needs and purposes of the here and now, but they lack a moral sense.

To invest law with ultimate values, with a dimension of morality and purpose transcending the transient context of the temporal and spatial, requires a grounding in the absolute. This can come only from the sole source of absoluteness, namely God. Thus we arrive at the concept of *dat Elokit*—Divine Law.[14]

None of the defects of natural or conventional law apply to Divine Law. On the contrary: Divine Law, ordained and revealed by God, deals not only with right conduct but also with right knowledge. It distinguishes between the true and the false, offering certainty in all matters, whether they be general or particular. It informs about ultimate ends and destiny, and enables man to realize these, offering the concomitant satisfaction that accompanies the knowledge of truth.

Only Divine Law can specify absolute rules for all cases and circumstances, and only it can define the true meanings of value judgments for terms like "proper," "virtuous," "temperate," "mercy," "cruelty," etc.—definitions which may possibly run counter to the subjective opinions held by some, most or all men. Only Divine Law, by virtue of its origin in Divine wisdom, possesses the qualities of absoluteness and permanence, and thus it alone—and none other—can inculcate a reliable and appropriate commitment prompting an innate desire for the truly becoming and aversion for the truly unbecoming. Likewise, only Divine Law can assure ultimate justice in terms of truly appropriate recompense or punishment, and it alone can consider internal acts and motives as much as empirically perceived ones. Thus it is only with Divine Law that one can speak of moral values and criteria.

Divine Law, then, seeks to establish and improve not only the material interests of people, but also soundness of belief. It takes pains to inculcate correct notions of God and reality. It seeks to make man wise, to give him understanding, to arouse his attention so as to lead him to know the whole of that which exists in its true form.[15]

Two comments at this point:

(1) Human law is generally based on practical reason. Divine Law transcends human law and is supra-rational. This is not to say, however, that Divine Law negates, ignores or belittles the underlying rationale of human law. On the contrary: It recognizes, complements and supplements human law by extending itself into areas where human reason and intelligence are unable to tread! Many precepts of Divine Law would have been discovered, adopted and practiced even without any revelation, for no other reason but that practical thought, common sense, dictates their observance.

Our rabbis thus taught: "'You shall do *mishpatai* (My ordinances)' (*Leviticus* 18:4)—i.e., those precepts prescribed by the Torah which, even if they had not been prescribed by Scripture, should by right (of reason) have been written, such as the prohibitions about robbery, incest, idolatry, blasphemy, and bloodshed."[16] That is, even if such matters (generally referred to as *mishpatim*)[17] had not been ordained by Divine Law, it would still have been appropriate to ordain these by human law.[18] Indeed, there are basic principles of decency and appropriate behavior which we could learn and derive even from simple observation of the behavior of certain animals![19]

Divine Law thus divides into two categories: a) *mitzvot sichliot*—rational precepts, laws possessed of self-evident rationale and purpose which would have been legislated even without revelation (such as those mentioned in the preceding paragraph), and b) *mitzvot shimiot*—revealed precepts, laws to which we submit by virtue of their being ordained by the Divine wisdom, and generally speaking of a religious or ritual nature. Human reason would not devise the latter on its own; they are imposed upon us by Divine command, and neither the approval nor the disapproval of these is decreed by reason. These precepts, too, have a cause and purpose, though these are unknown to us owing either to the deficiency of human knowledge or the weakness and limitation of human intellect. As opposed to *mishpatim*, these are called *chukkim* (statutes; decrees), and include the dietary laws, the laws of purity and impurity, the prohibition of wearing an admixture of wool and linen (*sha'atnez*), and so forth. To laws of this kind our Sages apply phrases like, "These are the things which I [God] decreed upon you, and you are not permitted to dwell upon them (i.e., to question or second-guess them)"; "The evil disposition and the nations of the world taunt Israel about them"; etc.[20]

(2) The rational laws (which parallel natural and conventional laws) display self-evident pragmatism. As *human* laws, however, as independent laws dictated by practical reason alone (and thus outside the context of Divine Law or revelation), they are devoid of *moral* content. No doubt they are practical, utilitarian, indeed essential to social order, peace and harmony; but no more. Ultimate value judgments of good and evil, just and unjust, moral and immoral, do not apply to them. On their own they are man-made, with all the defects and deficiencies implied thereby (as explained above).

In this context we can understand the following ruling in Maimonides' code of Torah Law:

> A non-Jew who accepts the seven commandments of the Noachide Code and observes them scrupulously is of the pious of the nations of the world and has a portion in the world-to-come. This, however, applies only if he accepts and performs them as precepts ordained by the Holy One, blessed be He.... But if he observes them as *reasoned conclusions*, then he is not deemed... of the pious of the nations but of their wise ones.[21]

The meaning and implication of this ruling is obvious. There are two ways of looking at the precepts of the Noachide Code: a)

There is the *traditional* view dating these precepts back to Divine revelation and ordinance in the days of Adam and Noah (and reaffirmed in the revelation to Moses);[22] or b) One can adopt them simply as rational precepts to which human reason inclines.[23]

If the Noachide Code is observed in the latter sense, this would mean to simply follow self-interest in terms of adopting a utilitarian code of behavior. This is not the same as submitting to moral principles. One cannot, therefore, apply to it such concepts as morality or piety, and thus one is not deserving of any reward (beyond the benefits of social order and harmony which these laws tend to produce). A person like that is indeed wise for realizing the self-rewarding value of natural and conventional law, but he is not of the pious.

If, again, the code is observed in the first (the traditional) sense, as revealed law, this implies submission to higher moral principles, to the Divine Will and Law—regardless of any self-interest. One can, therefore, apply to it concepts of morality and piety, and thus it renders one deserving of a special reward beyond the "fringe benefits" of social order and harmony which these laws produce. Such a person is both wise and pious.

In both ancient and modern philosophy we find definitions for man as a "rational animal" and a "social animal." The implication is that man is essentially an animal, albeit endowed with a rational faculty and social dependency. In this view, human reason is seen as nature's way of making up for the animal instinct or prowess which man lacks, thus providing him with a substitute in order to survive and sustain himself.

From this perspective, we can well understand and appreciate the rationale of the need for a social contract to guide and control human behavior. By the same token, however, this view, based as it is on human thinking, negates all concepts and values of morality or ethics. It provides pragmatism (for better or worse, whatever the circumstances will suggest), but not abiding guidelines or principles.

Revealed religion sees man altogether differently. There are indeed many similarities and analogies between man and animal. Man, by his very nature, does betray animalistic characteristics and tendencies which appear to support the former view. However, all these similarities are purely homonymous. In fact man is *essentially* different from animal, in *every* sense—spiritually, mentally and even physically.[24]

Man is by nature a *moral* being, born with a conscience—i.e., a consciousness of right and wrong, good and evil. This natural conscience may be like a blank tape or disk, filled in or recorded by the educational process and environmental influences, but it is there from birth, an integral part of the human reality. The detailed functioning of this human "computer" or "recorder" depends on the programming—whether we record the relative values of the opinions around us (which are subject to ever-changing conditions and situations), or the absolute values of an *a priori* system of ethics rooted in revelation.

Our ability to form social contracts, or the fact that we do so, does not assure us of a special identity. In a zoo or circus, too, one can find well-trained animals, and even law and order among the animals, albeit imposed by the sheer force of their keepers, trainers or guards; but the inhabitants remain brute animals nonetheless. Revelation alone assures us of a unique and distinct identity as humans, distinguished not only quantitatively but more so qualitatively, by virtue of our moral consciousness and reality.

Appendix

Question from the audience: Your presentation appears to place all emphasis on the rational faculty of man—rational decisions, etc.—and does not seem to allow for the emotional aspect of man. Surely the emotional nature of man is also part of his reality and should be given its due. How would you reconcile this?

Answer: You are quite right in emphasizing the importance of the emotional side of man. It should not, and cannot, be underestimated. Man's emotions play a most important role in all aspects of his behavior. In fact, it is man's *emotional* aspect, and not his intellect, that moves him to act; that is, our emotions are the motor power prompting us to act upon anything.[25] However:

(1) The motor causes a vehicle to move, but the vehicle still needs a driver to guide its direction. A car can move without a driver, but when left on its own it will sooner or later crash, or, at least, move

in the wrong direction. Our rational faculty is the driver (who on his own cannot achieve the action of the vehicle), while our emotions are the motor (which on its own will lead us nowhere). Emotions thus are important, but also dangerous. On their own they have no direction, criss-crossing in every which way, even moving in self-contradictory and self-destructive circles. Only mind, reason and intelligence can set meaningful goals and purposes, and prepare ways to achieve these.

The two must then work together: intellect determining guidelines and convincing the emotions to follow them and act upon them.

(2) Maimonides discusses[26] an interesting question: Who is greater—the *chasid* (saintly person), whose natural inclinations and dispositions prompt him to act morally and to perform the good, out of innate longing and desire (thus the emotions moving him automatically), or the *tzaddik* (righteous person), whose natural inclinations and dispositions crave, and arouse within him, immoral desires and deeds, but who fights these longings, subdues his passions, and with self-restraint (motivated by reason) succeeds in acting morally?

Each of these two has his own advantage and disadvantage: The *chasid* has achieved a level of self-perfection, instinctively pursuing the good and avoiding evil; on the other hand, however, it comes to him naturally, without any struggle, and thus beyond any exercise of his freedom of choice—in a sense, beyond moral consciousness. The *tzaddik* is continuously struggling, forced to exercise his freedom of choice, thus continuously and freely submitting to moral authority and self-elevation; on the other hand, the existence of his vexing desires for the improper seems to denote an immoral disposition and psychic corruption. Which, then, is preferable?

Maimonides answers by referring to our earlier distinction between *mitzvot sichliot* (rational, self-evident laws or precepts) and *mitzvot shimiot* (supra-rational, revealed laws or precepts). With regard to the rational precepts, he says, we must not only accept them as Divine commands but also work on ourselves until we are imbued by their truth to the point of observing them in a natural, instinctive way; that is, that we develop our emotions to the point of natural desire and pursuit of the good, and natural aversion to evil (the disposition of the *chasid*). With regard to the supra-rational—

the purely religious or ritual—precepts, we should recognize that their violation would not be irrational, harmful or unpleasant *per se* (from a human intellectual and pragmatic perspective), but we must submit to the higher authority of the Divine Will which transcends human reason and understanding (the disposition of the *tzaddik*).

Maimonides quotes as proof text the following statement of the Midrash:[27] "Whence do we know that one should not say, 'I cannot bear to wear *sha'atnez* (mixture of wool and linen),' 'I cannot bear to eat the flesh of swine,' or 'I cannot bear to engage in an illicit relationship,' but that one *should* say, 'I could and would, but what can I do as my Father in Heaven has imposed these prohibitions upon me'? Because Scripture says, 'I have separated you from the nations, that you be unto Me' (*Leviticus* 20:26)—i.e., to keep aloof from sin and accept the Kingdom of Heaven." The Commentary of Rabad adds: " 'unto Me'—for My (God's) sake, and not because of your own understanding and decision." Maimonides notes that this passage refers specifically to *revealed* laws as opposed to the self-evident rational precepts.

The emphasis on rational decisions does not, therefore, exclude emotional involvement. Both are essential. The first step, however, is rational knowledge and understanding of the principles discussed earlier.

NOTES

1. *Ta'anit* 23a. See *Bava Batra* 16b, and Maimonides, *Perush Ha-Mishnah, Avot* 1:6.
2. See R. Joseph Albo, *Sefer Ha-Ikkarim* 1: chap. 5. *Cf.* Maimonides, *Moreh Nevuchim* 1: chap. 72.
3. *Berachot* 58a; *Yerushalmi, Berachot* 9: end of 1.
4. See references in note 3; and Maimonides, *Mishneh Torah, Hilchot De'ot* 1:1.
5. *Moreh Nevuchim* 2: chap. 40.
6. For sources in secular philosophy on the concepts discussed here and later on (social contract; natural law; conventional law; Divine Law; etc.), see C. Morris, ed., *The Great Legal Philosophers* (University of Pennsylvania Press, 1959); and J. C. Smith and D. N. Weisstub, *The Western Idea of Law* (London, Toronto, Sidney: Buttersworth, 1983); especially *s.v.* Aris-

totle, Aquinas, Grotius, Hobbes, Locke, Bentham and Dabin. (It is interesting to note that there are striking similarities between the treatments of natural-conventional law and Divine Law in Aquinas and R. Albo.)

7. *Moreh Nevuchim* 2: chap. 40. See *Sefer Ha-Ikkarim* 1: end of chap. 5.
8. *Sefer Ha-Ikkarim* 1: chap. 5.
9. Ibid.
10. *Avot* 3:2; *Avodah Zarah* 4a.
11. *Sefer Ha-Ikkarim* 1: chap. 7.
12. Ibid., chap. 8.
13. *Moreh Nevuchim* 2: chap. 40.
14. On this, and the following, see *Sefer Ha-Ikkarim* 1: chaps. 7-8.
15. *Moreh Nevuchim* 2: chap. 40.
16. *Sifra* (and Rashi) on *Leviticus* 18:4; *Yoma* 67b.
17. Rashi on *Genesis* 26:5, and Maimonides in *Shemonah Perakim*, chap. 6, refer to the Scriptural term of *mitzvot* to have this meaning.
18. See Rashi on *Genesis* 26:5.
19. *Eruvin* 100b.
20. Rav Saadia Gaon, *Emunot V'De'ot* 3: chaps. 1-2. *Moreh Nevuchim* 3: chap. 26. *Shemonah Perakim*, chap. 6.
21. *Mishneh Torah, Hilchot Melachim* 8:11. Some commentators assumed this ruling to be an original insight of Maimonides himself (see *Kessef Mishneh, ad loc.*), while others tried to trace it to earlier sources (see *Yad Yehudah* on *Asarah Ma'amarot, Chikkur Din* 3:21, note 23). The discovery of an ancient manuscript of *Mishnat R. Eliezer* (New York, 1933) has provided us with the actual rabbinic source (see there, chap. 6, 121), as verified by Maimonides himself in a responsum—*Teshuvot Ha-Rambam*, ed. J. Blau, no. 148 (vol. 1, 282*f.*; and see also the supplementary notes, ibid., vol. 3, 163).
22. See Maimonides, *Perush Ha-Mishnah, Chullin* 7:6.
23. See *Mishneh Torah, Hilchot Melachim* 9:1; *cf.* Rabbi Y. Kapach's notes on his edition of *Moreh Nevuchim* 3:26, note 5.
24. See *Shemonah Perakim*, chap. 1; *cf.* Maimonides, *Milot Ha-Higayon*, chap. 13.
25. See *Moreh Nevuchim* 2: chap. 4; *cf.* J.I. Schochet, *Mystical Concepts in Chassidism*, chap. 3, p. 75, note 64.
26. *Shemonah Perakim*, chap. 6.
27. *Sifra*, end of *Kedoshim* (cited by Rashi on *Leviticus* 20:26).

Meir Tamari

The Challenge of Wealth: A Jewish Perspective

IN JUDAISM, as in all socioreligious movements, economic activities give rise to basic religious and moral problems which have to be solved in some fashion. Broadly speaking, these problems fall into two major categories which encompass both the scope of economic activity and its moral legitimacy:

(1) The importance of economic activity vis-à-vis the demands of religion, e.g., that a man devote time to prayer, study and meri-

---

MEIR TAMARI is Chief Economist in the Office of the Governor at the Bank of Israel, where he has worked since 1960. His work includes tracking current trends in the Israeli economy and the creation and supervision of major research projects. He studied at the University of Cape Town (B. Com.) and City University, London (Ph.D.), and lectured for many years at Bar-Ilan University, Israel. His special interest is small business and in this field he has worked as a consultant to numerous federal governments and international agencies. He is a popular lecturer at universities throughout Europe and North America and has been the keynote speaker at an International Small Business Congress in Amsterdam.

Parallel with his career, Dr. Tamari has been continuously involved with Jewish youth wherever he happened to be, giving talks and courses on Zionism, Bible, Chasidic teachings, and Israeli social issues. Among his many publications is a landmark volume entitled With All Your Possessions: Jewish Ethics and Economic Life.

torious deeds. In essence this is a problem of allocation of time between economic and religious activity.

(2) Since the production and accumulation of economic goods are basic human activities, religion must express an attitude toward them just as it does toward all man's other activities. The fact that wealth and the search for it are often fostered by greed and envy, and often result in injustice, theft and even bloodshed, makes the need for a religious attitude even more imperative. Furthermore, the knowledge that economics is not restricted to individual acts, but involves communities and nations as well, does not allow religion to ignore the issues related to it.

At the outset, therefore, we have to consider Judaism's response to these problems in order to verify the legitimacy of economic activity for a Jew who wishes to remain true to his Judaism.

Allocation of Time between Religious and Economic Needs

Since time is a limited resource, man has to ration it between satisfying his economic and religious needs. A basic restraint which Judaism places on time spent in economic activity is the forbidding of such activity during certain periods of the year. The Jewish calendar is indeed replete with days requiring complete abstinence from labor, commerce or other economic activity, and there are other times when such activity is permitted but curtailed.

There is, however, a more fundamental and far-reaching limitation on the time involved in economic activity which has the added distinction of being peculiar to Judaism. This is the obligation of religious study. This is an obligation which is binding not only for priests, rabbis and scholars, but for the ordinary person as well; nor is it limited to a particular period of time in a person's life. Every individual, irrespective of age, knowledge, or economic status, is required to devote unlimited time to learning—so that essentially one is obligated to study day and night until one's dying day. All other activities, since they detract from the time devoted to Torah study, are considered wasteful and a sign of misconduct.

Carrying this concept to its logical, if extreme, conclusion, there developed a school of thought which views all time devoted to economic activity as illegitimate since it is time taken away from studying, even though such activity was otherwise considered legitimate. According to this view, God will provide man with the necessities of life if man devotes his life to study.[1] However, the majority opinion of Jewish thinkers was summed up by Maimonides when he ruled that a man should divide his time equally into three parts: one third devoted to the study of Torah, one third devoted to earning a living, and one third to eating and sleeping, etc.[2]

It is clear, therefore, that devoting time to study is an essential tenet of Judaism even though it limits economic activity. Historically, this has led to the search for occupations that allow one to devote time to study, either because they do not require much time, or because they can be pursued in places where there are concentrations of Jews, which makes such study feasible. For example, Maimonides recommends that a man should go into commerce, rather than farming, because commerce allows him far more time for the study of Torah.[3]

Economics—Road to Ruin or Path to Sanctity?

Man's economic desires are treated by Judaism in exactly the same way as all other basic human drives. They are not seen as something to be destroyed, but rather as something which man must sanctify, and become sanctified thereby. This attitude is a reflection of man's partnership with the Deity, a continuation of the process of Creation. In such a partnership, the holy sparks which reside in man transform his ordinary everyday acts into communion with God.[4] Therefore, accumulating and keeping economic assets are considered by Judaism as legitimate, permissible and beneficial activities, sanctified by the observance of God's commandments, yet restricted.

Judaism's daily prayers contain requests not only for Divine forgiveness, for peace, for healing of the sick, etc., but also for an equitable and bountiful livelihood earned through honest and moral means. For instance, on the holiest day of the Jewish year, *Yom Kippur*, the Day of Atonement, perhaps the pinnacle of Jewish life, the High Priest offered a special prayer in the Temple. This prayer includes, as one of its major components, the request for a year of plenty, a year in which the people will not be dependent on others for their livelihood, and will enjoy material plenty.

The fact that these requests are not only included, but also highlighted, in the public prayer on this important and solemn occasion stands in glowing contrast to the glorification of poverty in other faiths and creeds. The Bible does not exhort against engaging in economic activities or accumulating material goods. No accusing fingers are pointed at those engaged in normal economic activities for the acquisition of material goods. Nor are there imperatives of asceticism and poverty for the spiritual good of man.

Despite the legitimacy of economic activity and the enjoyment of material goods, Judaism does not allow their unlimited accumulation and use. Both the achievement of economic wealth and its use are strictly limited and channeled by Judaism, for the individual and for the group. This does not flow from an exalted view of poverty or an other-worldly philosophy, but rather from the view that all of man's actions, including these, are subject to the ethical, moral and religious demands of the Torah. That the sphere of economic activity is a major vehicle for achieving sanctity may be seen in the fact that well over one hundred of the 613 commandments in the Torah are related to it. The Sages of the Talmud said, "He who is desirous of achieving sainthood, let him live according to the tractates of the Talmud regulating commerce and finance."[5]

"The Earth Is the Lord's and the Fullness Thereof"[6]

The basic premise of the Jewish economic framework is that all wealth originates from God alone. God in His infinite mercy makes sufficient economic resources available to man. That the wealth belongs to God Who has given it to man for his physical well-being is essentially a concept of economic stewardship for the temporary holders of wealth. Since Judaism is community-oriented as well as individual-oriented, the group at all levels—communal, national and international—is partner in some fashion to each individual's wealth. Perhaps two Biblical institutions can demonstrate this three-way partnership of God, the individual and society:

(1) The observance of the Sabbatical year requires that the Land of Israel lie fallow every seventh year, and that man eat only of the natural produce of the ground. Moreover, in those years man is required to renounce legal ownership over his land so that everything growing thereon is available to all and sundry.

Periodically, the Jew reaffirms his trust in God's mercy by not plowing, sowing, etc., and by relying only on the natural increase of the untilled ground, not only in the seventh year, but in the eighth as well. True, man is required to labor incessantly for his livelihood and to transform raw material into food, clothing, and shelter. Yet the Jew is taught that his material welfare is in fact given to him by God and therefore has to be used according to the Divine Will.[7]

"To any farmer, the first fruits of his endeavor are a special kind of crop..."

(2) To any farmer, the first fruits of his endeavor are a special kind of crop—there is in general a special relationship to one's first business deal, to one's first profit, to one's first asset and even to less tangible achievements in other spheres of life. The Jew is obligated to present his first fruits to the priest before he is able to eat of the new crop. However, what highlights the concept of dependence and thankfulness is not so much the bringing of the fruit, but

the text recited by the farmer in gratitude to God when he brings it. Here the Jew relates how an insignificant little family went down to Egypt and was enslaved and persecuted. Only through the love of God, and His power over the forces of nature, was this family redeemed from slavery, carried through the desert, and brought into its own land. And it was this grace of God which gave him not only the land, but its fertility, crops and the first fruits. The farmer was, in the final analysis, quite indebted for his own success.[8]

This recognition of man's dependence on the grace of God for his economic welfare and the obligation associated with that recognition are translated in Judaism into a legal framework and binding daily practices. The Torah provides definitions of what is permissible and what is forbidden, as well as regulations governing how, when and where the permitted acts may be performed. It is this definitive and regulatory legal framework to which we must turn for the implementation of the conceptual framework.

"And Thou Shalt Do that Which Is Righteous and Just in the Sight of the Lord..."[9]

No society or economy can persist long without rules which limit theft and fraud. It is easy, therefore, to accept Maimonides' view that Jewish rules prohibiting economic crime and dishonest means of earning a living are rational requirements for society's survival.[10] In the main, however, Judaism has viewed these concepts as far more than mere necessary social wisdom. They have been considered as part of a God-given moral social order.[11] One is forbidden to steal simply because God says so. This makes not stealing a religious act, and not merely something which flows from society's mores and concepts of economic morality. Halachic regulations consider honesty in economics an absolute and required rule, not only a benefit. Moreover, the concept of stealing has been extended far beyond its accepted meaning in humanistic morality. The halachic definition of theft is not dependent on the damage done to the injured party, nor to the relative economic status of the parties concerned; it is forbidden to steal even an item of economic insignificance.[12]

It is prohibited to put good fruit on top of bad, or brush an animal's hair in such a way as to make him look more valuable than he really is.[13] There is an extensive code for the repair and maintenance of scales, developed so that the customer cannot be cheated.[14] One is not even allowed to "steal" another's opinion, to deceive through implication. In other words, many of those things that we assume are legitimate advertising techniques are in fact forbidden.[15]

Weak and powerless members of society have to be protected in their economic activities. They may be lacking full knowledge of the law; they may not have the funds or the knowledge necessary to obtain their rights; and they may be afraid to demand those rights, even when they know them. So the widow and the stranger, the poor and the orphan are singled out for protection by Jewish law. One is not permitted to oppress them or defraud them, and one is not permitted to deal harshly with them in a way that takes advantage of their weak status.[16] All this, of course, is over and above the usual laws regarding moral behavior which apply to everybody.

There are many special circumstances under which other people, who do not fall into these special categories, need protection. The rabbinic Sages, in commenting on the Biblical injunction, "Thou shalt not put a stumbling block in the path of the blind,"[17] understood this as forbidding the giving of unwise advice, or the provision, even legally, of articles which lead to physical or moral detriment.[18] Professions such as counseling, brokerage, accounting, advertising, etc., as well as legal dealing in weapons, drugs or pornographic literature, would find severe restraints placed upon them by the acceptance of the rabbinic laws which flow from this concept.

A man is not permitted to use his property in a way which can cause harm or do damage to another person's body or property.[19] A tree planted alongside a neighbor's plot is in effect stealing, through its roots, another's wealth. Certain industries and professions, which are associated with pollution, noise and human traffic, "steal" another's peace and quiet, fresh air and health, and therefore are forbidden or restricted to certain areas. If an ox has caused fatal damage, its flesh cannot be eaten even when the ox is slaughtered ritually, so as to teach us the severity of causing damage to others.

It should be noted that Jewish law does not accept the Roman concept of "Let the buyer beware." Instead it places the onus for preventing misrepresentation, damage and loss solely on the seller. As an example, a vendor is assumed to guarantee the goods he sells even without an explicit statement to that effect, and the injured party can claim redress for fraud, irrespective of the time which has elapsed or the value of the transaction.[20]

"And Thy Brother Shall Live with Thee..."[21]

Not only is wealth to be earned in a moral way, but society—both the group and the individuals in it—has rights with regard to private Jewish property. Although Judaism accepts the idea that man owns his own property, he is not its sole master.[22] The rabbis of the Talmud, reflecting a thought process which was already then two thousand years old, claimed that Sodom's sin was its inability to share its wealth with strangers, the weak and the poor.[23] The giving of charity is not considered to be an act of special kindness on the part of the "haves" to the "have-nots." The "have-nots" have by right a stake or share in the property of the "haves," since it was given to the latter partially for that purpose. It is no coincidence that the Hebrew word for charity (*tzedakah*) stems from the same linguistic root as the word for justice (*tzedek*). What is given to the poor is not an act of mercy or of righteousness, but an act of justice. Since the community has an obligation to provide food, shelter and basic economic goods for the needy, it has a moral right and duty to tax its members for this purpose. It must regulate matters so as to protect the interest of its weakest members.

This wealth-sharing requirement includes non-monetary acts as well. One is not allowed to verbally oppress the convert, the widow, the orphan or the stranger by reminding them of their special situation. A creditor is not allowed to intrude on the privacy of the debtor, even when he is collecting his debts. Neither is he allowed to take for a security deposit items essential for the sustenance of the debtor or for the earning of his livelihood.[24]

Furthermore, the *Halachah* produced the concept of "the spirit of the law" (literally "beyond the boundary of the law") to educate and train us to forego, voluntarily, economic gains which may legally be ours, in order to allow weak or lesser members of society to maintain themselves. For example, many famous rabbinic personalities closed their stores after a few hours of trading so as to prevent gross competition with their less-learned competitors. These rabbis forfeited the competitive edge allowed them by the Torah itself which enjoins doing business with rabbis when feasible.

The duties and obligations toward one's neighbors go beyond the scope of charity, and include acts of kindness—acts, according to Jewish thought, which are to be done even to those who are undeserving of them. One example is the commandment to make interest-free loans. This is distinct from the injunction against taking interest, as well as from the obligation to give charity. It is an act of kindness (*gemilut chesed*) granted both to the rich man who is temporarily in financial straits and to the poor man trying to improve his economic situation.[25]

Another example of the Torah's regulating trade for the sake of kindness is the law of *bar metzra*. According to Jewish law, a person whose land and property adjoins that of another person automatically has the first right to purchase such property. Since the purchase is to be at the market price, the seller suffers no loss. At the same time, the buyer gains, since the expansion of his property is often an economic advantage. This is a concept in which "one loses nothing and the other one gains."[26] Thus Jewish economic philosophy acknowledges the demands of charity and welfare in the wider sense. These demands often lead to a deliberate distortion of the market mechanism.[27]

"Justice, Justice Shalt Thou Pursue..."[28]

A cardinal tenet of Judaism is the centrality of justice. Justice is an attribute of God. It is displayed in His conduct of the world, and the active pursuit of justice is enjoined upon man. The establishment of a just legal system and courts of law is one of the Seven Noachide Laws seen by Judaism as binding on all men. This justice knows no class distinction: it does not favor the rich and the powerful, nor does it distort itself for the sake of the poor and the weak. Judges are not allowed to fear the wealthy nor favor the poor, or succumb to bribery in all its varied and ingenious forms.

The centrality of justice provides the stable legal system which is an essential prerequisite for any economic activity. This justice is perfectly symmetrical: Creditors have an obligation to grant interest-free loans; but the debtor has an obligation to repay his debt and not to waste the loans given to him. Employees have the right to receive prompt payment of their wages; yet they also have an obligation to perform their work properly. Neither buyer nor seller enjoys special privileges in the marketplace.[29] Furthermore, there is a clear demarcation between justice, on the one hand, and mercy and charity, on the other. This can have important implications for the modern welfare state.

The concept of the free loan can perhaps best serve to illustrate this demarcation in the economic sphere. Consider the case of a debtor who cannot repay his loan. One could argue that since the lender is presumably wealthier than the debtor, he should forego his claim as a creditor. This would be an act of charity and might seem to be the desired way to act.

Such charity, however, distorts justice. It ignores the obligations of the debtor and foists onto the creditor a supposed moral obligation simply because he committed a praiseworthy act by granting the interest-free loan in the first place. As a result of this unpremeditated and involuntary charity, the moral basis of the debtor and creditor is distorted. The borrower on the one hand could tend to make his investments casually and wastefully, knowing that he could perhaps evade repayment altogether. The lender, viewing the loan as charity, could simply be reinforcing the irresponsible behavior of the borrower. This is a pattern often found not only in welfare states but also in economies where subsidized public-sector funds are made available to entrepreneurs. The main creditor, the State, is often prepared to waive its debts or assume the debts of the defaulting corporations. This leads to uneconomic investments and their perpetuation, and also to a willful and immoral management of public funds.

The halachic view is that the creditor need not take upon himself all the social and economic problems of the borrower. Therefore the debtor has to meet his obligation even at the cost of losing all his property.[30] At the same time the community has an obligation, in which the creditor shares as a member, to help the debtor socially and financially.

It is important to note that the Jewish legal system makes a clear demarcation between crimes against property and capital crimes. Murder, adultery and idolatry were punishable by death, without any possibility of monetary settlement.*

On the other hand, no prisons ever existed for debtors, and no jail sentence was imposed for theft or embezzlement; punishment was limited to restitution and fines. Capital punishment, banishment or bodily mutilation for theft were never recognized. While private property entails rights which must be equitably and strictly enforced, such rights were never considered sacred or absolute.

NOTES

1. *Talmud Bavli, Berachot* 35b.
2. *Mishneh Torah, Hilchot De'ot*, chap. 5; *Hilchot Talmud Torah*, chap. 1; Maimonides' Letter to his son.
3. *Mishneh Torah, Hilchot De'ot.*
4. Nachmanides' Commentary on the Torah; *Leviticus*, chap. 19; S.R. Hirsch, *Horeb*, Section 5, 480.
5. *Talmud Bavli, Bava Batra* 175b.
6. *Psalms* 24.
7. *Exodus* 23:11; *Leviticus* 25:2-5. Commentary of *Sefer Ha-Chinnuch* and *Klei Yakar.*
8. *Sefer Ha-Chinnuch, Mitzvah* 506.
9. *Deuteronomy* 6:18.
10. Maimonides, *Shemonah Perakim*, chap. 6.
11. *Exodus* 20; Commentary of the Malbim.
12. *Shulchan Aruch, Hilchot Genevah*, Section 348. Also Mishnah *Bava Batra*, chap. 10, *mishnah* 9.
13. *Shulchan Aruch, Hilchot Ona'ah*, Section 228.
14. Mishnah *Bava Batra*, chap. 5, *mishnah* 11. Also *Shulchan Aruch, Hilchot Ona'ah*, 231.
15. Mishnah *Bava Metzia*, chap. 6, *mishnah* 11. Also *Shulchan Aruch, Hilchot Ona'ah*, 228.

---

* The Torah allows capital punishment only by verdict of the *Sanhedrin*, the Jewish supreme court. During the *Sanhedrin*'s functioning, more than two thousand years ago, capital convictions were so rare that any *Sanhedrin* which ordered more than one execution in seventy years was considerd "murderous."[31]

16. *Exodus* 22:20-21 and 23:4-9; *Leviticus* 19:9-10, 33-34 and 25:25; and *Talmud Bavli, Gittin* 52a.
17. *Leviticus* 19:14.
18. Commentary of Rashi on above verse. Also Mishnah *Avodah Zarah,* chap. 1, *mishnah* 2.
19. Mishnah *Bava Kama,* chap. 2, *mishnah* 6.
20. *Talmud Bavli, Bava Metzia* 14a.
21. *Leviticus* 25:36.
22. I. Herzog, "Law of Property," *The Main Institutions of Jewish Law,* vol. 1.
23. Malbim on *Genesis* 18:20. Also Talmud *Ketubot* 103a and *Bava Batra* 12b.
24. *Exodus* 22:25-27; *Deuteronomy* 24:10-14.
25. *Sefer Ha-Chinnuch, Mitzvah* 66. *Shulchan Aruch* 97, 1.
26. *Mishneh Torah, Hilchot Shechenim,* chaps. 5, 12, 13, 14.
27. M. Tamari, *Competition, Prices and Profits* (Bar-Ilan University) (Hebrew).
28. *Deuteronomy* 16:20.
29. *Shulchan Aruch, Hilchot Ona'ah,* Section 227.
30. *Shulchan Aruch* 97, 23.
31. Mishnah *Makkot* 7a.

Eliezer Zeiger

Torah, Science and Human Knowledge

JUDAISM TEACHES us that the Torah is the blueprint of the world.[1] This implies that the Torah contains a complete description of the universe. Judaism also teaches that the Torah provides us with the comprehensive sets of norms that prescribe human conduct. This implies that the Torah tells us who we are, what is the world that surrounds us and how we should live. Science too provides modern man with a description of the universe. Scientific concepts have become an essential component of human thinking; and technology, the brainchild of science, dominates the human environment of the twentieth century.

Many religious Jews firmly believe that Torah knowledge suffices for all their needs, and choose to ignore science as a source of knowledge. Conversely, many secular people confine their description system to the scientific domain which, they claim, provides the only rational description of the universe. In this essay, I shall pro-

---

ELIEZER ZEIGER is Professor of Biology at the University of California. A specialist in plant physiology, he studied at the University of Buenos Aires, Argentina (B.Sc.), and the University of California at Davis (B.Sc.), and held Professorships at the University of Chile at Santiago; Stanford; the University of Stirling, UK; and the Hebrew University of Jerusalem. He has published some fifty scientific articles and two major textbooks, and has organized numerous workshops and cooperative research programs. Professor Zeiger is a popular lecturer in South America on Torah/Science topics.

pose that Torah and science are, in fact, compatible description systems of the universe and that human life is vastly enriched when both Torah and science are tapped as sources of knowledge and inspiration.

Since both Torah and science offer comprehensive descriptions of the world, proposing that the two description systems are valuable and legitimate requires justification. In addition, the adoption of both as legitimate systems poses important questions. How shall we deal with instances in which these systems provide us with contradictory descriptions? Furthermore, since the description of the universe which we adopt is bound to affect our actions in the world, which system should have preeminence in case of conflict? These and other related questions are the subject of this essay.

A Tale of Two Maps

We are all familiar with city maps. If I wanted to visit a new friend, I would look at a map to find out how to drive to his house and what is the shortest route. A city map is thus a description, or representation, of the city. But city workers installing a new transmission tower would use another type of map—a topographic map in which all points in the city with the same altitude (with respect to sea level) are joined by a line.

A person who is unfamiliar with maps might be baffled if told that the two maps are descriptions of the same city, because their contents would look completely different. Yet a complementary use of the two maps could be very helpful. For example, using the street map I might select the shortest route between two points, but by studying the topographic map I might find that my selected route includes a road with a very steep gradient that my old car could not negotiate. Detailed comparisons of the two maps could also reveal apparent contradictions. For example, I might find that a certain street shows up in the street map as completely straight, but looking at the topographic map I can see that the street would have such a pronounced grade that driving through it would be very dangerous for any car. Lombard Street in San Francisco has such characteristics; it is so steep that it has been built with curves in opposite directions every few yards, to make it possible to negotiate it. If the street map I am looking at does not show that kind of detail and Lombard Street is represented as an ordinary street, and if I have never seen the actual place, I could suspect that one of the two maps is in error.

Torah and science offer us descriptions of the universe that can be thought of as conceptual maps. The maps look very different but both of them describe properties of the same universe. We can readily envision situations that justify the complementary use of both maps. For example, if one wants to learn about the miracles performed by God to free the Jewish people from slavery in Egypt, one would use the Torah map. On the other hand, if one liked to go bird-watching and wanted to become familiar with the different bird species in the area, one would use a bird taxonomy guide rather than the Talmud.

The two maps also show some seemingly conflicting descriptions. Classical conflicts involve the age of the world and the phylogenetic relationships between different living beings. These apparent conflicts pose a problem for a critical person who wants to use both maps. Can either of the maps be in error? If one wished to choose one of the descriptions as the most reliable one, what criteria should be used to make a decision? We can gain insight about these questions by reflecting upon the intrinsic properties of the Torah and science maps.

The Scientific Method

The scientific method is the basic tool used for the construction of the science map. When a scientist has a question, he uses the scientific method to find an answer. In turn, the scientific community uses the same rules to validate the answer. If most scientists think that the answer does not fulfill the basic criteria of the scientific method, the answer will not be accepted, even if the scientist who presented the answer is fully convinced that it is correct. Thus, scientific facts are validated by consensus. Furthermore, an answer widely accepted by the scientific community at one time might be shown to be incorrect by subsequent investigation, in which case the answer will no longer be accepted as valid. Thus, scientific facts accepted as true at one time can be shown to be incorrect at another time. Often, a given question gets one answer from one segment of the scientific community and a different one from another group of scientists. These controversies can go on for a long time, until one of the answers gets further verification and it is accepted by consensus.

The procedure used to obtain answers is the backbone of the scientific method. Usually the question under investigation arises from previous observations made in a quest for answers to other questions. The investigator then thinks about possible answers for the new question and tentatively chooses the one that seems to be correct. At that point, the scientist starts to work on the verification of the tentative answer. In the theoretical sciences, verification usually involves analytical work using principles that have already been proven correct. In the biological sciences, the tentative answer will usually be tested by experimentation. For example, it is a common observation that apples have a sweet taste. A scientist might ask the question: What component of the apple causes the sweet taste? To find an answer, a scientist can subject apples to chemical analysis and identify as many chemical components as possible. He then chooses one of them as the putative factor responsible for the sweetness. His answer can then be tested by tasting water to which only the putative chemical compound has been added and verifying whether that solution tastes sweet. Further verification can be obtained by synthesizing that compound from simple molecules in the laboratory and showing that, without apples or any of their components being involved, the sweet taste can be elicited. The scientific process is then likely to proceed in several directions. Organic chemists might synthesize families of chemicals that have some of the structures of the original ones, but lack others, and engage in research to determine the minimal chemical structure needed for a sweet taste. Botanists might start a comparative study of the chemical composition of other fruits related to the apple to see if they also have that compound. Human physiologists might study the taste buds of the mouth and ask how the sweet taste is perceived, and how the stimulus is transmitted to the brain. This process leads to the progressive building of the scientific map.

It is important to note that the apparently straightforward procedure described in our example depends on some very complex requirements. Although "apple" is a well-known element of the scientific map, it has actually been established in the map by a scientific discipline called plant taxonomy. If a botanist visits a previously unexplored area of the Amazon and finds a wild tree that has fruit that looks like apples, he will not simply call it an apple tree; he will first go through an elaborate verification procedure to determine if the fruit is identical to the element of the scientific map that by consensus is called apple, or if the similarity is only superficial and he is actually looking at something that has a different name on the map, or has no name at all and requires a new one. Note also that the initial chemical analysis used to separate different components of apples relies on decades of research that has classified and named natural compounds and, equally important, has led to the design of methodology *and* instrumentation that provide the basis for new analysis. Because of this intricate relationship, every new answer in science depends on and, to a large extent, is generated by a previously acquired body of knowledge. That basic property of the scientific process is often overlooked, leading to the incorrect belief that a new answer is solely defined by the context of its generating question.

With these elements in mind, we can attempt to characterize the main components of the scientific method:

(1) Given a question, scientists find an answer whose verification generates the phenomenon that elicited the question. (The putative chemical compound dissolved in water tastes sweet like an apple.)

(2) The answer should invoke the minimum number of assumptions (there is no need to assume that the taste of an apple would depend on the political party in power) and offer the simplest solution (in the first trial, do not postulate that three different compounds are required for the sweet taste when, in principle, a single one could do the job).

(3) A valid answer depends on a number of explicit *and* implicit assumptions which emerged in previous stages of the scientific process. If, at some point, any of the supporting assumptions is proven wrong, the original answer is no longer valid. (If subsequent investigation shows that a machine that was used to analyze the apple was calling something compound A when it was later shown to be

compound B, all previous work with that machine needs to be revised, including the study of apples.)

Corollary of (3). This dependence of each answer of the scientific map on previous answers that emerged from independent investigations involving different assumptions imposes a relativity on scientific knowledge that is often overlooked by scientists and laymen alike. Contrary to common belief, a vast amount of research can go on, based on an answer assumed to have solid support but actually resting on insufficient evidence. It is, however, a fundamental strength of the scientific process that it has built-in procedures which should eventually expose those weaknesses, leading to a revision of all the pertinent body of knowledge.

(4) Current scientific knowledge (the science map) is the accumulation of interrelated answers obtained over the course of many centuries. The rigorous documentation which is an essential part of the scientific process makes it possible to backtrack and determine the supporting evidence for any given answer, and such a task would ultimately lead to simple premises based on a few, undemonstrated assumptions. Theoretically, if one could trace back all current elements of the scientific map to their generating questions and their verification, we would ultimately find no elements in the map and a single initial question. It is outside the scope of this essay to speculate on what that question would be....

This brief description of some properties of the scientific method should clarify how the elements of the science map are defined, and underscore some limitations of human knowledge as shaped by science. Further issues on the relativity of science are discussed in other essays included in this volume (see, for instance, the article on quantum physics by Rabinowitz and Branover); here I would like to probe another aspect of the science map, one which relates to the properties of the mapmaker.

How Do We Know What We Know?

The quality of maps varies and new, more accurate maps are made from time to time. The quality of a map depends on the precision of the instruments used to gather the needed information and on the skills of the mapmaker. The same is true for the scientific map. On the other hand, all maps are made by human beings, and so we can ask: Are there biological properties of the human being that impose general limitations on the process of mapmaking?

This question takes us into the realm of human cognition. One scientific discipline that deals with this problem is called epistemology. The problem of cognition has occupied many philosophers and it will not be reviewed here. Instead, I will concentrate on recent developments in the field of biological epistemology, addressing questions on the biological properties of the human being which affect knowledge. In particular I want to discuss the work of a Chilean biologist, Humberto Maturana.

Maturana is a neurobiologist who in the 1950s conducted classical experimental work on vision in frogs. Some of his results led him to ponder the relationship between the outside signal stimulating the eye and its perception by the living organism. This endeavor led Maturana to a completely different realm of research that culminated in a new theory of biological organization and the basis of knowledge. Space limitations restrict my discussion of Maturana's work to a few central concepts; the reader is referred to one of his books for a more complete overview of his theories.[2]

Maturana's Concept of the Biological Organization

The definition of life is a difficult undertaking. Maturana makes an important contribution to that problem by proposing that the most basic characteristic of living beings is the continuous and dynamic maintenance of their organization. Maturana and his co-worker Varela coined the word *autopoiesis* to describe this ongoing "self-production" which they propose to be the basic property of life.*

As in many instances of brilliant definitions, the statement might

---

* There is an interesting parallel between Maturana's concept of autopoiesis, in which living beings are continuously "creating" their organization, and the Torah teaching that not only did God create the universe at the beginning of time, but that He is constantly recreating it at every moment.[3]

appear trivial when first encountered. But careful reflection can reveal the power of this analysis: This criterion allows me to distinguish a living being from a machine. For example, a very common definition of living organisms is "those that reproduce themselves." However, I can encounter a machine that, using techniques of robotics, makes another machine just like itself. According to the criterion of reproduction, that machine is alive; according to Maturana's criterion it is not, because a machine cannot actively maintain its organization. (Some of the most advanced robots have some capacity for self-repair but only to the extent that their software has been specifically programmed to that effect.) Furthermore, once manufactured, the machine becomes a fixed structure, whereas living beings are constantly changing *while* maintaining their organization.

Analysis of the processes involved in the maintenance of the living organization shows that an essential requirement for success is that organisms function as *closed systems*, that is, organization is maintained in a well-defined space which has clear-cut boundaries. In a cell, such a boundary is provided by its membranes, which show specialized properties allowing the cell to remain structurally closed while making possible the exchange of matter and energy with its environment.

The Human Nervous System Is Also a Closed System

Maturana extended this biological analysis to the nervous system, which is built of a very large number of interconnected neurons. This vast network of neurons is in turn connected to the muscles and the brain. When viewed as a unit, the nervous system can also be characterized as *operationally closed*.[4] In other words, the activity of the nervous system is expressed in internal changes of and interactions between neurons that only result in further changes and interactions between them.

As opposed to the concept of the cell as a closed system, which is readily grasped on intuitive grounds, the concept of operational closure of the nervous system is difficult to grasp because it contradicts the *representational* view of the operation of the nervous system. This popular point of view states that the nervous system is an instrument providing the organism with information needed to generate adequate behavior in response to environmental signals. In this view, the environment inputs its characteristics into the nervous system and the nervous system outputs appropriate responses that generate behavior. In fact, this representational description only states *what appears to be the case* when an observer watches the behavior of an organism.[5] However, the nervous system does not acquire representations of the environment; rather, environmental perturbations *trigger* changes in activity in the neuronal network which, when coupled to motor responses, generate behavior.

This structural coupling between organisms and environment can be illustrated with an example. Consider a garage door that can be opened by remote control, using an infrared sensor. The system includes: a device which emits infrared light and is used by the driver of the car; an infrared light sensor which is on the outside of the garage door; an electrical circuit which connects the sensor to a mechanical motor attached to the inside of the door; and the motor proper which drives a pulley capable of raising or lowering the door. With respect to the action of opening or closing the garage door, it will be evident that the unit-system is composed of the door, the pulley, and the motor. It will be further evident that such a unit does not perceive the infrared light activating the sensor; it only responds to an on-off switch that changes its state in response to an electrical stimulus. In fact, if the sensor were instead a microphone or a coded keypad, the garage-door unit would still open or close if properly activated. Yet an observer who is unfamiliar with the situation and sees the driver of the car aiming the infrared device at the sensor and the door opening, might think that the garage door is actually sensing the infrared signal, and further infer that the same activating device could open any garage door.*

The coupling between the infrared device, the electrical circuit and

---

* The reader is invited to apply a similar analysis to an airplane and The reader is invited to apply a similar analysis to an airplance and its pilot. (Tip: Is the pilot "flying" the plane?) For a similar discussion on structural coupling and the handling of a submarine, see note 2, 136-137.

the garage door provides a useful analogy to the coupling between the environment, the nervous system and the motor muscles of a human being. Neither the garage door nor the nervous system perceives the surrounding environment, yet we move aside when we see an obstacle in our path without any representation of that obstacle reaching our brain. The basis of such avoiding behavior is a series of coupled responses involving the eyes, the nervous system, the brain and the muscles that take us away from the obstacle. In terms of the operation of the nervous system, however, the obstacle-signal only triggers state-changes in the neurons, without any violation of their operational closure. Because of the central role of the nervous system and the brain in cognition, the operational closure of the nervous system has important implications about human knowledge.

In his writings, Maturana has discussed many lines of empirical evidence that can be used as proof that the nervous system is a closed system (see note 2 and references therein), but space limitations preclude their review here.

Some Biological Aspects of Cognition

The concept of operational closure of the nervous system poses an important question about cognition. We can understand that the structural coupling between organisms and the environment makes adequate behavior possible without the need for an actual representation of the environment in the brain. But how can human beings describe their surroundings without any access to representations of the environment?

The answer to that question is that, through language, human beings generate a linguistic domain of descriptions. This linguistic domain allows for the separation between the observer and the observed and it is one area where representations exist. Human beings live in continuous, recursive interactions between the domain of their actions and the domain of their descriptions. Both domains are embedded in language and in the biological properties of the organism that set their boundaries and define their relationships.[6] Both cognition and the science map are components of the human descriptive domain and therefore are also constrained by these biological properties.

It is important to recognize that the linguistic domain of descriptions also generates a coupling rather than a true representational system like a photographic film. Thus, in isolation, a person cannot make a valid distinction between perception (a description of the outside environment) and hallucination (an internal representation that has no direct relationship to the "outside"). We can only distinguish between perceptions and hallucinations because of the operation of yet a different domain, that of *consensus,* or the cognitive agreement that is achieved through the interaction between human beings. Isolated human beings cannot distinguish between perception and hallucination because of the inescapable constraint imposed by the operational closure of the nervous system. However, human beings are essentially social beings and language is a fundamental social phenomenon. Hence, since all human actions are embedded in language, all actions are ultimately social actions. In the descriptive domain, I can distinguish my inner world from the outside environment and from interactions with other human beings; I validate those distinctions through consensus.

Maps and the Mapmaker

We now return to the question of how maps are shaped by the biological properties of the mapmaker. The structural closure of human beings imposes an absolute barrier to knowledge. Language makes possible the generation of a descriptive domain that allows the uncoupling from the action (being) domain, thus generating a cognitive context. The scientific map is constructed within this linguistic domain and it is shaped by the human properties (and limitations) described above. Yet science is optimally suited to generate cognition in a context of structural closure. By posing questions with the least number of assumptions and then testing putative answers with the scientific method as a means of interaction with the ultimately unknowable universe, the elements of the scientific map are painstakingly put in place.

The process is illustrated in the well-known parable of the several blind scientists who were trying to identify an elephant. Each one touched one part of the animal and came up with a different hypothesis about the unknown object; eventually they pooled their observations and agreed on the right answer. Besides its illustration of the intrinsic cognitive blindness of human beings, the parable underscores another aspect of the effectiveness of science in the shaping of reality: the remarkable power of the scientific method to generate consensus among structurally-closed observers. Because of that power, people from different cultures living in distant places can make a few assumptions and conduct a similar experiment that will generate what people will *agree* are the same results. Very few human activities are capable of generating such an unambiguous consensus.

On the other hand, we should not overlook the fact that, in the parable, we are told at the outset that the blind scientists are all touching an elephant. In the making of the science map, no higher-level observer tells the scientists what they are dealing with; the map is only a relative construct inferred from observations which are taken as reality only insofar as their validation remains consistent with empirical verification. Furthermore, the shaping of reality is as much determined by the properties of the observers as it is by the properties of what is observed, and its ultimate validation criterion is actually consensus.

Torah and Cognition

Judaism teaches us that the whole Torah, both Written and Oral, was given by God to Moshe *Rabbenu** at Sinai, and that God is infinite and immutable. The Torah map encompasses a body of knowledge that explains the nature of the universe and prescribes human conduct in all aspects of life. In contrast with the science map, which is generated within the human cognitive domain, the Torah map originates from a higher-level reality, God, which created the human condition yet transcends it altogether. In Judaism, transmission of Divine knowledge to humans is called prophecy or revelation. The Torah deals with prophecy in great detail, not only in the Pentateuch and the Talmud but also in halachic sources,[7] in which we are taught how to distinguish between true prophets and false ones. On the other hand,

* Moses, our teacher.

prophecy cannot be found in the science map, because such a phenomenon cannot be apprehended by the scientific method as currently understood.

The origin of the Torah map from outside the human cognitive domain has major implications. In Torah, the answer *precedes* the question and originates outside the human cognitive domain. In the science map, the question always precedes the answer and the answers are generated *within* the human cognitive domain (in fact, answers from outside that domain are explicitly ruled out). Furthermore, scientific answers are subject to revision and can change at any time, if a different answer is validated by consensus. Torah, on the other hand, is not affected by time; after its revelation at Sinai its validity remains immutable throughout the generations. (The manifestation, or expression of Torah, however, is strongly dependent on consensus, hence the critical importance of Jewish unity.) Also, because Torah originates from a source that is external to the human cognitive domain, the absolute limits imposed on cognition by the operational closure of the nervous system do not operate in the Torah map.

A Tale about the Blind and the Sighted

Our preceding discussion allows us to evaluate some interesting cognitive relationships between Torah and science. People today are exposed to both the Torah and the science maps and often argue about their intrinsic validity. Many are convinced that their preferred map is the only valid one.

From a cognitive point of view, this argument brings to mind the following hypothetical situation: There is a small community that is virtually devoid of communication with the rest of the world. A genetic disease which is prevalent in this community has rendered about half of its members blind. The community members with normal vision routinely describe many features of their environment, such as colors and shapes. The blind people are used to hearing about these features and take them as valid despite the fact that they have never seen them themselves. But at some point, a philosophically inclined blind person objects: "How do I really know whether these people, who describe things which I have never seen, really *know* what they are talking about? I can perceive countless features of the environment using my senses; why should I believe that my environment is different because other people claim it to be? In fact, I should only rely on what *I* know is out there, on what my senses tell me is so." This blind person actively lobbies for his position and succeeds in convincing all the other blind people that his is the correct one. From then on, the community is separated into two groups with conflicting cognitive views.

Let us further suppose that the sighted members have an ancient document which has passed from generation to generation, explaining the origin and history of that community. Of course the blind people, unable to read it, dismiss it along with all the other unverifiable perceptions of the sighted people. With time, some talented blind people succeed in designing increasingly sophisticated instruments which measure properties of the environment in a way that blind people can discern. Some of these measurements will reveal "colors" as different wavelengths of energy emitted by objects, which seem similar to what the sighted people claim they see as colors, but these features receive different names in the map of descriptions of the blind people because they have originated from a different cognitive domain. Further progress in the building of this description map by the blind people allows them to make some inferences about their past that, because of their different cognitive origin, contradict the description found in the ancient document that the sighted people read every week in their community meetings. At this point, the blind people conclude that *their* instruments provide the only valid description of reality in that community.

This hypothetical community provides a metaphor for a context in which a cognitive domain depending on a nervous system that exhibits operational closure cannot encompass a reality that exists beyond the boundaries of its biological organization. The metaphor also shows that, from a cognitive point of view, the blind people would have no means to validate the existence of the community of sighted people and their perceptions. Similarly, the distinct properties of the Torah and science maps preclude a scientific validation of the Torah, because of restrictions arising from the nature of the scientific method (the phenomenon of Divine revelation cannot be empirically generated) and from epistemological constraints (the Torah's contents originated from outside the boundaries of human cognition). The Divine origin of the Torah, however, should not be interpreted to suggest a lack of rigor within the Torah map. On the contrary—the Torah map satisfies the highest standards of precision and internal consistency.

"Many people are convinced that their preferred map is the only valid one."

Human Limitations and the Absoluteness of Torah

The Divine origin of the Torah poses an important question: How does the limited human mind deal with the infinite dimensions of God? We can gain insight about this question from a teaching of the Talmud which states that "the Torah speaks in the language of the sons of man."[8] For example, there are many Biblical passages telling us about acts of God in which human organs or functions, such as hands or sight, are used. Yet, Judaism teaches explicitly and forcefully about the incorporeality of God. Maimonides (the Rambam) explains that the attributes indicating corporeality have been used by the Torah in order to make clear the existence of God, because the human mind cannot conceive of existence without corporeal attributes.[9] Thus, the absolute truth of Torah has been *encoded* in human language, in order to make it accessible to human cognition. In this conversion of the Absolute into the limited human context, cognitive constraints are imposed on the *manifestation* of Torah in the human descriptive domain. These limitations are made abundantly clear in the Talmud, reflected in the cases where the Sages give conflicting opinions about a given issue. We are repeatedly taught that these apparent conflicts do not reflect "right" or "wrong" opinions, but are rather different interpretations having identical validity. From a cognitive standpoint, we can understand such a process as an expression of a situation in which the limited human mind is facing the infinite wisdom of God. The simultaneous acceptance of different views represents a way of learning offered by the Talmud, in which the limited human mind can approximate the ever-elusive Absolute understanding.

Free Will Is Only Possible When the Absoluteness of Torah Is Hidden

From a Torah standpoint, there is another important reason requiring that the Divine essence remain hidden in the world. After receiving the Torah at Sinai and wandering in the desert for forty years, the Jews who were about to enter the Promised Land received a parting message from Moshe *Rabbenu*. He told them what would happen if they followed the ways of Torah, and what was in store for them if their hearts turned away from God: "... I have set before you life and death, blessing and curse; therefore choose life...."[10] Jews are thus commanded to love God out of their own volition and are given complete free will to choose between Godliness and evil. The Torah also teaches that, for free will to be possible, God manifests Himself in the world through *natural* ways,[11] except for the most exceptional circumstances, such as the ten plagues in Egypt or the giving of the Torah at Sinai.

The requirement of natural order in the world for the exercise of free will can be understood upon reflection of what would be the consequences of an overt manifestation of God's omnipotence. If

Divine punishment were irrevocably coupled with bad actions, and Divine reward always accompanied those that follow the path of righteousness, we could readily predict that every rational human being would adopt the ways of Torah. But that is not the case; we are taught that God does not desire that human devotion arise from such Divinely-imposed behavior. Rather, we are given free choice to love and fear God, of their own volition. A world based on natural laws appears to be the optimal setting for the maximal exercise of freedom of choice.

These conditions specified in the Torah map, which make free will possible, are fully consistent with the cognitive relations between the Torah and the science maps. Human cognition is shaped by language and by the operational closure of the human nervous system. Torah has been made accessible to human beings through Divine revelation, and it can only enter human cognition by being encoded in human language. In this coupling between the absoluteness of Torah and the limited dimensions of human cognition, Torah in the human domain acquires finite boundaries, which include limitations to its understanding and uncertainties in its interpretation. In addition, the giving of the Torah was designed to leave human free will completely unimpaired. This constraint demands the concealment of the existence of God from the world and the Divine handling of the world via natural means. The inaccessibility of the Torah map by the scientific method satisfies another condition for the exercise of free will.

The science map, on the other hand, is built by inferences based on observations generated by the scientific method. Both the questions and answers which shape the science map are generated within the human cognitive domain, and this domain shows absolute limits imposed by the operational closure of the human nervous system; extrapolation beyond those limits violates the principles of the scientific method.

A longing to know has been an intrinsic human characteristic since the dawn of history. Science provides one answer to that longing and offers a systematic, reproducible and documented description of the universe. However, exclusive choice of the scientific map confines people to the boundaries of the cognitive human domain, and forces them to live with the intrinsic, temporal and conceptual relativity of the science map.

A longing to transcend one's limitations, including the cognitive ones, is also a primal human trait. The Torah offers human beings access to Divine truth, which provides an understanding that transcends cognitive limitations. Access to the Torah map demands belief in prophecy, a requirement that clashes with the pervasive empiricism of our times. More importantly, access to the description of the universe contained in the Torah map demands the simultaneous adoption of high ethical standards, a condition that some people seem unwilling to accept.

The above characterization of the Torah and science maps allows us to answer the basic question: Is there a need for two descriptive frameworks of the universe? Our analysis provides an unambiguous positive answer to that question. The Torah gives us a description system that transcends human limitations and is unaffected by temporal changes and relativism, and science provides us with an empirical description of the natural laws of the universe. Adoption of the two maps therefore fulfills both our longing to know and our longing to transcend.

Na'aseh V'nishma and the Tale of Two Maps

When the Jewish people were offered the Torah at Sinai, they answered: *Na'aseh v'nishma* (We shall do and we shall hear).[12] What is the meaning of that statement? The *na'aseh* part can be readily understood; the Jewish people promised to follow all the commandments of the Torah. The meaning of *nishma,* our Sages explain, is that the Jewish people promised to understand the Torah. Such a dual commitment invites some reflection. A commitment to act involves behavior based on an unqualified acceptance of the authority of the Torah in daily life, as manifested in the rules of *Halachah.* A commitment to understand, on the other hand, implies rational thought and theoretical involvement. One aspect of that involvement is also connected with the activities of daily life; we are commanded to thoroughly understand the rational aspects of *Halachah.*

This is illustrated by the first positive commandment listed by Maimonides in his *Mishneh Torah*: "... to know that there is a First Being...."* We are not commanded to *believe* that there is a God, but to know it. Clearly, our rational mind is to be involved in the fulfillment of that commandment. Another component of that understanding refers to the part of the Torah map pertaining to the description of the universe, as encoded in the Pentateuch and interpreted by our Sages in the Talmud. This is a context in which the Torah and science maps converge: Both descriptions of the universe provide an opportunity for us to become closer to God with our rational minds. In the Talmud, we learn the teachings of our Sages on the Divine wisdom; in the science map, we understand the laws of nature, which are the manifestation of the creative power of God.

Science and Infinity

I became aware of another relationship between the Torah and science maps through my research work. When I was a Ph.D. student in biology (before I had returned to the practice of Jewish religion), I was trained under the implicit assumption that the science map contained the potential to explain all the features of the universe. At that time, in the late 1960s, the biological sciences were in the midst of a conceptual revolution caused by dramatic advances in molecular biology: the discovery of the structure of DNA, the nucleic acid that holds the hereditary information in living organisms, and the "breaking" of the genetic code, which translates the DNA's information into the proteins that control cellular metabolism. These advances allowed scientists to understand some basic biological processes, a development that led to the belief that all the remaining secrets of life were within reach, and that, given enough time and resources, science could explain every aspect of the universe.

I started my research work in cell physiology under the convic-

---

* "The basic principle of all basic principles, and the pillar of all sciences, is to realize (Hebrew: *lada'at*, to know) that there is a First Being Who brought every existing thing into being. All existing things, whether celestial, terrestrial, or belonging to an intermediate class, exist only through His true existence."[13]

tion that in a few generations our understanding of the universe would approach completion. As my work progressed, I became aware of a peculiar aspect of the research process. I had carefully selected a scientific question and was fortunate to find an answer. What I had not anticipated was that, side by side with that answer, several new questions became evident. I first assumed that this was a temporary phenomenon, ensuing from the fact that I had started a relatively new line of research, and I proceeded to carefully select the best available next question. To my surprise, the finding of the next answer produced a similar array of new questions, a feature that has continued to characterize my scientific work. With time, I became aware of a sharp contradiction between the point of view I had been trained with, which implied that the number of answers would inexorably exceed the number of questions until most features of the universe became clear, and the puzzling fact that, in my work, I was generating many more questions than answers. Furthermore, I am under the distinct impression that such a phenomenon is not restricted to my own work but that it is a widespread feature of the scientific process. How is it possible that, despite the fact that the number of living scientists working today exceeds the total number of scientists in all previous generations, and that the body of scientific knowledge has grown to unforeseen dimensions, scientists continue to generate more questions than answers? Is that consistent with the point of view that science is characterizing a finite universe and that an essentially complete map will eventually become available? The persistent predominance of questions over answers would rather suggest that the scientific process is actually characterizing an *infinite* universe, and, therefore, a complete scientific map of the universe is a theoretical impossibility.

Within that perspective, the Torah and science maps converge in facing the greatest challenges for human cognition: the grasping of the infinite dimensions of God and of His Creation. We read in the *Chumash* that when Moshe *Rabbenu* asked God to show him His glory, he was told, "You cannot see My face, for man shall not see Me and live,"[14] but Moshe was allowed to see God's "back."[15] From a cognitive point of view, we can interpret these passages as stating that our cognitive organization would collapse if God's infinity were to be apprehended. But we are graced with glimpses of God's "back," which in Torah is embodied in the *encoded* manifestation of God's essence. In the scientific map, we can glimpse at God's "back" in the domain of descriptions of the natural world. Neither map gives us access to God's "face," that is, complete and absolute knowledge, because of the respective cognitive limitations described previously. Each map, on the other hand, can provide us with some insight into Divinity. This is the basis of our contention that human life is vastly enriched when both Torah and science are tapped as sources of knowledge and inspiration.

The Preeminence of the Torah Map

The cognitive relationships between the Torah and science maps also provide us with criteria for the appraisal of apparent conflicts between the two descriptions of the universe. Some of the discrepancies might arise from the different properties of each map. For example, in one of his *Sichot*, the Lubavitcher Rebbe, *shlita*, alludes to a controversy between the Babylonian and Jerusalem Talmud regarding the influence of prayer on the determination of the sex of a child in gestation.[16] The Babylonian Talmud states that prayer can affect the sex of an embryo up to forty days after conception,[17] while the Jerusalem Talmud teaches that prayer might be of avail until much later; according to one opinion, even when the mother has already gone into labor.[18] Besides disagreeing with each other, both sources contradict the scientific map, which states that the sex of a child is fixed at the time of fertilization. The Lubavitcher Rebbe explains the discrepancies between the Jerusalem and Babylonian Talmud in terms of the manifestation of the Divine essence in the present world and in the postmessianic era. After the Redemption, all restrictions on the manifestation of the Divine essence will be removed; hence in the postmessianic era prayer will be effective at all times. The Rebbe, *shlita*, further explains that the Babylonian Talmud, written in Babylonia, manifests mundane limitations to a much greater extent than the Jerusalem Talmud, which reflects the reality of the world-to-come. We thus find a gradient of limitations in the three maps: the science map deals strictly with the physical plane and hence states that the sex of the child is fixed at fertilization; the Babylonian Talmud introduces the first level in the removal of physical limitations heralded by Judaism in the acknowledgment of Divine Providence and sets the current limit for the influence of prayer at forty days after conception; the Jerusalem Talmud is completely embedded in the world-to-come, in a manifest reality of Divine sovereignty in the universe, and hence states that prayers can be effective up to the time of labor. In this instance, then, apparent contradictions are resolved when the different validation criteria of the respective maps are taken into consideration.

In other instances we might be unable to offer a good explanation for apparent contradictions, such as the discrepancy between the age of the world according to the Torah map (5748 years, as of this writing) and that stated by the science map, running in the billions of years. We may or may not be able to solve this contradiction in the future but we need not be disturbed about it. Each datum is a valid statement within the framework of its respective description map, and the cognitive foundation of each map rests on different premises. Thus we might expect that in certain cases the maps would provide different representations of the same phenomena. If we are convinced that each map is rigorously constructed and carefully validated, we can accept these apparent contradictions as a logical consequence of the use of different description systems.

On the other hand, it is important to recognize that, for an observant Jew, the Torah map has undisputed preeminence over the science map. This preeminence ensues from fundamental considerations. First, the Torah map is absolute, eternal and all-encompassing. Because of these properties, the acceptance of the truth of the Torah map must embody every aspect of both the Written and Oral Torah. In other words, any selectivity in the acceptance of one aspect of the Torah map and not another is inconsistent with the cognitive origin of the Torah. The same premise is the basis of the preeminence of the Torah over the science map, which is relative and always subject to changes. Second, the Torah map provides a precise ethical code which cannot be separated from its description of the universe. Thus, acceptance of the description of the universe found in the Torah demands a concomitant acceptance of its ethical code. In contrast, science is completely silent about human conduct and therefore intrinsically indeterminate about ethical values. The overriding importance placed by Judaism on ethical values further justifies the preeminence of the Torah map over the science map.

The relevance of a clear understanding of the preeminence of Torah goes beyond theoretical considerations. For example, circumcision is a cornerstone of Jewish life and has also been conventionally praised by the medical sciences as a healthy practice. Yet in the last few years the American media have publicized concerted efforts made by some circles to discredit circumcision on presumed medical and ethical grounds. Were Jewish acceptance of the command of circumcision dependent on its scientific validation, these developments could (God forbid) weaken the determination of Jews to carry out this commandment. But the foundation of circumcision is the Torah, irrespective of the prevailing scientific point of view. Thus, although the confluence of the Torah and science maps is always a source of rejoicing, the Jewish way of life is based on Torah.

Efforts to understand the relationship between Torah and science are ingrained in the Jewish tradition. For example, Maimonides wrote in depth about the relationship between Torah and philosophy,[19] which was the most advanced science of those times. Some thinkers have stated that his *Moreh Nevuchim* represents Maimonides' efforts to "conciliate" Jewish religion and philosophy. Such an interpretation is plainly incorrect; Maimonides had a paramount grasp of Torah and he fully understood the preeminence of Torah over any other area of human discourse. Yet he took great care to prove the unity of God on philosophical grounds and to relate the Torah to fundamental principles of philosophy. Careful reading of *Moreh Nevuchim* clearly reveals that a major goal of Maimonides was to use philosophy, the most advanced science at his disposal, as a tool to further our understanding of the essence of God. Several centuries later, we face the challenge of following Maimonides' guidance in the use of science for the service of God.

NOTES

1. *Bereshit Rabbah* 1:2. Here Torah refers not only to the Five Books of Moses, but includes the complete Written and Oral Jewish tradition as well.

2. H.R. Maturana and F.J. Varela, *Tree of Knowledge, the Biological Roots of Human Understanding* (Boston and London: Shambhala Press, 1987).
3. *Nehemiah* 9:6; Maimonides, *Moreh Nevuchim*, trans. Pines (Chicago: University of Chicago Press, 1963), chap. 169.
4. Maturana and Varela, *Tree of Knowledge.*
5. Ibid.
6. H.R. Maturana and F.J. Varela, *Autopoiesis and Cognition* (Boston: D. Reidel, 1980).
7. Maimonides, *Mishneh Torah, Hilchot Yesodei Ha-Torah*, chap. 7.
8. Babylonian Talmud, *Yevamot* 71a; *Bava Metzia* 31b.
9. Maimonides, *Moreh Nevuchim*, trans. Pines (Chicago: University of Chicago Press, 1963), chap. 126.
10. *Deuteronomy* 30:19.
11. Babylonian Talmud, *Shabbat* 53b; *Zohar* 1:201b; *Pesachim* 64b.
12. *Exodus* 24:7.
13. Maimonides, *The Book of Knowledge*, trans. Moses Hyamson (New York: Feldheim, 1981), chap. 1, part 1.
14. *Exodus* 33:18-20.
15. *Exodus* 33:22.
16. *Likkutei Sichot*, vol. 3, 69-70.
17. *Berachot* 60a.
18. Jerusalem Talmud, *Berachot* 9:3.
19. Maimonides, *Moreh Nevuchim*, trans. Pines (Chicago: University of Chicago Press, 1963).

Glossary

The following glossary provides a partial explanation of some of the Hebrew, Yiddish and Aramaic words and phrases used in this book. The spelling and explanations reflect the way the specific word is used herein. Often, there are alternate spellings and meanings for the words.

AMORA (AMORAIM): (A.) the Sage(s) whose opinions comprise the GEMARA.

BAR METZRA: (A.) a neighbor who has the right of preemption.

BEIT HA-MIDRASH: a house of study.

BERACHAH: a blessing.

BERESHIT: the Book of Genesis.

CHASID: a person devoted to the service of God and ethical perfection; a follower of the teachings of the Ba'al Shem Tov.

CHASIDUT: a religious and social movement founded by Rabbi Israel Ba'al Shem Tov in the eighteenth century, which taught that purity of heart was more essential than Torah study and eschewed ascetic practices, stressing joy as the tool with which to serve God.

CHESED: lovingkindness.

ERETZ YISRAEL: the Land of Israel.

GAON: a very learned man; a genius.

GEMARA: commentary on the MISHNAH (together they comprise the Talmud); a volume of the Talmud.

GEMILUT CHESED: benevolence.

GET: a bill of divorce according to Jewish law.

HALACHAH: Jewish law.

HANASI: the prince.

HASHEM: God.

KABBALAH: Jewish mysticism.

KINDERLACH: (Y.) children.

KOHEN: a member of the priestly family descended from Aaron, brother of Moses.

L'HAVDIL: a phrase meaning literally "to differentiate," that is, not to mention the sacred and profane in the same breath.

MASHGIACH: the dean of students in a YESHIVA who acts as a spiritual guide and adviser.

MASHIACH: the Messiah.

MIDRASH: a collection of non-literal interpretations and homiletic teachings of the Sages.

MISHNAH: the Oral Law, the primary basis of the Talmud.

NEFESH: the lowest of the three levels of soul, according to some Kabbalists.

NESHAMAH: the highest of the three levels of soul, according to some Kabbalists.

NIDDAH: a woman who has become impure due to menstruation.

NISAN: the Hebrew month corresponding to March/April.

PARASHAH: the weekly Torah portion.

RABBAN: (A.) our teacher, an honorary title.

RABBENU: our teacher.

ROSH YESHIVA: the dean of a YESHIVA.

RUACH: the intermediate of the three levels of soul, according to some Kabbalists.

SEFER: a book; a sacred book.

SEFIRAH (SEFIROT): a technical Kabbalistic term to describe the emanation(s) through which Hashem manifests Himself.

SHA'ATNEZ: a garment which contains a mixture of wool and linen, the wearing of which is prohibited by the Torah.

SHABBAT: the Sabbath.

SHEMOT: the Book of Exodus.

SHLITA: a Hebrew acronym for the words: "May he live long and happily, Amen!"

TALMID CHACHAM: a scholar; a learned man.

TANNA (TANNAIM): (A.) Jewish scholar(s) and teacher(s) in the time of the Mishnah.

TEFILLIN: phylacteries.

TZEDAKAH: righteousness; charity.

TZEDEK: righteousness; justice.

YESHIVAH: an academy of Torah study.

ZAVAH: a woman who has become impure due to a discharge of blood, not during the time of her menstrual period.

ZOHAR: the Book of Brightness, the chief work of the KABBALAH.